Notes upon Russia

A Translation of the Earliest Account of that Country, Entitled 'Rerum moscoviticarum commentarii'

VOLUME 2

SIGISMUND VON HERBERSTEIN
EDITED BY RICHARD HENRY MAJOR

CAMBRIDGE UNIVERSITY PRESS

Cambridge, New York, Melbourne, Madrid, Cape Town, Singapore,
São Paolo, Delhi, Dubai, Tokyo

Published in the United States of America by Cambridge University Press, New York

www.cambridge.org
Information on this title: www.cambridge.org/9781108008082

© in this compilation Cambridge University Press 2010

This edition first published 1852
This digitally printed version 2010

ISBN 978-1-108-00808-2 Paperback

This book reproduces the text of the original edition. The content and language reflect the beliefs, practices and terminology of their time, and have not been updated.

Cambridge University Press wishes to make clear that the book, unless originally published by Cambridge, is not being republished by, in association or collaboration with, or with the endorsement or approval of, the original publisher or its successors in title.

CAMBRIDGE LIBRARY COLLECTION
Books of enduring scholarly value

Travel and Exploration

The history of travel writing dates back to the Bible, Caesar, the Vikings and the Crusaders, and its many themes include war, trade, science and recreation. Explorers from Columbus to Cook charted lands not previously visited by Western travellers, and were followed by merchants, missionaries, and colonists, who wrote accounts of their experiences. The development of steam power in the nineteenth century provided opportunities for increasing numbers of 'ordinary' people to travel further, more economically, and more safely, and resulted in great enthusiasm for travel writing among the reading public. Works included in this series range from first-hand descriptions of previously unrecorded places, to literary accounts of the strange habits of foreigners, to examples of the burgeoning numbers of guidebooks produced to satisfy the needs of a new kind of traveller - the tourist.

Notes upon Russia

The publications of the Hakluyt Society (founded in 1846) made available edited (and sometimes translated) early accounts of exploration. The first series, which ran from 1847 to 1899, consists of 100 books containing published or previously unpublished works by authors from Christopher Columbus to Sir Francis Drake, and covering voyages to the New World, to China and Japan, to Russia and to Africa and India. This volume, first published in 1852, contains an English translation of the second part of the account by Sigismund von Herberstein (1486–1566) of his visits to Russia in 1517 and 1526 as Ambassador of the Holy Roman Emperor. He published his 'Rerum Moscoviticarum Commentarii' in Latin in 1549, and it is the earliest detailed Western description of the land and people of Russia. Here Herberstein describes the geography and history of the country, with more fascinating details about the people and their customs. The book also includes an index to both volumes.

Cambridge University Press has long been a pioneer in the reissuing of out-of-print titles from its own backlist, producing digital reprints of books that are still sought after by scholars and students but could not be reprinted economically using traditional technology. The Cambridge Library Collection extends this activity to a wider range of books which are still of importance to researchers and professionals, either for the source material they contain, or as landmarks in the history of their academic discipline.

Drawing from the world-renowned collections in the Cambridge University Library, and guided by the advice of experts in each subject area, Cambridge University Press is using state-of-the-art scanning machines in its own Printing House to capture the content of each book selected for inclusion. The files are processed to give a consistently clear, crisp image, and the books finished to the high quality standard for which the Press is recognised around the world. The latest print-on-demand technology ensures that the books will remain available indefinitely, and that orders for single or multiple copies can quickly be supplied.

The Cambridge Library Collection will bring back to life books of enduring scholarly value (including out-of-copyright works originally issued by other publishers) across a wide range of disciplines in the humanities and social sciences and in science and technology.

WORKS ISSUED BY

The Hakluyt Society.

NOTES UPON RUSSIA.

VOL. II.

M.DCCC.LII.

THE GRAND PRINCE VASILEY IVANOVICH.
From Herberstein's Rerum Moscoviticarum Commentarii.

NOTES UPON RUSSIA:

BEING A TRANSLATION OF THE

Earliest Account of that Country,

ENTITLED

RERUM MOSCOVITICARUM COMMENTARII,

BY THE BARON

SIGISMUND VON HERBERSTEIN,

AMBASSADOR FROM THE COURT OF GERMANY TO THE GRAND
PRINCE VASILEY IVANOVICH, IN THE YEARS
1517 AND 1526.

TRANSLATED AND EDITED,

With Notes and an Introduction,

BY

R. H. MAJOR,

OF THE BRITISH MUSEUM.

VOL. II.

" — if thou list to know the Russes well,
To Sigismundus booke repayre, who all the trueth can tell."
Turbervile, 1568.

LONDON:
PRINTED FOR THE HAKLUYT SOCIETY.
M.DCCC.LII.

THE HAKLUYT SOCIETY.

SIR RODERICK IMPEY MURCHISON, G.C.St.S., F.R.S., Corr. Mem. Inst. Fr., Hon. Mem. Imp. Acad. Sc. St. Petersburg, &c., &c., PRESIDENT.

THE EARL OF ELLESMERE. } VICE-PRESIDENTS.
CAPT. C. R. DRINKWATER BETHUNE, R.N., C.B.

JOHN BARROW, ESQ.
REAR-ADMIRAL SIR FRANCIS BEAUFORT, K.C.B.
CHARLES T. BEKE, ESQ., Phil. D., F.S.A.
THE LORD ALFRED S. CHURCHILL.
WILLIAM DESBOROUGH COOLEY, ESQ.
BOLTON CORNEY, ESQ., M.R.S.L.
THE RIGHT REV. LORD BISHOP OF ST. DAVID'S.
THE VISCOUNT EASTNOR.
SIR HENRY ELLIS, K.H., F.R.S.
RICHARD FORD, ESQ.
JOHN FORSTER, ESQ.
R. W. GREY, ESQ., M.P.
JOHN WINTER JONES, ESQ.
SIR CHARLES LEMON, BART., M.P.
P. LEVESQUE, ESQ.
SIR GEORGE T. STAUNTON, BART., M.P.
HENRY D. WOLFF, ESQ.

R. H. MAJOR, ESQ., F.R.G.S., HONORARY SECRETARY.

ADVERTISEMENT.

SINCE the publication of the first volume of the present work, the Editor has been kindly favoured by the Prince Alexis Lobanoff Rostovski, of Berlin, with the following four points of additional information (respectively marked I, II, III, IV) touching the bibliography of those writers who preceded the date of Herberstein's first embassy to Russia in 1517.

I. The existence of a traveller in Russia, previously unknown to the Editor, named

GUILLEBERT DE LANNOY,

whose family derived its origin from the small town of Lannoy, in Flanders.

Guillebert de Lannoy was born about 1386, and seems to have early adopted the career of arms. In 1413-14, he made a journey through Prussia, Russia, Lithuania, and Poland; and in 1421, being dispatched to the east on various commissions, principally from Henry V. of England, passed through Poland, on his way to Egypt and Syria. He left an account of these and his other travels, which was first published by the "Societé des Bibliophiles de Mons", in No. 10 of their publications, with the title—

Voyages et Ambassades de Messire Guillebert de Lannoy, chevalier de la toison d'or. Seigneur de Santes, etc., etc. 1399-1450. Mons, 1840 (or rather 1842);

under the editorial care of Mr. C. P. Serrure, from a manuscript in his library.

For our information respecting this edition, and the incorrectness in its date, we are indebted to an edition, by the learned Joachim Lelewel, of those portions of De Lannoy's work in which he relates his travels in Prussia, Russia, Lithuania, and Poland. It is entitled—

Guillebert de Lannoy et ses Voyages en 1413, 1414, et 1421. Commentés en Français et en Polonais par Joachim Lelewel, Bruxelles et Posen, 8vo.

To the preface of this work we would also refer the curious reader for observations on the manuscript originals, which it would be tedious for us to dwell upon in this advertisement.

II. Two editions of Æneas Sylvius' work, on Prussia and Livonia. The first, entitled—

Enee Silvii episcopi Senensis de situ et origine Pruthenorum—De Livonia ejusque ortu et situ, etc. Sine anno et loco; but, according to Brunet, Cologne, about 1470.

The second edition referred to by the Prince, occurs in the "Æneæ Silvii opera Geographica et Historica". Helmstadii, 1699, 4to., pp. 272-83.

ADVERTISEMENT. iii

III. An edition of Marco Polo, published at Venice in 1847, entitled—

I Viaggi di Marco Polo Veneziano tradotti per la prima volta dall' originale francese di Rusticiano di Pisa e corredati d' illustrazioni e di documenti da Vincenzo Lazari. Venezia, 1847, 8vo.

The Editor's attention was also kindly directed to this publication by the Vicomte de Santarem, and by Dr. Henderson, a member of the Hakluyt Society. The latter gentleman in his letter states, that " it appeared towards the close of the scientific meeting, which was held at Venice in the autumn of 1847, and which was commemorated by a medal in honour of Marco Polo, and by the erection of his bust in one of the galleries of the Ducal Palace."

IV. An edition of Herberstein, in the first volume of " Historiæ Ruthenicæ Scriptores exteri sæculi xvi. Collegit et ad veterum editionum fidem edidit Adalb. de Starczewski." Berolini et Petropoli, 1841-42, 2 vols., 8vo., without note or comment.

The curious and interesting documents appended to this work have been selected, not only as matter supplementary and akin to the Commentarii, but because the originals of them appeared in the interval between the period of Herberstein's first journey to Russia, and the publication of his great work in 1549; while the longest and most important, viz., that by Paulus Jovius, is given as an appendix to most of the early Latin editions. They were first published collectively in Ramusio's " Navigationi et

Viaggi", and afterwards "gathered in parte and done into Englyshe by Richarde Eden", as he himself expresses it, in his "History of Travayle in the West and East Indies, etc." The first edition of Eden was in 1555, but for the convenience of the reader, on account of the improvement in the language and spelling, the present reprint is given from the edition of 1577.

MOSCOVIA QVATE
DITVR, ARX VOCATVR EX
rum ædium num

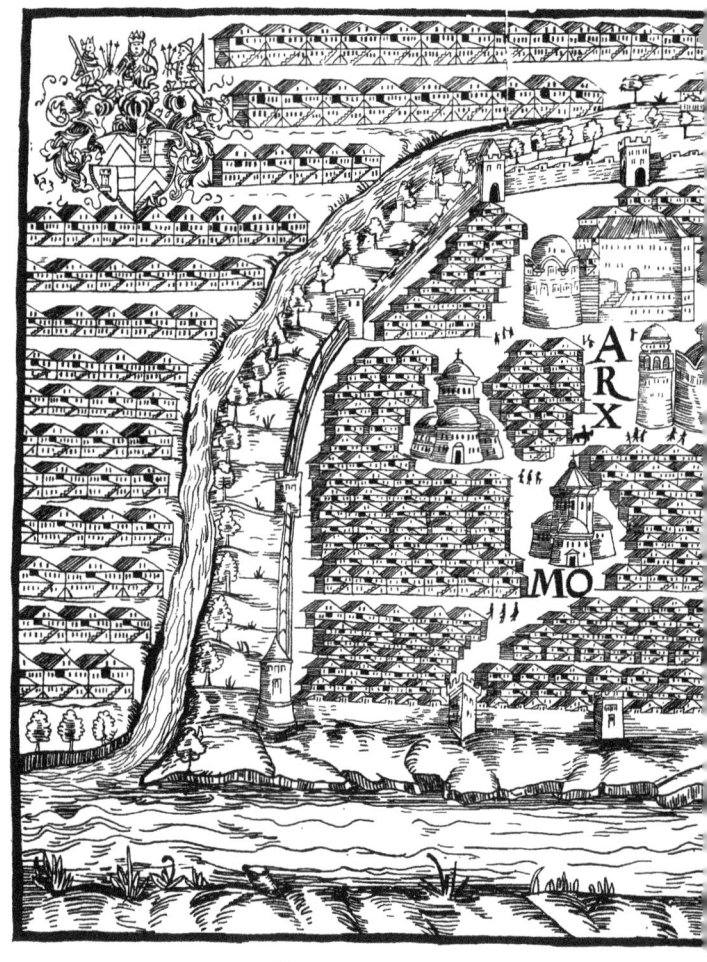

HOC FLVVIO EIVSDEM
OCCAM, RHA, ET

VS MOENIBVS INCLV
RA MOENIA INGENS LIGNEA-
us, ciuitas dicitur.

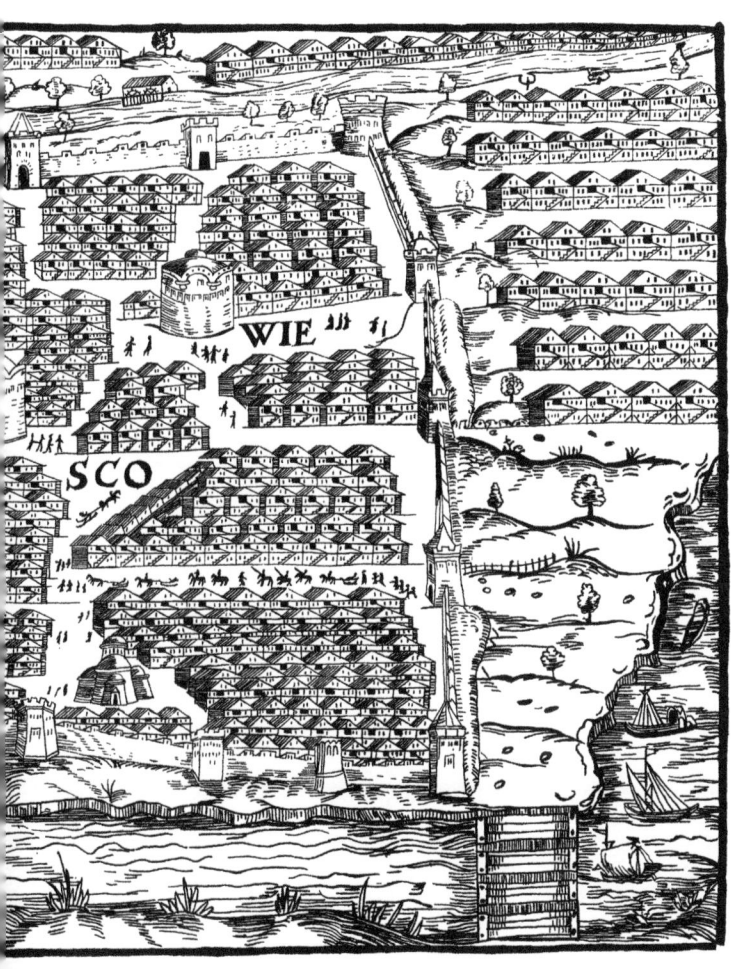

NOMINIS NAVIGATVR IN
CASPIVM MARE.

NOTES UPON RUSSIA.

I shall now undertake the "Chorography" of the prin-
CIPALITY AND LORDSHIP OF THE GRAND DUKE OF MUSCOVY, TAKING
MOSCOW, THE PRINCIPAL CITY, AS THE STARTING POINT; AND PRO-
CEEDING THENCE, I SHALL DESCRIBE THE SURROUNDING AND MORE
FAMOUS PRINCIPALITIES ONLY, FOR IN SO GREAT AN EXPANSE I HAVE
NOT BEEN ABLE TO TRACE EXACTLY THE NAMES OF ALL THE PRO-
VINCES. THE READER MUST, THEREFORE, CONTENT HIMSELF WITH
THE NAMES OF THE CITIES, RIVERS, MOUNTAINS, AND SOME OF THE
MORE REMARKABLE PLACES.

THE city of Moscow then, the capital and metropolis of Russia, together with the province itself, and the river which flows by it, have but one and the same name, and in the vernacular language of the people are called Mosqwa. Which of the three gave its name to the other two is uncertain; but it is likely that the name was derived from the river. For although the city itself was not formerly the capital of the nation, yet it is evident that the name of Muscovites was not unknown to the ancients. The river Mosqwa, moreover, has its source in the province of Tver, nearly seventy wersts above Mosaisko (a werst is nearly the length of an Italian mile), not far from a place called Oleskno, and measuring thence a distance of ninety wersts, flows down to the city of Moscow, and having received some streams into itself, flows eastward into the river Occa. It begins, however, to be navigable six miles above Mosaisko, at which place materials for building houses and other purposes are placed on rafts and brought down to Moscow. Below the city the merchandize, etc., imported by foreigners, is brought up in ships. The navigation is, however, slow and difficult, on account of the numerous turnings and windings with which the river is indented, especially between Moscow and the city of Columna, situated on the bank of the river about three miles from its mouth, where, by its many long windings, it increases the length of the passage by two hundred and seventy wersts. The river is not very abundant in fish, for indeed, with the exception of mean and common sorts, it has none at all. The province of Moscow also is not over extensive or fertile, for the sandy soil which covers it and which kills the corn with the least excess of dryness or moisture, is a very great obstacle to fertility. To this must be added the immoderate and excessive inclemency of the atmosphere, for as the severity of the winter overpowers the heat of the sun, the seed which is sown cannot in some places reach maturity. For the cold is sometimes so intense there, that in the same manner as with us in summer time the earth splits into clefts with too much heat, so with them it does so from the extreme cold, and water thrown into the air, or saliva spit from the mouth, freezes before it reaches the ground. We ourselves, when we arrived there in the year 1526, saw some boughs of fruit-bearing trees that had entirely perished with the rigour of the preceding winter, which had been so severe that year, that many couriers (whom they call gonecz) were found frozen in their carriages. There were some men driving cattle tied together with ropes from the neighbouring districts to Moscow, who, overpowered by the excessive cold, perished together with the cattle. Several itinerants also, who were accustomed to wander about the country with bears taught to dance, were found dead in the roads. The bears also, stimulated by hunger, left the woods and ran about hither and thither through the neighbouring villages and rushed into the houses, while the rustic multitude, terrified at their aspect and strength, fled and perished miserably out of doors with the cold. This excess of cold is sometimes equalled by the too great heat, as in A.D. 1525, when nearly everything that had been sown was burnt up by the immoderate heat of the sun; and such a want of provision followed that drought, that what could previously be bought for three dengs, would afterwards cost twenty or thirty. A great many districts, and woods, and corn-fields, were seen burnt up by the excessive heat. The smoke of this so filled the country, that the eyes of those who walked out were severely injured by it; and besides the smoke, a certain darkness supervened, which blinded many.

It is evident from the trunks of large trees which still exist, that the whole country was not long since very woody; but although the husbandmen give care and labour to the cultivation of trees, all except such as grow in the fields are brought hither from the neighbouring provinces. There is abundance of corn and common vegetables, but none of the sweeter kinds of cherries or nuts (except filberts) are found in the whole country. They have indeed the fruits of other trees, but they are insipid. They cultivate melons with particular care and industry. They put earth mixed with manure into beds of a good depth, and set the seed in them, by which plan it is equally protected against immoderate cold or heat; for if the heat should happen to be too great, they prevent it from suffocating the seed by making little spiral chinks in the earth, which has been thus mixed with manure, while in excessively cold weather the warmth of the manure itself affords protection to the buried seed.

There is no honey in the province of Moscow, nor is there any game, except hares. Their cattle are much smaller than ours, but not without horns, as a certain person has written,[1] for I have seen there oxen, cows, goats, and rams, all horned. The city of Moscow has a very eastward position among the

[1] This assertion is made by Miechow (*Tract.* ii, lib. 2).

other cities of the north, which we easily perceived in our journey thither; for when we left Vienna, we proceeded direct to Cracow, and thence travelled nearly a hundred German miles northward; at length the road turning eastward, we reached Moscow, situated, if not in Asia, at any rate on the very extreme confines of Europe, where it joins Asia, of which circumstance I shall say more hereafter in my description of the Don.

The city itself is built of wood, and tolerably large, and at a distance appears larger than it really is, for the gardens and spacious court-yards in every house make a great addition to the size of the city, which is again greatly increased by the houses of smiths and other artificers who employ fires. These houses extend in a long row at the end of the city, interspersed with fields and meadows. Moreover, not far from the city, are some small houses, and the other side of the river some villas, where, a few years ago, the Prince Vasiley built a new city for his courtiers, called Nali (which in their language means "pour in"), because other Russians were forbidden to drink mead and beer, except on a few days in the year, and the privilege of drinking was granted by the prince to these alone; and for this reason they separated themselves from intercourse with the rest of the inhabitants to prevent their being corrupted by their mode of living. Not far from the city are some monasteries, which alone appear like a great city to persons looking from a distance. Moreover, in consequence of the great extent of the city, it is confined by no settled boundary, nor has it any useful defences in the shape of walls, fosses, or ramparts. The streets are, however, blocked up in some places by beams thrown across them, and are guarded by watchmen placed there at early nightfall, so that no one is allowed access by that way after a stated hour; and any who are taken after that by the watchmen are either beaten, stripped, or thrown into prison, unless they happen to be persons of distinction or respectability : and even these are generally accompanied home by the watchmen. Such watches are generally set wherever there is an open entrance into the city, for the Mosqwa flows by one side of the city, and the river Jausa, which flows into it under the city itself, has such steep banks, that it scarcely admits of being forded. In this latter river many mills have been erected for the public use of the city, which seems to be mainly defended by these rivers; with the exception of a few stone houses, churches, and monasteries, it is entirely a city of wood. The number of houses which it is said to contain is scarcely credible. For they say, that six years before my arrival at Moscow, the houses were counted by an order of the prince, and that the number exceeded 41,500. This city is so broad and spacious, and so very dirty, that bridges have been constructed here and there in the highways and streets and in the other more distinguished parts. There is a fortress in it built of burnt tiles, which on one side is washed by the Mosqwa and on the other by the River Neglima [Neglinaia]. The Neglima flows from certain marshes, but is so blocked up before the city around the upper part of the fortress, that it comes out like stagnant water, and running down thence, it fills the moats of the fortress, in which are some mills, and at length, as I have said, is joined by the Mosqwa under the fortress itself. The fortress is so large, that it not only contains the very extensive and magnificently built stone palace of the prince, but the metropolitan bishop, the brothers of the prince, the peers, and a great many others, have spacious houses of wood within it. Besides these, it contains many churches, so that from its size it might itself almost be taken for a city. This fortress was at first surrounded only by oaks, and up to the time of the Grand Duke Ivan Danielovich was small and mean in appearance. It was he, who, by the persuasion of Peter the metropolitan, first transferred the imperial residence to this place. Peter had originally selected that place from love of one Alexius, who was buried there, and who is said to have been famous for miracles; and after his death, being buried in this place, miracles were likewise done at his tomb, so that the place itself acquired such a celebrity, from a certain notion of its sacredness and religious character, that all the princes who succeeded Ivan thought that the seat of empire ought to be held there. For on the death of Ivan, his son of the same name retained his seat there; and after him, Dimitry; and after Dimitry, that Vasiley, who married the daughter of Withold, and left behind him Vasiley the Blind. Of him was born Ivan, the father of that prince, at whose court I was ambassador, and who first surrounded the fortress with a wall; and his descendants, nearly thirty years after, have brought the work to completion. The ramparts and battlements of this fortress, as well as the prince's palace, were built of brick, in the Italian style, by Italians, whom the prince had sent for from Italy with the offer of large remuneration. There are also, as I have said, many churches in it, nearly all of wood, except the two handsomest, which are built of brick. One of these is consecrated to the Blessed Virgin, the other to St. Michael. In the church of the Blessed Virgin are buried the bodies of the two archbishops who were the cause of the prince's transferring thither the seat of empire and the metropolis; and principally on that account they have been enrolled among the number of the saints. The other church is used as a burial-place for the princes. There were also many churches, being built of stone, at the time that I was there.

The climate of the country is so wholesome, that, from the sources of the Don, especially northwards, and a great way towards the east, no plague has raged there in the memory of man. They sometimes, however, have a disorder of the bowels and head, not unlike the plague, which they call "the heat": those who are seized with it die in a few days.

That disorder was very prevalent when I was at Moscow, and took off one of my servants; but from the people being accustomed to live in so wholesome a climate, if the plague at any time be raging in Novogorod, Smolensko, or Plescow, from fear of contagion they exclude from their own country any people who come thence to them.

The people of Moscow are more cunning and deceitful than all others, their honour being especially slack in business contracts,—of which fact they themselves are by no means ignorant, for whenever they traffick with foreigners, they pretend, in order to attain greater credit, that they are not men of Moscow, but strangers.

The longest day in Moscow in the summer solstice, is said to be seventeen hours and three quarters. I could not, at that time, ascertain from any body the exact elevation of the pole, although one man told me, but upon uncertain authority, that he had heard it was fifty-eight degrees. At length I myself made a venture with the astrolabe, and on the ninth day of June, at noon, observed that the sun was at fifty-eight degrees. From which observation it was deduced, by the reckoning of men skilled in these things, that the elevation of the pole was fifty degrees, and that the longest day was seventeen hours and one quarter.

Moscow having received the first place in this description, I shall proceed to the other provinces subject to the Grand Duke, taking them in order as they lie eastward, whence going round by the south, and west, and north, we shall in due course come down again to the equinoctial east.

First comes the great city, Vladimir, which has a fortification of wood attached to it. This city, from the time of Vladimir, who was afterwards called Vasiley, to the reign of Ivan Danielovich, was the metropolis of Russia. Between the Wolga and the Occa, there are two great rivers, situated thirty-six German miles eastward from Moscow, in a spot so fertile, that from one bushel of wheat often twenty, and sometimes thirty bushels, may be produced. The river Clesma [Kleasma] washes the city; in other respects it is begirt with large extensive woods. The Clesma, moreover, rises four German miles from Moscow, and is alike famous for, and rendered useful by, the numerous mills upon it; it is navigable twelve miles, as far as the town of Murom, situated on the bank of the Occa, into which river it falls. There was formerly a principality, situated amidst vast forests, twenty-four miles due east from Vladimir, inhabited by a people called Muromani, and which abounded in furs, honey, and fish.

Lower Novogorod is a large wood-built city, situated on a rock at the confluence of the Volga and Occa, with a stone fortification, built by the present monarch, Vasiley. They say that it is forty German miles east from Murom; and if so, Novogorod will be a hundred miles from Moscow. The country equals Vladimir in fertility and abundance. It forms the boundary, in this direction, of the Christian religion; for although the Prince of Muscovy has beyond this Novogorod a fortress named Sura, yet the intermediate people, who are called Czeremissi, do not follow the Christian, but the Mahometan religion. Moreover, there are other people, called Mordwa, mixed with the Czeremissi, who occupy a great part of the country this side of the Volga, as far as Sura. The Czeremissi live northwards beyond the Volga, and to make a distinction from them, those that live above Novogorod are called the Upper or Mountain Czeremissi; not, indeed, from any mountains, for there are none, but rather from the hills which they inhabit.

The river Sura divides the dominions of the Prince of Russia and the King of Kazan. Coming from the south, it bends its course eastward twenty-eight miles below Novogorod, and flows into the Volga. At the confluence of the two rivers, Prince Vasiley has built, on the further bank, a fortress, which he has named after himself, Vasilovgorod, which has subsequently become the hotbed of many misfortunes. Not far hence is the river Mosqwa, which also flows from the south, and falls into the Occa above Murom, not far from the town of Cassimovgorod, which the Prince of Moscow has given up as an abode for the Tartars.

The women of the latter people, by a certain art, stain their nails a black colour, for the sake of beauty, and constantly go about with their heads uncovered and their hair dishevelled. Eastward and southward of the river Mosqwa are immense forests inhabited by the Mordwa people, who have a dialect of their own, and are subject to the Prince of Moscow. Some maintain that they are idolaters, while others say that they are Mahometans. They dwell in villages scattered here and there, and cultivate the ground. Their food is game and honey, and they abound in valuable skins; they are especially hardy men, for they have often bravely repulsed those Tartars who rove about in quest of plunder. They are nearly all foot soldiers, remarkable for their long bows, and very skilful in archery.

The province of Rezan is situated between the Occa and the Don, and has in it a wood-built city not far from the bank of the Occa. There was formerly a fortress in it, called Jaroslaw, of which nothing now remains but the ruins. Not far from that city the river Occa forms an island, called Strub, once a large duchy, whose prince was subject to no one. South-east, or as some maintain, north-east[1] of Moscow, stands the city of Columna. After that Rezan, which is thirty-six miles distant from Moscow. This province is more fertile than all the other provinces of Russia, for they say that in it each grain of wheat produces sometimes two or more ears, and the stalks grow so thick that horses cannot

---

[1] Columna is situated, as Herberstein correctly states, south-east of Moscow.

easily pass through it, nor the quails fly out of it. There is a great abundance there of honey, fish, birds, and wild beasts; and the fruits are far superior to the fruits of Moscow. The people are most daring and warlike.

The Don flows out of the province of Moscow up to this fortress, and nearly twenty-four German miles beyond it; it passes near a place called Donco, where the merchants going to Azov, Caffa, and Constantinople, load their ships. This they do generally in autumn in the rainy season, for the Don is not full enough of water at other times of the year to bear laden vessels. The Grand Duke Vasiley, who had married the sister of Ivan Vasileivich, Grand Duke of Moscow, and had by her Ivan and Feodor, once ruled over Rezan. When Vasiley died, his son Ivan succeeded him; and his sons by the daughter of the knes, Feodor Babitz, were Vasiley, Feodor, and Ivan. On the death of their father, the two eldest of these contended for the dominion, and fought a battle on the plains of Rezan. One of them died in this battle; and the victor not long after died on the same plains, where an oaken cross was erected to his memory. The youngest of the three brothers, who still survived, on learning their death, made alliance with the Tartars, and took forcible possession of the principality for which his brothers had contended, and which was hitherto in the possession of his mother. Having done this, he applied to the Duke of Moscow for permission to govern, as his ancestors had done, unchecked by any one in the free tenure and possession of the principality. While he was making this proposal, the Grand Prince heard that he was seeking in marriage the daughter of the king of Taurida, with whom the prince was then at war. Wherefore, when the prince sent for him, he, through fear, hesitated and delayed to go. At length, by the persuasion of Simon Crubin, one of his counsellors, he went to Moscow, where he was seized by the prince's command, and placed under custody, but not in prison (*liberis custodiis*). The prince then deposed his mother, and threw her into a monastery, and took possession of the citadel and the principality; and to prevent any subsequent revolt on the part of the people of Rezan, he dispersed a great portion of them through different colonies, so that the strength of the entire principality was loosened and broken. Moreover, in 1521, when the Tartars pitched their camp before Moscow, Ivan escaped from custody in the tumult, and fled into Lithuania, where he still continued in exile [when I was in Russia?].

The town of Tula is nearly forty German miles distant from Rezan, but thirty-six southward from Moscow; it is the last city one comes to before reaching the desert plain. It contains a stone citadel built by Vasiley Ivanovich. A river of the same name flows by it. Another river, called the Uppa, washes the citadel on the east, and joining the river Tula, flows into the Occa, nearly twenty German miles above Worotinski. Not far from its mouth is the fortress of Ovoyov'. The town of Tula, moreover, had its own prince in the time of Vasiley.

The very famous river Don, which divides Europe from Asia,[1] rises nearly eight miles south and a little by east from Tula,—not in the Riphæan [*i. e.*, Ural] mountains, as some have stated, but in the Ivanovosero, that is, the Great Lake of Ivan, which in length and breadth stretches over about 1,500 versts, and takes its rise in a wood which some call Okonitzkilies, others Jepiphanovlies. From this lake, the two great rivers, the Schat and the Don, take their rise. The Schat flows westward, and after receiving the river Uppa, flows in a north-west direction into the Occa. But the Don in its first course flows due east, and runs between the kingdoms of Kazan and Astrachan, six or seven German miles from the Volga; it then takes a southward course, and forms the

[1] This notion of Herberstein, that the Don separated Europe from Asia, accounts for his elsewhere describing Moscow as situated in Asia.

marshes which have received the name of the Palus Mœotis. The nearest city to its source is Tula; but on the shore nearly three miles above its mouth is the city of Azov, which was originally called Tanas. Four days' journey above this is the town of Achas, situated on the same river (called in Latin, Tanais), which the Russians call the Don. This place is so remarkable for its abundance of excellent fish, and also for its pleasantness,—each side of the river being laid out and cultivated with considerable industry, in the fashion of a garden, with a variety of plants and most delightful roots, and a great number of fruit-bearing trees,—that it is impossible to praise it too highly. There is also such an abundance of game there, which they kill with their arrows without much trouble, that persons travelling through the country want nothing else to support life, except fire and salt for cooking. In these parts they do not reckon by miles, but days' journeys. So far as I could form a conjecture, the Don is nearly eighty German miles from its source to its mouth, going in a straight line. Nearly twenty days' sail from Donco, where, as I said, the Don is first navigable, we come to Azov, a city which is tributary to the Turks; and, according to them, is five days' journey from the Isthmus of Taurica, otherwise called Precop. Here is a famous emporium of many nations, who come thither from different parts of the world; and as free access is permitted to all people of every country, with abundant liberty of buying and selling, so also on going out of the city are all permitted to do what they please with impunity.

As to the altars erected by Alexander and Cæsar, or their ruins, which several writers describe as being in these parts, I have not been able to learn anything for certain, either from the natives, or others, who have very frequently travelled in those places. The soldiers also, whom the prince is accustomed to have there in garrison every year to reconnoitre and repress the excursions of the Tartars, have told me when I have made inquiries upon the subject, that they have neither seen nor heard anything of the sort. They confessed, however, that about the mouth of the Lesser Don, four days' journey from Azov, near the site of Velikiprevos, in the holy mountains, they have seen some statues of marble and stone. The Lesser Don, moreover, rises in the principality of Sewerski, whence the Donetz is called Sewerski, and falls into the Don three days' journey above Azov. Those who travel by land from Moscow to Azov, cross the Don near the old and ruined city of Donco, and turn southwards and a little by east, where, if a straight line be drawn from the mouth of the Don to its source, you will find that Moscow is in Asia, and not in Europe.—[See note, page 11.]

Misceveck is a marshy place, in which there was formerly a fort, the remains of which yet exist. There are still some people who dwell in huts near this place, who in times of danger take refuge among those marshes, or flee into the fortress. Misceveck lies nearly sixty German miles south of Moscow, and nearly thirty from Tula. The river Occa rises nearly eighteen miles to the left of Misceveck. It first flows eastward, then northward, and lastly, towards the summer east (as they themselves call it); and thus the Occa shuts in Misceveck with a figure of nearly a semicircle, and then flows by many towns, namely, Worotin, Cologa, Cirpach, Corsir, Columna, Rezan, Casimovgorod, and Murom, and finally enters the Volga below Lower Novogorod, and is enclosed on both sides with woods, which are extremely abundant in honey. All the lands which it waters are most fertile. The river is very celebrated, especially for its abundance of fish; and its fish is preferred to those of the other rivers of Russia, particularly those which are taken near Murom. It has, moreover, some kinds of fish peculiar to itself, which are called in their language Beluga,—a fish of a wonderful size without fins, with a large head and mouth,—

Sterlet, Schevriga, Osseter,—the three last are a kind of sturgeon,—and Bielaribitza, which is a little white fish of most excellent flavour. It is supposed that the greatest part of these come down thither from the Volga. Moreover, they say, that two other rivers take their rise at the sources of the Occa, namely, the Sem and the Schosna. The Sem flows through the principality of Sewera, and passing by the town of Potivlo, falls into the river Desna, which last river runs through the town of Czernigov, and joins the Dnieper below Kiev. The Schosna, however, makes its way directly into the Don.

Corsira is a town on the banks of the river Occa, six miles above Columna. It formerly had a governor, who held it in his own right; but being reported to Prince Vasiley as one who conspired against his life, he was invited, under a plausible pretext from the prince, to join him in the chase. He armed himself (for some one advised him not to go unarmed), and went to the prince during the hunt. He was not admitted, however; but was ordered to be taken, under the charge of Michael Georgiovich, the prince's secretary, to the neighbouring town of Czerpach, and there to be confined. On his arrival, the prince's secretary desired him, according to the usual custom, to drink to the prince's health. When he found himself thus caught in a snare, which he had no means of escaping, he sent for a priest, drained the cup, and died. By this infamous crime, Vasiley became possessor of the town of Czerpach, which lies eight miles from Corsira, on the banks of the Occa, near which there are iron mines situated in a plain.

Coluga is a town on the river Occa, thirty-six miles from Moscow, and fourteen from Czerpach. They make there cleverly carved cups of wood, and other articles for domestic purposes of the same material, which are exported thence into the various provinces of Russia, as well as into Lithuania, and other surrounding countries. The prince is accustomed to place garrisons every year in this spot, against the incursions of the Tartars.

Worotin is a city and fort, bearing the same name as its principality. It lies three miles above Coluga, not far from the bank of the Occa. The principality was formerly possessed by the Knes Ivan Worotinski, a warlike man, and excelling in various accomplishments, through whose generalship the Prince Vasiley had often won distinguished victories over his enemies. In the year 1521, however, when the King of Taurida crossed the Occa, and, as has been already said, invaded Russia with a large army, the Knes Dimitry Bielski, a young man, was sent with an army by the prince to check and repel him; but he, neglecting the wise counsels of Worotinski and others, disgracefully took to flight at the first sight of the enemy. After the departure of the Tartars, the prince made diligent inquiries respecting the authors of the flight, but acquitted Andrew, the prince's own brother (who really had been the cause of it), and others; while Ivan Worotinski not only fell under the prince's severest displeasure, but was seized and driven out of his principality. He was, it is true, finally discharged from custody, but only on the condition that he should never leave Moscow. I have myself seen him at Moscow among the principal men at the prince's court.

Sewera is a great principality, whose citadel, Novogrodek, not long since was the seat of the Sewerian princes, before they were ejected from the principality by Vasiley. It lies a hundred and fifty German miles due south from Moscow, the road passing through Coluga, Worotin, Serensko, and Branski; and the principality extends as far as the Dnieper. It contains some vast deserts, with fields interspersed here and there; there is, however, a large wood in the neighbourhood of Branski. It contains many forts and towns; the most celebrated of which are Staradub, Potivlo, and Czernigov. The land is fertile wherever it is cultivated.

The woods are extremely abundant in squirrel and martins, and also in honey. The people are very warlike, through their constant engagements with the Tartars. Vasiley Ivanovich, however, reduced this principality, like many others, into subjection to himself, in the following manner: Vasiley had two nephews, sons of his brothers,—one surnamed Semetzitz, who possessed the fortress of Novogrodek, while the other held the city of Staradub. At the same time a certain prince named Dimitry possessed Potivlo. Now Vasiley Semetzitz, who was strong in arms, and a terror to the Tartars, was so strongly infected with the lust of power, that he coveted the whole principality for himself, and could not rest until he had brought Vasiley of Staradub to a most abject condition, and then driving him away, he took possession of his province.

After succeeding in this attempt, he attacked Dimitry in a different manner. He traduced him to the prince as one who was plotting treachery. The prince, indignant at this, ordered Vasiley to seize Dimitry by any contrivance, and to send him forthwith to him to Moscow. Vasiley accordingly contrived to have Dimitry waylaid while hunting; and stationed horsemen at the gates of his town to seize him if he should endeavour to flee thither; and being thus captured, Dimitry was taken to Moscow and thrown into prison. His only son, Dimitry, took this injury so much to heart, that he immediately fled to the Tartars, and with the view of effecting a more speedy and heavy revenge for the wrong done to his father, he abjured the Christian faith, was circumcised, and became a Mahometan. During his stay amongst the Tartars, he chanced to fall violently in love with a very beautiful girl, and as he could not gain possession of her by any other means, he privately carried her off without the consent of her parents. The servants who were circumcised with him, made this known to the girl's relations, and they suddenly attacked him one night, and put both him and the girl to death by a discharge of arrows. When Prince Vasiley heard of the flight of Dimitry's own son to the Tartars, he ordered the father to be placed in still closer confinement, and when the old man shortly after heard of the death of his son in Tartary, he died worn out with grief and imprisonment in that same year, 1519. All this was done through the agency of Vasiley Semetzitz, at whose instigation the prince had previously seized his relative, the lord of Corsira, and slain him in prison. But as it often occurs that they who lay snares for others fall into them themselves, so it happened to this Semetzitz. For he also was accused to the prince of the crime of rebellion, and was summoned on that charge to Moscow, but refused to go thither unless he first received letters of safe conduct, ratified by the oath of the prince and the metropolitan. Upon his receiving these, which were formally made out and sent to him, he went to Moscow on the 19th of April 1523, and was honourably received by the prince, who even offered him presents; but a few days after he was seized and thrown into prison, and was still kept in confinement [at the time that I was there]. They say that the reason of his being imprisoned was, that he had sent letters by the governor of Kiev to the king of Poland, expressing a wish to desert to him; and that the governor, when he became acquainted with his base intention towards his prince, resigned his charge of the letters, and sent them immediately to the prince of Moscow. Others, however, ascribe a more likely reason, viz., that as Semetzitz was the only one in all the empire of the prince of Muscovy who now remained in possession of fortified towns and principalities, the latter, in order the more easily to eject him, and for the greater safety of his own government, invented against him the charge of treason, as a means of removing him. In allusion to this, a certain jester went about carrying brooms in the streets at the time that Semetzitz went into Moscow, and on being asked what he meant by this, answered, that the prince's dominions were not yet cleansed, but that now the fitting time was come for sweeping all garbage out of the empire. Ivan Vasileivich first added this province to his dominions after he had routed the army of Alexander, the grand-duke of Lithuania, at the river Vedrosch.

The princes of Sewera, moreover, derive their race from Dimitry, grand-duke of Muscovy. Dimitry had three sons, Vasiley, Andrew, and George. Of these, Vasiley, as the eldest, succeeded his father in the kingdom; and from the other two, Andrew and George, the princes of Sewera have derived the origin of their race.

Czernigov is thirty miles distant from Kiev, and as much from Potivlo. Potivlo is a hundred and forty German miles distant from Moscow, sixty from Kiev, and thirty-eight from Branski. This latter lies beyond a large wood, twenty-four miles in breadth.

Novogrodeck is eighteen miles from Potivlo, and fourteen from Staradub. Staradub is thirty-two miles from Potivlo.

In going through the desert of Potivlo into Taurida, one meets with the rivers Ina, Samara, and Ariel,—the two last of which are rather broad and deep, and travellers are sometimes detained a long time in crossing them, upon which occasions it will often happen that they are surrounded and captured by the Tartars. Next come the rivers Koinskawoda and Moloscha, the passage across which is effected by a novel kind of ferry boat. They bind together bundles of small wood into faggots, and place themselves and their goods upon them, and thus by paddling and availing themselves of the stream, they are carried to the opposite side. Others fasten faggots of this kind to the tails of horses, which, by a plentiful use of the whip, they force to drag them over to the opposite shore.

Ugra is a deep and muddy river, which rises in a wood not far from Drogobusch, and empties itself into the Occa, between Coluga and Vorotin. This river formerly divided Lithuania from Moscow.

Demetriovich is a fortified town lying eighteen miles south-west from Viesma, and about twenty from Vorotin. Smolensko is an episcopal city situated on the river Dnieper, and on the eastern bank of the river it has a fortress constructed of oak, containing a considerable number of houses like a city. On that side of it which stretches towards the hill (for on the other side it is washed by the Dnieper), it is protected with ditches, and in addition to these, with sharp stakes, which form a barrier against the attacks of the enemy. Vasiley Ivanovich very often attacked this place in the most desperate manner, but never could take it by force. At length he gained possession of it through the treachery of the soldiers, and of a certain Bohemian who was governor, and of whom we have spoken before in the account of Michael Linski. The city lies in a valley, is surrounded on all sides with fertile hills, and is begirt by immense forests, from which is derived a great supply of furs of various kinds. In the citadel there is a church dedicated to the blessed Virgin, and other buildings constructed of wood. In the suburbs there are considerable ruins of monasteries built of stone. In going southwestwards from Moscow towards Smolensko, a journey of eighteen miles will bring you first to Mosaisko; twenty-six miles more to Viesma; eighteen more to Drogobusch; and another eighteen to Smolensko: the whole journey making eighty German miles, although the Lithuanians and Russians reckon it a hundred. I have myself, however, travelled through these places three times, and never found the distance more than eighty miles. While Vasiley reigned over this principality, Vithold, grand-duke of Lithuania, took it from the Russians in the year 1413. Vasiley Ivanovich took it from Sigismund king of Poland, on the 30th of July, in the year 1514.

Drogobusch and Viesma are fortified towns built of wood,

situated on the Dnieper, and were formerly under the sway of the princes of Lithuania. By the town of Viesma runs the river of the same name, which at no great distance, viz., two wersts, falls into the Dnieper, and vessels laden with merchandise are carried down by it to the Dnieper and back again from the Dnieper to Viesma.

Mosaisko also is a fortified wood-built town, in the neighbourhood of which is a great abundance of hares of various colours, and the prince is accustomed to hold an annual hunt there. Sometimes also he receives ambassadors from different princes there, as was the case while we were at Moscow, when he received the Lithuanian ambassadors; and it was to this place also that we were summoned from Moscow to receive our discharge, after having fulfilled the instructions of our respective princes. I may further add that, in the time of Vithold, the boundaries of the dominion of the princes of Muscovy extended to about five or six miles beyond Mosaisko.

Biela is a principality, with a fortified city of the same name, on the river Opscha. It is situated amidst vast forests, more than sixty German miles to the west of Moscow, thirty-six from Smolensko, and thirty from Toropetz. Its rightful princes in former days were the descendants of Gidemin, but in the time of Casimir king of Poland, the sons of Jagellon gained possession of this principality, for at that time Vasiley, otherwise called Bielski, the prince of Biela, deserted to Ivan, Vasiley's father, and surrendered both himself and his property to him. In his removal, he also left his wife behind him in Lithuania, and as we have before said, married another woman in Russia. By the latter he had three sons, whom I saw at the court of the prince; and one of them, named Demetrius, was held in great esteem and honour from respect to his father's rank. These three brothers, however, although they lived upon the paternal inheritance which they received from their father from Biela, and derived their support from the yearly revenues supplied from Biela, dared not go thither, for the prince of Muscovy had deprived them of the lordship of the principality, and usurped the title to himself.

Rsova of Demetrius is a fortified city, lying twenty-three miles due west of Moscow. This fortress, from which the prince usurps to himself a title, is situated on the river Volga, and commands a very extensive domain. There is also another Rsova, called the deserted, a hundred and forty miles from Moscow, twenty from Velikiluki, and as many from Plescov. Beyond Rsova, some miles to the westward, is a wood called Volkonski, from which four rivers take their rise. In this wood is a marsh, named Fronov, out of which flows a river of no great size, and after a course of about two miles, falls into a lake, named Volgo. From this lake it again emerges, increased by a multitude of streams, and is called Volga from the name of the lake. After passing through many marshes, and receiving into itself many rivers, it empties itself by five-and-twenty, or, as some say, seventy mouths into the Caspian sea (called by the Russians Chvalensko Morie), and not into the ocean, as a certain author has written.[1]

The Volga is called Esk by the Tartars, and Rha by Ptolemy, and is so near to the Don that it is said they are only seven miles apart from each other. We shall speak in the proper place of the cities and towns by which it passes. In the same wood, about ten miles from the marsh of Fronov, is the village of Dnyepersko, near which rises the Borysthenes, called by the natives the Dneiper, but which we here call Borysthenes. Not far from that place is the monastery of the Holy Trinity, where rises another river smaller than the former, called Niepretz, a name given to it by way of a diminutive. Both these rivers, however, meet between the source of the Borysthenes and the marsh of Fronov, and

[1] Miechov, *Tractatus de duabus Sarmatiis.*

the merchandise of the Russians is shipped at this place and carried into Lithuania, and the merchants usually put up at the monastery or at the inn.

I have, moreover, discovered that the Rha and the Borysthenes do not rise from the same source as some think. This I have learned from others, especially from the positive statement of several merchants who have trafficked in those parts. The course of the Borysthenes is as follows:—first, it flows southward past Viesma, then bending eastward, it passes by the towns of Drogobusch, Smolensko, Orscham, and Mohilev; then again turning southward, it passes by Kiev, Circassia, and Otzakov, and finally, falls into the ocean at a point where the sea seems to take the form of a lake; and Otzakov is, as it were, on a corner at the mouth of the Borysthenes. Our own route lay from Orscham to Smolensko, and we brought our baggage by ship as far as Viesma, where there was so great an inundation, that a monk conveyed Count Nugaroli and me a great distance through the woods in a fishing boat, and the horses accomplished the greater part of their journey by swimming.

The lake Dwina is nearly ten miles distant from the sources of the Borysthenes, and as many from the marsh of Fronov. Westward out of it there flows a river of the same name, at a distance of twenty miles from Vilna. It afterwards turns northwards, and falls into the German Ocean (called by the Russians, Vareczkoie Morie), near Riga, the capital of Livonia. It washes Vitepsko, Polotzko, and Dunenburg; but does not flow through Plescov, as a certain author has said. The Livonians call this river, which is for the most part navigable, Duna.

Lovat, the fourth river, is not at all to be compared with the other three. It rises either between the lake of Dwina and the marsh of Fronov, or out of the marsh itself, for I could not completely explore its source, although it is not far from the source of the Borysthenes. This is the river to which, according to their records, the Apostle St. Andrew brought a little boat by dry land from the Dnieper. It has a course of nearly forty miles, flows by Velikiluki, and falls into the lake Ilmen.

Volock is a fortified city twenty-four miles due west from Moscow, nearly twelve from Mosaisko, and twenty from Tver. The prince usurps to himself the title to this place, and usually amuses himself here every year with the sport of hunting hares with falcons.

Velikiluki is a fortified city a hundred and forty miles west of Moscow, nearly sixty from Great Novogorod, and thirty-six from Polvezko. It is on the road from Moscow into Lithuania.

Toropecz is a fortified city between Velikiluki and Smolensko, on the borders of Lithuania. It is nearly eighteen miles distant from Luki.

Tver, or Otwer, formerly a most extensive domain, and still one of the great principalities of Russia, is situated on the river Volga, thirty-six miles south-west from Moscow. It has a great city, through which the Volga flows, with a fortress on that bank from which Tver looks towards Moscow; while at the opposite point the river Tvertza falls into the Volga. It was by this river that I came into Tver by water, and on another day sailed up the Rha [or Volga].

This city, moreover, was the seat of a bishopric in the lifetime of Ivan, the father of Vasiley, and at that time the Grand Duke Boris ruled over the principality of Tver. Ivan Vasileivich, prince of Muscovy, married his daughter Mary, and had by her his first-born son, Ivan, as has been related above. When Boris died, his son Michael succeeded him, but was afterwards driven from the principality by his sister's husband, the Grand Duke of Muscovy, and died in exile in Lithuania.

Tersack is a town ten miles from Tver. One half of it used to be under the government of Novogorod, the other under that of Tver, and was thus under the command of two lieutenant-governors. Two of the rivers already mentioned take their rise there, namely, the Tvertza and the Sna,—the latter flows westward to Novogorod, the former takes an eastward course.

Great Novogardia is the most extensive principality in all Russia. It is called in the language of the country, Novogorod, meaning new city or new fortress. For whatever is surrounded with a wall, defended with oak stakes, or in any way enclosed, they call *gorod*. The city of Novogorod is large, and traversed by the navigable river Volchov, which rises out of the lake Ilmen scarcely two versts above the city, and falls into the lake Neva, which they call Ladoga, from the town in its neighbourhood. Novogorod is a hundred and twenty miles south-west from Moscow, though some reckon it only a hundred; thirty-six from Plescov; forty from Velikiluki; and as many from Ivanovgorod. But in former times, when this city was flourishing and under its own jurisdiction, it possessed a very extensive domain, which was divided into five parts. Each of these divisions not only referred all matters of public or private importance to the ordinary competent magistrate of its own district, but could transact business or conveniently traffic with other of the citizens only in its own municipal boundary; nor was any one allowed to summon another in any matter before any other magistrate of the same city. It was at that time the greatest commercial town in all Russia, for an immense crowd of merchants resorted thither on all sides from Lithuania, Poland, Sweden, Denmark, and Germany itself; and the citizens increased their riches and their stores from this repeated concourse of many nations. Indeed, at the present day, the Germans are allowed to have their own treasurers or registrars. Its dominion extends for the most part eastward and northward; it used nearly to reach to Livonia, Finland, and Norway. The merchants of that place earnestly begged me, after I had travelled thither from Augsburg in one and the same carriage, to leave them the vehicle in which I had accomplished so great a journey, that they might place it in their church, as a perpetual memento of the occurrence. Novogorod had also the principalities of Dwina and Vologda on the east, and on the south the town of Tersack, not far from Tver. And although these provinces, from being filled with rivers and marshes, are unproductive, and cannot conveniently be inhabited, nevertheless, the princes who used to rule over these districts would make great profit of the furs, honey, wax, and fish, with which this country abounded. The princes not only themselves constituted by their own will and pleasure the authority which they held, but increased it by subduing the neighbouring nations upon any pretext, and compelling them to pay tribute in their own defence, as if such tribute were levied upon some fairly constituted principle.

From this sort of connexion with nations, whose assistance the people of Novogorod have been obliged to use in preserving their republic, it has arisen that the Russians boast that they maintain their own governors in that country; while the Lithuanians, on their part, acknowledge that they are tributary to them.

At the time that the archbishop himself was directing the affairs of this principality, with his counsel and authority, Ivan Vasileivich, duke of Muscovy, invaded it, and oppressed it seven long years with a disastrous war. At length, in the month of November, A.D. 1477, he overcame the Novogradians in a battle on the river Scholona, and compelled them to surrender on certain conditions, and appointed a governor over the city in his own name. But thinking that he did not yet hold absolute sway over them, and finding that he could not obtain it without arms, he went to Novogorod under the religious pretext that the people wished to forsake the Russian ritual, and that he would bind them to its observance; and under this pretence he took possession of the city, and reduced it to submission. He despoiled the archbishop, the citizens, merchants, and foreigners, of all their goods, and carried away three hundred carriages, laden, according to some accounts, with gold, silver, and jewels, to Moscow. Indeed, I myself made diligent inquiries at Moscow about this business, and heard that a far greater number of carriages were taken away laden with booty. And no wonder, for after the city was taken, he took the archbishop and all the richest and most powerful men with him to Moscow, and sent his own subjects as new colonists into their estates. Consequently, out of their possessions he derived annually an immense revenue into his treasury beyond the ordinary returns. Out of the proceeds of the archbishopric he only granted a small portion of the returns to a certain bishop then appointed by himself, and at his death the episcopal see was for a long time vacant. At length, in consequence of the urgent request of the citizens and of his subjects, that they might not always be without a bishop, he instituted one again at the time that we were there.

The people of Novogorod formerly offered their chief worship and adoration to a certain idol named Perun, which was placed on the spot where now stands the monastery named Perunski, after the same idol. When subsequently they received baptism, they removed it from its place, and threw it into the river Volchov; and the story goes, that it swam against the stream, and that near the bridge a voice was heard, saying, "This for you, O inhabitants of Novogorod, in memory of me"; and at the same time a certain rope was thrown upon the bridge. Even now it happens from time to time on certain days of the year, that this voice of Perun may be heard, and on these occasions the citizens suddenly run together and lash each other with ropes, and such a tumult arises therefrom, that all the efforts of the governor can scarcely assuage it.

It is also related in their annals, that when the people of

Novogorod were besieging Corsun, a city of Greece, with a grievous siege of seven years' duration, their wives becoming weary of their solitary life, and being also doubtful of the safety or return of their husbands, married their slaves. At length the city was taken, and the victorious husbands returned from the war, bringing with them the bronze gates of the conquered city, as well as a great bell, which we ourselves saw in their cathedral church. The slaves endeavoured to repel by force the masters whose wives they had married. Their masters, in great indignation, at the suggestion of some one, laid down their arms, and took thongs and ropes in their hands, as the proper mode of dealing with slaves, at which the latter became terrified, and fled. They betook themselves to a place still called Chloppigrod,—*i. e.*, the Slaves' Fortress,—and defended it. They were conquered, however, and received the merited punishment from their masters.

The longest day in the summer solstice at Novogorod is eighteen hours and more. The climate is much colder even than that of Moscow. The people used to be very courteous and honourable; but now, doubtless from the Russian contagion introduced by the people who emigrated thither from Moscow, they are become most degraded.

The lake Ilmen, which in ancient Russian documents is named Almer, and which others call Limidis, lies two wersts above Novogorod. It is twelve German miles long and eight broad, and receives, besides others, two rather famous rivers, the Louat and the Scholona, which latter rises in another lake. Another river takes its rise in lake Ilmen, viz., the Volchov, which flows through Novogorod, and after a course of six-and-thirty miles enters lake Lodoga. It is sixty miles broad and nearly a hundred long, interspersed with some islands. It discharges the large river Neva, which flows westward nearly six miles into the German sea. At its mouth lies Oreschak, called by the Germans

Nuremburg, situated in the middle of the river. It is under the dominion of the Muscovite.[1]

Russ, formerly called Ancient Russia, is an ancient little town under the government of Novogorod, from which it is twelve miles distant, and thirteen from lake Ilmen. It has an artificial river, which the townspeople have formed, in a large ditch like a lake, and from it each man has water brought down by channels to his own house, and prepares salt.

Ivanovogorod is a fort built of stone, on the bank of the river Nerva, by Ivan Vasilievich, from whom it took its name. Opposite to it, on the other bank, is a fort of the Livonians, named Nerva, from the said river. The river Nerva flows between these two forts, and divides the domain of the people of Novogorod from that of the Livonians. The river Nerva, moreover, which is navigable, rises in that lake which is called by the Russians Czutzko or Czudin, by the Latins Bicis or Pelas, and by the Germans Peiifues. After receiving two rivers into itself, namely, the Plescov and the Velikareca, which comes from the south, it passes by the town of Opotzka, leaving Plescov on the right. The navigation from Plescov to the Baltic would be easy, were it not obstructed by some rocks which lie near Ivanovogorod and Nerva.

The city of Plescow is situated on the lake from which the river of the same name emerges. This river flows through the middle of the city, and after a course of six miles falls into the lake which the Russians call Czutzko. Plescov is the only city in all the Muscovite's dominions which is surrounded by a wall. It is divided into four parts, each of which is surrounded with its own walls. This has led some into the error of saying that it was surrounded with a quadruple wall. The domain or principality of this city is called,

---

[1] Oreschak, or Orekhov, was the ancient name for Schlusselburg, situated at the point where the Neva flows out of lake Ladoga.

in the language of the people, Pskov or Obskov. It was formerly very extensive, and had its own jurisdiction; but in the year 1509, Ivan Vasileivich took possession of it through the treachery of some priests, and reduced it to servitude. He also took away the bell, by the ringing of which the senate used to be summoned to the parliament of the republic; and by dispersing the citizens through the colonies, and sending Muscovites into their place, he utterly abolished their liberty. Hence it followed, that in place of the more refined and, consequently, more kindly manners of the people of Plescov, were introduced those of the Muscovites, which are more debased in almost everything. For there was always so much integrity, candour, and simplicity in the dealings of the Plescovians, that they dispensed with all superfluity of words, for the purpose of entrapping a buyer, and briefly stated the case exactly as it stood. I would here mention by the way, that the Plescovians still wear their hair parted in the middle,—not in the Russian, but in the Polish fashion. Plescov lies thirty-six miles westward from Novogorod, forty from Ivanovogorod, and as many from Velikiluki. You must pass through this city in going from Moscow and Novogorod to Riga, the metropolis of Livonia, which is sixty miles distant from Plescow.

The country of Votska lies twenty-six, or, at the most, thirty miles north-west of Novogorod, leaving the fort of Ivanovogorod on the left. In this country it is related as a miracle, that all animals, of whatever kind, that are brought into it, change their colour to white. This place seems to demand that I should make a slight allusion to the places and rivers near the sea, as far as the borders of Sweden. The river Neva, as I have already said, divides Livonia from the Russian's dominions, from which, if leaving Ivanovogorod you go along the seashore northward, you come to the river Plussa, at whose mouth lies the fortress of Iamma. Twelve miles from Ivanovogorod, and as many from Iamma, which are four miles from each other, is the fort of Coporoia and a river of the same name. Thence to the river Neva and the fort Oreschak are six miles. From Oreschak to the river Corela, whence the city takes its name, seven miles. Twelve miles thence you come at last to the river Polna, which divides the territory of the Russian from Finland, which country is called by the Russians, Chaniska-Semla, and is under the dominion of the kings of Sweden.

There is another Carela besides that already named. It is a province which has its own territory and dialect, and lies sixty miles more or less north of Novogorod. Although it demands tribute from some of the neighbouring nations, it is nevertheless itself tributary to the king of Sweden, and also to the Muscovite, by reason of the dominion of Novogorod.

The island of Solovki lies to the northward in the sea, eight miles from the continent, between the Dwina and the province of Carela. Its distance from Moscow has not been ascertained, on account of the frequent marshes, woods, and vast deserts, which intervene. Some, however, state it to be three hundred miles from Moscow, and two hundred from Bieloiesero. There is abundance of salt prepared in this island. There is a monastery there, into which it is considered a great crime for any woman married or unmarried to enter. There is also a great fishery, of a sort of fish called by the native *selgi*, which we think are herrings. They say that in the summer solstice the sun shines here constantly, with the exception of two hours in the twenty-four.

Dimitriov is a fortified city twelve miles a little northward of west from Moscow. George, the grand-duke's brother, at that time possessed it. It is watered by the river Jachroma, which flows into the river Sest. The Sest receives also the Dubna, and empties itself into the Volga. This convenience of river navigation is the cause of the great wealth of the merchants of the country, who are thus enabled, without much trouble, to convey their merchandize from the Caspian by the Volga into different parts, and bring it up even as far as Moscow.

Bieloiesero is a fortified city, situated on a lake of the same name. The Russian word Bieloiesero, means "White Lake". The city, by the way, does not stand in the lake itself, as some have said, but is surrounded on all sides with marshes, so that it seems to be impregnable. For this reason, the princes of Russia are accustomed to store up their treasures there. Bieloiesero is a hundred miles north of Moscow, and the same distance from Great Novogorod. Indeed, there are two roads from Moscow to Bieloiesero; one, the nearest, by Uglitz, for the winter time; the other by Jaroslav, for the summer. Both of these roads, however, on account of the frequent marshes and woods, intersected with streams, are difficult to travel by, unless by making bridges of ice to pass over,—so that from the obstacles presented by these places the miles are reckoned shorter. In addition to this difficulty of travelling, this frequent occurrence of marshes, woods, and interlacing streams, causes the country to be uncultivated, and to have no cities built in it. The lake itself is twelve miles long, and as many broad; and it is said that three hundred and sixty rivers empty themselves into it. Only one, the Schocksna, emerges from it, and falls into the Volga fifteen miles above Jaroslav, and four below Mologa. The fishes which pass from the Volga into this river and lake, improve; nay, the longer they remain in it, the finer they become. The fishermen have such skill in recognizing them, that when they catch fish that have returned from this river into the Volga, they can tell how long they had been in it. The inhabitants of this place have a dialect of their own, although now nearly all of them speak Russian. Their longest day in the summer solstice is said to be nineteen hours. I was told by a person of no small reputation, that he had made a rapid journey from Moscow to Bieloiesero in the spring, when the trees were budding, and that after he had crossed the river Volga, he performed all the rest of his journey in carriages, for everything was covered with snow and ice. And although the winter is longer there, yet the fruits ripen, and are gathered at the same time as in Moscow. At an arrow-shot from the lake of Bieloiesero is another lake, producing sulphur; and a river which rises out of it, carries the sulphur down with it in abundance, like foam on its surface. Through the ignorance of the people, however, there is no use made of it.

The fortified city of Uglitz stands on the shore of the Volga, and is twenty-four miles distant from Moscow, thirty from Jaroslav, and forty from Tver. The citadel is on the south bank of the Volga, while the city stands on both sides.

Chloppigrod,[1] the place to which I have said before that the slaves of Novogorod fled, is two miles distant from Uglitz. Not far from it is seen a fort, now in ruins, on the Mologa. This river has a course of eighty miles after leaving the territory of Great Novogorod, and falls into the Volga. At its mouth is a fortified city of the same name;

[1] This town no longer exists, and its very site is a matter of antiquarian inquiry; and although Herberstein describes it as having been so important in his time, that the largest fair in all Russia used to be held in it, the very fact of its existence would but for him—as far as we can learn—have been lost to history.

It is true that Zedler, in the fifth volume of his *Grosses Universal Lexicon*, which was published in 1733, when Chloppigorod no longer existed, speaks of it as "a Russian town in the principality of Rosdow, on the Volga, between Novogorod, Veliki, and Rosthow. It is populous, carries on a good trade, and is celebrated for its fairs for all kinds of commodities." The authority is not given, but there is a strong reason to suppose that the account was unsuspectingly taken from Herberstein himself.

A dissertation was written on the subject by Count Alexei Mussin Puschkin (Moscow, 1810, 4to.), in which he adduces arguments to show that such a town had really existed, and not far from the position described by Herberstein, but somewhat more westerly, namely, where the village of Starij Cholopije now stands.

and two miles from thence, on the bank of the same river, stands the church only of Chloppigrod. The fairs (which I have elsewhere alluded to) are more frequent in that place than in the whole Russian dominions; for the Tartars, and many other nations from the east and north, resort thither to barter with the Swedes, Livonians, and Russians. There is scarcely any use made of gold or silver amongst these nations; but they exchange ready-made dresses, needles, knives, spoons, hatchets, and other such things, mostly for skins.

Pereaslav is a fortified city twenty-four miles somewhat eastward of due north from Moscow. It stands on a lake, in which, as at the island of Solovki, those little fish, the selgi, are taken, of which I spoke above. The land is tolerably fertile and productive; and, after harvest, the prince is accustomed to amuse himself there with hunting. There is in the same country a lake from which salt is obtained by evaporation. Those who go from Castroma, Jaroslav, and Uglitz, to Little Novogorod, pass through this city. It is impossible to make any calculation of the roads in these parts, on account of the great number of marshes and woods. There is there also a river called Nerel, which rises from a certain lake, and falls into the Volga above Uglitz.

Rostov is a fortified city and an archiepiscopal see. After Great Novogorod, it is held with Bieloiesero and Murom amongst the principal and most ancient of the principalities of Russia. The road thither from Moscow is direct through Pereaslav, from which it is ten miles distant. It stands on the lake, which gives rise to the Cotoroa, a river which, after passing by Jaroslav, falls into the Volga. The nature of the soil is fertile, and the country is particularly abundant in fish and salt. This territory used to belong to the second sons of the grand-dukes of Russia; but their posterity have very recently been thrust out and banished by Ivan, the father of Vasiley.

Jaroslav is a fortified city on the bank of the Volga, twelve miles from Rostov, on the direct road from Moscow. The country is tolerably fertile, especially in the parts near the Volga. Like Rostov, it belonged to the second sons of the princes, but was forcibly taken by the same monarch; and although there still remain dukes of the province called *knesi*, yet the prince usurps the title to himself, the country being granted to the knesi as to subjects. The country is held by three knesi, however, descended from the second-born princes, whom the Russians call Jaroslavski. The first is Vasiley, who conducted me to and fro from my dwelling to the prince. The second is Simeon Federovitz, named Kurbski, from Kurba, his inheritance. He is an old man, and very reduced in body, from the remarkable abstinence and severity of life which he has adopted since the time that old age began to come upon him. For many years he has abstained from eating meat. He only eats fish on Sunday, Tuesday, and Saturday; but on Monday, Wednesday, and Friday, at fast time, he abstains from these. The grand-duke used sometimes to send him with an army through Permia into Jugaria to the great emperor, to subdue distant nations; and he has accomplished a great part of the journey on foot on account of the quantity of snow; and when the snow was melted, after crossing the mountain of Petchora, performed the remainder in boats. The last is Ivan, surnamed Possetzen, who, in the name of his prince, went as ambassador to the Emperor Charles in Spain, and returned with us. He was so poor, that (as we know for a certainty) he borrowed clothes and a kolpack (which is a head-dress) of somebody else to travel in. He must have been greatly mistaken, therefore, who wrote to the effect, that this man could in any necessity send thirty thousand horse soldiers to his prince out of his own territory or inheritance.[1]

[1] In the Russian chronicles, where allusion is made to this prince, he appears to have been described under the name of Ivan Ivanovich,

The province, city, and fortress of Vologda, in which the bishops of Permia hold their see, though without jurisdiction, took their name from a river of the same name. The city stands north-west of Moscow in a line from Jaroslav. It is fifty German miles from Jaroslav, and nearly forty from Bieloiesero. The whole country is marshy and woody, so that travellers can take no exact account of the road, on account of the numerous marshes and windings of the rivers. The further you go, the more marshes, rivers, and woods, you encounter. The river Vologda flows northward by the city, and eight miles below the city is joined by the river Suchana, which rises from a lake named Koinski. It then takes the name of Suchana, and flows north-west. The province of Vologda was formerly under the jurisdiction of Great Novogorod, where they say the prince used to lay up a great part of his treasure, as from the nature of the place it was a strong fortification. In the year in which we were at Moscow, there was so great a scarcity of provision, that one bushel of the corn, which they use, was sold for fourteen dengs, which otherwise used to be sold in Moscow for four, five, or six, dengs.

The Vaga is a river well stocked with fish. It rises between Bieloiesero and Vologda, amidst marshes and the densest forests, and flows into the river Dwina. The people who live by the river exist by hunting, for they have scarcely any bread. Black and ash-coloured foxes are caught there. It is, moreover, but a short journey thence to the province and river of Dwina.

more properly Feodorovich Jaroslavski Sassekin, or Zassekin. The surname, Possetzen, stands in the original for the word Posadnik, which means the governor of a district. The writer here alluded to is Johann Fabri, to whose book reference is made at page 120 of the introduction to the present work, as being recommended to Herberstein and his companions as an indispensable guide in making the observations required of them in their journey. The prince Zassekin was one of the ambassadors alluded to on the same page as being joined by Herberstein on their return to Moscow by way of Vienna.

The province of Ustyug took its name from a fortified city situated on the river Suchana. It is a hundred miles from Vologda, and a hundred and forty from Bieloiesero. It was formerly situated on the mouth of the river Jug, which flows from south to north. Afterwards, on account of the convenience of the locality, it was removed nearly a mile above the river's mouth, but still retains its old name. For in Russian Usteie is a mouth; whence Ustyug is the mouth of the Jug. This province used to be subject to Great Novogorod. Little or no bread is used there; their food consisting of fish or game. They have salt from the Dwina. They have their own dialect, but more frequently speak Russian. There are not many sable skins there, nor are they very excellent. They abound, however, in the skins of other beasts, especially black foxes.

The province and river of Dwina took their name from the confluence of the rivers Jug and Suchana; for Dwina signifies two or double in Russian. After a course of a hundred miles, this river falls into the Northern Ocean, where it washes Sweden and Norway, and divides them from the unknown country of Engroneland. This province lies in the very north, and was formerly under the jurisdiction of the people of Novogorod. It is reckoned to be three hundred miles from Moscow to the mouth of the Dwina; although, as I have before said, in the countries beyond the Volga, no calculation can be made of the roads, on account of the numerous marshes, rivers, and vast woods. We are inclined, however, to reckon it, from conjecture, as scarcely two hundred miles; since from Moscow to Vologda, and from Vologda to Ustyug, one goes somewhat in an easterly direction; but from Ustyug by the Dwina due north. There are no towns or forts in this province, except the fort of Colmogor and the city of Dwina, which stands nearly midway between the source and the mouth of the river, and the fort of Pienega, which stands at the very mouth of the Dwina. It is said to contain many villages, however, which lie wide apart, on account of the barrenness of the soil. The people earn their livelihood by fish, game, and the skins of beasts, which are abundant of all kinds. In the maritime parts of this country they say that white bears are found, and those for the most part living in the sea; their skins are often brought to Moscow. I brought back two with me from my first embassy to Moscow. This country abounds in salt.

Journey to Petchora Jugaria, as far as the River Obi.

The territory of the Prince of Muscovy extends far to the east, and somewhat to the north, as far as the following places. A paper written in Russian upon this subject, containing the plan of this journey, was presented to me, which I have translated, and have here purposely subjoined; although those who go thither from Moscow would take a more frequented and a shorter road, by Ustyug and the Dwina, through Permia. The distance from Moscow to Vologda is reckoned at five hundred versts; from Vologda to Ustyug, along the right bank of the river, descending the Suchana, which joins it, is five hundred versts, which rivers are joined by the river Jug near the town of Streltze, two versts below Ustyug; this river comes from the south, and is computed to be more than five hundred versts in length from its source to its mouth. These two rivers, the Suchana and Jug, below their junction lose their former names, and take that of the Dwina; five hundred versts along the Dwina, bring us to Colmogor, at six days' journey below which the Dwina falls into the ocean by six mouths. The greatest part of this journey is made by water, for the land route from Vologda to Colmogor, crossing the Vaga, is equal to a thousand versts. Not far from Colmogor, the river Pienega, which flows from the east on one's right hand, falls into the Dwina, after a course of seven hundred versts. At a distance of two hundred versts from the Dwina, in travelling along the river Pienega, we come to a place called Nicolai, whence by a sail of half a verst, vessels are brought into the river Kulvio. This river takes its rise from a lake of the same name in the north, and is six days' journey in length from its source to its mouth, where it falls into the ocean. In sailing then along the right bank of the sea, we pass the following territories, namely, Stanwische, Calunczscho, and Apnu. Having sailed round the promontories of Chorogoskinosz, Stanwische, Gamenckh, and Tolstickh, we at length reach the river Mezen, along which, in six days' journey, we come to a village of the same name, situated at the mouth of the river Piesza, ascending which towards the south-east, after three weeks' journey, we arrive at the river Piescoya. After the ships have then traversed five versts through two lakes, two courses lie open to us; one of which, to the left, leads by the river Rubicho into the river Czircho; some take the other course, which is shorter, and runs direct from the lake into the Czircho, by which course in favourable weather a passage may be made in three weeks to the river and mouths of the Czilme, the great river of Petchora, which at that place is two versts in breadth. Sailing downwards thence, we come in six days' journey to the town and fortress of Pustoosero, near which the Petchora falls by six mouths into the ocean. The inhabitants of this place, who are very simple-minded, did not receive baptism till the year of our Lord 1518. From the mouths of the Czilme through Petchora, to the mouths of the river Ussa, is one month's journey. The Ussa takes its rise in the mountain of Poyas Semnoi, which lies on the left in the direction of the southeast: the river flows out of a huge rock of that mountain called Kamen Bolschoi. The distance from the sources of the

Ussa to its mouth is reckoned at more than a thousand versts. The Petchora flows from south to north; and the ascent of this river from the mouths of the Ussa to those of the river Stzuchogora, is a journey of three weeks. They who compiled this itinerary, said that they halted between the mouths of the Stzuchogora and the Potzscheriema, and deposited the provisions they had brought with them from Russia in the neighbouring fortress of Strupili, which is situated to the right in the mountains on the Russian shore. Beyond the rivers Petchora and Stzuchogora, as far as the mountain Camenipoias, reaching to the sea and its neighbouring islands, and the fortress of Pustoosero, are various innumerable races, who are called by the one common name of Samoged, which implies, "men who eat one another". In this country there is a great abundance of birds, and different kinds of animals, such as sables, martins, beavers, ermins, squirrels, and in the ocean the morse, of which I have spoken above, and also vess;[1] there are likewise white bears, wolves, hares, the equus woduanus,[2] and a fish named semfi,[3] with a great variety of others. These races do not come to Moscow, for they are savage, and avoid communion with other people, and civilized society. From the mouths of the Stzuchogora up to Poiassa, Artavische, Cameni, and the greater Poiassa, is a journey of three weeks. The ascent up the mountain of Camen occupies three days; after descending which, we come to the river Artavishche, then to the river Sibut, and afterwards to the fortress of Lepin on the river Sossa. The dwellers on this river are called Vogolici. Leaving the Sossa on the right, we come to the river Oby, which rises in the lake Kitaisko; the crossing this river occupies nearly a whole day, even with a rapid passage, for its breadth is so vast as

[1] It is difficult to conjecture what fish or mammal is here alluded to.
[2] Perhaps the equus hemionus, or dziggetai.
[3] Query, the schuyp, or acipenser schypa of Guedenstadt, a species of sturgeon.

to extend to nearly eight versts. The Vogolici and Ugritzschi dwell upon the banks of this river. In ascending the river Oby, it is three months' journey from the fortress of Obea to the river Irtische, where the Sossa falls into it. In these parts are the two fortresses of Jerom and Tumen, governed by the Knesi Juhorski, who are said to be dependants of the Grand Duke of Muscovy. There are many animals there, and a great variety of furs.

From the mouths of the river Irtische to the fortress of Grustina is a journey of two months, and thence to the lake of Kitai by the river Oby, which, as I have said, has its sources in that lake, is more than three months' journey. From this lake come many black men who speak one common language, and who bring with them a variety of merchandize, which they barter with the Grustintzi and Serponiotzi: these latter people derive their name from the fortress of Serponov Lucomoryae, situated in the mountains beyond the river Oby. It is said that a certain marvellous and incredible occurrence, and very like a fable, happens every year to the people of Lucomoryae, namely, that they die on the 27th of November, which among the Russians is dedicated to St. George, and come to life again like the frogs in the following spring, generally on the 24th of April. These people hold a novel and otherwise unusual kind of intercourse with the Grustintzi and Serpovtzi; for when their stated period for dying or sleeping is approaching, they deposit their merchandize in a certain spot, which is taken away in the interim by the Grustintzi and Serpovtzi, who leave their own merchandize in exchange; but when the former come to life again, they require their own property to be given back if they find it has been taken at an unfair valuation, and hence occasion arises for many conflicts and quarrels among them. In descending the river Oby on the left, we come to the Calami nation, who migrated thither from the Obiosa and Pogosa. Below the Oby up to the

Golden Old Woman, which is situated at the confluence of the Oby with the ocean, are the rivers Sossa, Berezva, and Danadim, all of which have their rise in the mountain of Camen, Bolschega, Poiassa, and the neighbouring rocks. All the races which dwell between these rivers and the Golden Old Woman, are said to be tributary to the Prince of Russia.

Slata Baba, that is, the Golden Old Woman, is an idol situated on the mouths of the Oby on its further bank, in the province of Obdora. There are many fortresses scattered here and there along the banks of the Oby, and about the neighbouring rivers, the lords of which are all said to be subject to the Prince of Moscow. The story, or I should more correctly call it the fable, runs, that this idol of the Golden Old Woman is a statue, representing an old woman holding her son in her lap, and that recently another infant has been seen, which is said to be her grandson; they also say that she has placed certain instruments upon the spot, which constantly give forth a sound like that of trumpets. If this be the case, I think that it must arise from the vehement and constant blowing of the wind through those instruments.

The Cossin is a river which flows down from the mountains of Lucomorya; at its mouth is the fortress of Cossin, which was formerly possessed by the Knes Ventza, but now by his sons: from the sources of the great river Cossin to this point is a journey of two months. Moreover, from the sources of the same river, rises another river Cassima, which, after passing through the district of Lucomorya, flows into the great river Tachnin; beyond which are said to dwell men of prodigious stature, some of whom are covered all over with hair, like wild beasts, while others have heads like dogs, and others have no necks, their breast occupying the place of a head, while they have long hands, but no feet. There is also in the river Tachnin a certain fish, with a head, eyes, nose, mouth, hands, feet, and in other respects almost entirely resembling a man, but without voice, which, like other fish, affords excellent food.

Hitherto, whatever I have related, has been literally translated by me from a Russian itinerary, which has been placed at my service; and although in my narrative some things may appear to be fabulous and scarcely credible,—such as men being dumb, dying and coming to life again, the Golden Old Woman, men of monstrous shape, and fishes having the appearance of men,—yet I myself, in spite of diligent investigation respecting them, have not been able to get certain information from any one who has seen them with his own eyes, although by universal report they are held to be true; at the same time, in order to afford others a more ample opportunity of investigating these matters, I have been reluctant to omit anything, and have therefore quoted the very names of the places just as they are called by the Russians.

Noss is the Russian name for nose; hence this name is given to headlands protruding like a nose into the sea. The mountains near the river Petchora are called Semnoi Poyas, which signifies the girdle of the world or of the earth; for *poyas* in Russian signifies a girdle. The lake Kithai gives its name to the great Khan of Chathaia, whom the Russians call the Czar of Kythai. *Chan* amongst the Tartars signifies king.

The districts of Lucomorya, which lie on the sea-coast, are covered with wood, and the inhabitants do not dwell in houses. But although the author of the itinerary described most of the nations of Lucomorya as subject to the Prince of Moscovy; yet as the kingdom of Tumen is near to it, and the prince of that country is a Tartar, and is called in their native language the Tumenski czar, which means king in Tumen, and has not very long ago done great injury to the Prince of Moscovy, it is very probable from the vicinity that these nations are in reality subject to the latter prince.

On the river Petchora, of which mention has been made in the itinerary, is situated the city and fortress of Papin, or Papinovgorod; its inhabitants are called Papini. Beyond this river are some very lofty mountains stretching down to its banks, whose summits, from their continual exposure to the winds, are almost entirely destitute of grass or any other vegetation. Although these mountains are differently named in different places, they are commonly called the "Girdle of the Earth". In these mountains, the birds called gyr falcons make their nests, of which I shall speak below, when I come to the description of the prince's hunting. Cedar trees also grow there, in the neighbourhood of which are found very black sables. In the dominions of the Prince of Moscow there are no mountains seen but those which probably were regarded by the ancients as the Rhiphæan or Hyperborean mountains;[1] and as from the severity of the perpetual snow and ice they are very difficult to pass, they are supposed to constitute the unknown province of Engroneland. Vasiley Ivanovich, grand-duke of Muscovy, at one time sent two of his governors, named Simeon Feodorovich Kurbski (so called from his paternal estate, but sprung from the race of Jaroslav), and the Knes Peter Uschatoi, through Permia and Petchora, to explore the districts and subdue the nations beyond these mountains. Kurbski was still alive at the time that I was at Moscow, and told me, when I inquired about this expedition, that it took him seventeen days to ascend the mountain, and that after all he could not pass the summit, which, in the language of the country is called Stolp, meaning a column. This mountain extends to the ocean, as far as the mouths of the rivers Dwina and Petchora.

And let this suffice for the itinerary.

[1] The Oural mountains.

I now return to the Principalities of Moscow.

The principality of Susdal, with the fortress and city of the same name, which is an episcopal see, is situated between Rostov' and Vladimir. At the time that the imperial court was held at Vladimir, this was considered one of the chief principalities, and formed the metropolis of the neighbouring cities. At a later period, when the grand-duke's dominions had increased, and the seat of the court was removed to Moscow, the principality of Susdal became the *apanage* of the second sons of the princes; but their descendants were at length driven therefrom by Ivan Vasileivich. Two of these, namely, Vasiley Schinski and his brother's son, were still alive at the time I was at Moscow. In the city of Susdal is a famous convent of nuns, in which Solomea was shut up after her repudiation by Vasiley.

Amongst all the principalities and provinces of the Prince of Muscovy, Rezan claims the first place for richness of soil, and abundance of all kinds; next to it in fertility come Jaroslav, Rostov, Pereaslav, Susdal, and Vladimir.

Castromovgorod, which is a city with a fortress, is situated on the banks of the Volga, nearly twenty miles south-east of Jaroslav, and about forty from Lower Novogorod; the river from which the city takes its name, flows into the Volga at that point.

Galitz, another principality with a city and fortress, lies on the road from Moscow eastward in journeying by Castromovgorod.

The province of Viatka lies beyond the river Kama, at a distance of nearly a hundred and fifty miles south-east of Moscow; the shortest road to which is by Castromovgorod and Galitz; but this road is the most difficult, not only on account of the marshes and forests which lie between Galitz and Viatka, but on account of the tribes of Czeremisse, which rove about in search of plunder. Hence the road by Vologda and Ustyug, though longer, presents greater facilities and security for travelling. Viatka is one hundred and twenty miles distant from Ustyug, and sixty from Kazan. The district derives its name from a river, on whose banks are situated Klinova, Orlov, and Solovoda. Orlov lies four miles below Klinova. Six miles lower down to the west lies Solovoda. Cotelnitz is eight miles from Klinova on the river Rhecitza, which flows from the east between Klinova and Orlov, and empties itself into the Viatka. The region is marshy and barren, and forms a sort of asylum for fugitive serfs; it abounds in honey, wild beasts, squirrels, and fish. It was formerly under the dominion of the Tartars; and, indeed, up to the present day, the Tartars hold rule over the country on both sides of the Viatka, especially about its mouths, where it falls into the Kama. Journeys in that country are reckoned by *czunckhas*. The czunckha is equal to five versts. The river Kama empties itself into the Volga twelve miles below Kazan. The province of Siberia is watered by this river.

Permia is a large and extensive province lying at a distance of two hundred and fifty, or, according to some, three hundred miles directly north-east of Moscow. It has a city of the same name on the river Vischora, which ten miles below it flows into the Kama. It is scarcely possible to travel thither by land, except in winter, on account of the numerous marshes and rivers; but in summer, the journey thither is made with tolerable facility in boats by the Vologda, the Ustyug, and the river Vitzechda, which flows into the Dwina twelve miles from Ustyug. Those who travel from Permia to Ustyug must go in boats up the Vischora, and after making the passage of several rivers, have to transport their boats to other rivers, and so at length come down to Ustyug, at a distance of three hundred miles from Permia.

Bread is very seldom used in that province; and they pay their yearly tribute to the prince in horses and furs. They have an idiom of their own; they have also characters peculiar to themselves, which were invented by one Stephen, a bishop, who had been the means of confirming them in the faith of Christ, at a time when they were vacillating in the matter of religion: indeed, at a former period, while they were yet infants in the faith, they flayed a certain bishop who had made a similar attempt. This Stephen was afterwards enrolled amongst the number of the gods by the Russians, in the reign of Dimitry Ivanovich. There still remain many idolaters amongst them, scattered here and there in the woods, whom the monks and hermits who wander into those parts strive unceasingly to reclaim from their error and profitless worship. In winter they travel here, as in most parts of Russia, almost entirely in *artach*, which are a sort of oblong wooden shoes, nearly six palms in length, which they fasten on the foot, and perform their journeys with great speed. They use for beasts of burden large dogs, which are very useful for this purpose, with which they convey baggage in carriages, in the same manner as will be hereafter described in speaking of the deer. They say that that province borders eastward upon the Tartar province called Tumen.

The situation of the province Jugaria is shown by what has been already said. The Russians pronounce the word Juhra with an aspirate, and call the people Juhrici; this is Juharia, whence the Hungarians proceeded when they took possession of Pannonia, and subdued many provinces of Europe under their leader Attila. The Muscovites are very boastful of this name, because their subjects formerly devastated great part of Europe. George, called the Little, who was a Greek by birth, wishing, in the treatises which he wrote at the time of my first embassy, to extend the sway of his prince over the grand duchy of Lithuania, the kingdom of Poland, etc., described the Juhari as having been subjects of the Grand Duke of Muscovy, and as having located themselves on the Palus Mæotis [the Sea of Azov], but that they then wandered to Pannonia on the Danube, and thence derived the name of Hungary. He further stated, that Moravia was so named from a river which waters it; and that Poland took its name from *polle*, which signifies a plain; and that Buda derived its name from a brother of Attila. For my own part, I have at least desired to give the account as I have received it. They say that the Juhari up to the present time use the same dialect as the Hungarians, but whether this be true, I cannot say from my own knowledge; for though I have made diligent search, I have been unable to find any man of that country with whom my servant, who is skilled in the Hungarian language, might have an opportunity of conversing. These people pay a tribute to the prince in furs; and although pearls and gems are brought thence into Muscovy, they are not collected upon that coast, but are principally brought from the shores of the ocean near the mouths of the Dwina.

The province of Siberia borders upon Permia and Viatka; but I have been unable to learn whether it contains any cities or fortresses. In this province rises the river Jaick, which empties itself into the Caspian Sea. They say that this region lies waste on account of the neighbourhood of the Tartars; or, if it is cultivated in any part, it is where the country has been taken possession of by the Tartar Schichmamai. The natives use a dialect of their own. They trade principally in squirrel skins, which surpass in size and beauty those of other provinces; but we have not been able to see any great plenty of them in Moscow.

The people of Czeremissi dwell in the woods below Lower Novogorod. They have their own dialect, and follow the tenets of Mahomet. They are now subservient to the King of Kazan, although the greatest part of them were formerly tributaries of the Duke of Muscovy, whence they are still reckoned as Russian subjects. The prince had several of these people brought to Moscow on suspicion of rebellion, whom I saw when I was there; but as they were afterwards sent back to the borders towards Lithuania, they at length dispersed themselves into various parts. These people, who have no fixed abodes, inhabit a region stretching far and wide, from Viatka and Vologda as far as the river Kama. All of them, both men and women, are exceedingly swift in running, and very skilful archers, never laying down the bow out of their hands; and so great is the delight which they take in this exercise, that they will not give their children food until they hit a mark with their arrows.

Two miles from Lower Novogorod is a settlement of several houses, having the appearance of a municipal town, where salt used to be prepared. These houses were burnt some time since by the Tartars, but afterwards restored by order of the prince.

The Mordva are a people situated on the southern shore of the Volga below Lower Novogorod; they resemble the Czeremissi in all things, except that they are more frequently found dwelling in houses. And here let us terminate our digression as well as our description of the Muscovite empire.

I shall now subjoin some details respecting the neighbouring and surrounding nations, observing the order in which they came under my notice in travelling from Moscow eastwards. In this arrangement, the Tartars of Kazan come first; of whom, before I proceed to their peculiar characteristics, it is necessary that I should first make some general observations.

Of the Tartars.

Concerning the Tartars and their origin: besides what is contained in the annals of the Poles, and in the little books upon the two Sarmatias, much has been written by various authors, which it would be more tedious than useful to repeat here. I have, however, thought it right briefly to write down such things as I have learned from the Russian annals, and from the accounts given me by a great number of persons. They say that the Moabites, who were afterwards called Tartars, and who differed from the rest of mankind in language, manners, and dress, came to the river Calka; but that no one knew whence they came, or what religious doctrine they held. Although they were called by some Taurimeni, by others they were known as Pieczenigi, and by others under another name. Methodius, bishop of Patanczki,[1] says that they wandered out of the deserts of Ieutriskie, lying between the north and east, and gives the following as the reason of their emigration. He says, that a certain man of the highest rank amongst them, named Gideon, filled them with terror, by saying that the end of the world was at hand; and that they being led away by his preaching, and anticipating the destruction of the boundless wealth of the globe, made expeditions with an innumerable multitude to plunder the surrounding provinces, and cruelly ransacked the whole territory westward as far as the Euphrates and the Persian Gulf; and thus, after ravaging the provinces which lay in their way, routed at the river Calka, A.M. 6533 [A.D. 1025], the nations of the Polovtzi, who alone, with the assistance of the Russian

[1] Misspelt for Patarski, *i. e.*, of Patara. The substance of this passage appears to be taken from the ancient chronicler, known as the chronicler of Novogorod, but involves an evident anachronism, as Methodius the celebrated opponent of Origen, who died A.D. 311, could not have recorded the battle of Calka.

forces, dared to arrest their progress. On this subject, it is evident that the author of the little book, *De Duabus Sarmatiis*, was in error in speaking of the people of the Polovtzi, when he interpreted their name as meaning hunters; for *Polovtzi* means men of the plain; *poli* signifying a plain— *lovatz* and *lovtzi* both signifying hunters, the termination *tzi* and *ksi* not changing the signification, which does not depend upon the last, but upon the first syllables. But as it is a general custom with the Russians to add the generic syllable *ski* to this kind of words, the man has been deceived by this circumstance, so that Polovtzi ought to be interpreted "men of the plain", and not hunters. The Russians maintain that the Polovtzi were Goths, but I do not agree with that opinion. He who attempts to describe the Tartars will have to describe many races; for they derive this name from one sect alone, while they consist of various nations lying wide apart from each other. And now I return to the task I proposed to myself.

Bathi, proceeding with a strong force northwards, took possession of Bulgaria, which lies on the Volga below Kazan. In the following year, A.M. 6745 [A.D. 1237], following up his victory, he advanced into Muscovy and took the royal city, which surrendered to him after a siege which lasted a considerable time. He afterwards, however, broke his faith with respect to the terms upon which this surrender had been made; and proceeding onwards, carrying slaughter wherever he went, he desolated the neighbouring provinces of Vladimir, Pereaslav, Rostov, and Susdal—comprising many towns and fortresses—with fire, slaughtering the inhabitants or reducing them to servitude. He routed and slew the Grand Duke George, who had come out to meet him with a trained army; he also took Vasiley Constantinovitch prisoner, and put him to death: all which took place in the above-mentioned year 6745.

From that time nearly all the princes of Russia were inaugurated by the Tartars, and paid allegiance to them, until the time of Withold, Grand Duke of Lithuania, who valiantly defended his own provinces and those which he had taken possession of in Russia against the arms of the Tartars, and was a terror to all around him. The Grand Dukes of Vladimir and Muscovy, after they had once yielded allegiance and submission to the Tartar princes, continued therein up to the time of the present Duke Vasiley. The annals say that this Bathi was killed in Hungary by Vlaslav, king of the Hungarians (who on his baptism was named Vladislaus, and was enrolled amongst the number of the saints); for he had carried off the king's sister, whom he had accidentally met with during the spoiling of the kingdom, and the king, moved by love for his sister, and by the indignity of the deed, pursued him; but when he made his attack upon Bathi, his sister took up arms in the cause of the adulterer, against her brother, which so enraged the king that he slew his sister together with the adulterous Bathi. These things were done A.M. 6745 [A.D. 1237].

Bathi was succeeded in the empire by Asbec, who died A.M. 6834 [A.D. 1326], and was succeeded by his son Zanabeck, who, after slaying his brother in order that he might reign alone without apprehension, died in the year 6865 [A.D. 1357]. He was followed by Berdebeck, who after in like manner killing his twelve brothers, died in 6867 [A.D. 1359]. After him came Alculpa, who did not reign more than a month; for immediately after assuming the reins of government he was slain, together with his children, by a certain prince named Naruss. As the latter now became the possessor of the kingdom, all the princes of Russia came together to him, and did not depart till each of them had obtained the power of ruling independently in his own province. Naruss was slain in the year 6868 [A.D. 1360]. He was succeeded in the kingdom by Chidir, who was slain by his son Themerhoscha, who, gaining the kingdom by a crime, scarcely enjoyed it for a week; for being driven out by Temnick Manais, and fleeing beyond the Volga, he was slain by the soldiers who pursued him, in the year 6869 [A.D. 1361]. After these Thachamisch obtained the empire, A.M. 6890 [A.D. 1382], and going forth on the 26th of ·August with an army, he laid waste Muscovy with fire and sword. Being routed by Themirkutlu, he fled to Withold, Grand Duke of Lithuania. Themirkutlu reigned over the kingdom of Savai, A.M. 6906 [A.D. 1398], and died 6909 [A.D. 1401]. His son Schatibeck succeeded him in the empire, after whom came Themirassack, who led an immense army into Retzan with a view of depopulating Russia, and inspired such terror into the princes of Muscovy, that, despairing of victory, they threw down their arms and betook themselves to the protection of the saints. They immediately sent to Vladimir for a certain image of the blessed Virgin Mary, which was celebrated for having performed many miracles; and as this image was being brought into Moscow the prince went out to meet it with all the multitude, to give it an honourable reception; and first most humbly imploring it to repel the enemy, he brought it into the city with the greatest respect and veneration: and they say that by this act of worship they obtained grace from the Virgin, so that the Tartars did not advance beyond Retzan. And for a perpetual memorial of this event, a temple was erected on the spot where the image was waited for and received; and that day, which is called by the Russians *stretimue*, that is the day of meeting, is solemnly celebrated every year on the 26th of August. These things took place in the year A.M. 6903 [A.D. 1395].

The Russians relate that this Themirassack was of obscure birth, and rose to this high degree of dignity by plunder; they say also that he was an extremely clever thief in his youth, and that it was by one of these exploits that he derived his appellation; for having once stolen a sheep, and being caught by the owner, he received a violent blow from a stone which broke his leg, and as he bound it up with a piece of iron, the name he afterwards bore was given to him from the iron and from the lameness, for "Themir" signifies iron, and "Assack", lame. At the time that the people of Constantinople were sorely besieged by the Turks, he sent his son thither with auxiliary forces, who, after routing the Turks and forcing them to raise the seige, returned victoriously to his father in the year 6909 [A.D. 1401].

The Tartars are divided into hordes, amongst which the horde of Savolha stands first in numbers and in fame; for all the other hordes are said to have derived their origin from it. The word "horde" among them signifies a concourse or multitude. But although each horde has its peculiar name, such as the horde of Savolha, Precop, Nahaisa, and many others, and all are of the Mahometan religion, yet they are highly offended if they are called Turks, and consider it a reproach, but delight in being called Besermani, a name which the Turks also are pleased to be called by. But as the regions inhabited by the Tartars are scattered far and wide in various directions, so do they differ from each other considerably in manners and mode of life. The men are of middle stature, with a broad, fat face, with eyes turned in and hollow, wearing no hair but the beard, shaving the rest of their hair; the more distinguished persons only wear their hair, which is very black, and curling down to their ears; they are strong in frame and of a daring courage, preposterously depraved in the indulgence of their passions, and feeding contentedly on the flesh of animals in whatever manner they may have been killed, except pork, from which they are obliged to abstain by law. They are so patient under the want of food and sleep, that they will sometimes endure these privations for four days together, without in the least relaxing any needful exertion. Again, when they by chance have lighted upon something to eat, they gorge themselves beyond measure, leaving nothing uneaten; and with this kind of surfeit they make amends for their previous fasting. When thus overcome by food and labour they sleep continuously for three or four days, and while in this state of deep sleep the Lithuanians and Russians, into whose country they are accustomed to make sudden irruptions and carry away much booty, fall upon them, and, defenceless as they are, having no sentinels nor any order amongst them, by degrees overwhelm them. Moreover, if during a long ride they are troubled with hunger or thirst, it is a practice to lance the veins of the horses on which they sit, and relieve their craving by drawing their blood; and they think that this is an advantage to the animals. As they nearly all wander on uncertain tracks, they are accustomed to direct their course by the observation of the stars, especially the polar star, called in their language Selesnicoll, which means an iron nail.

They are particularly found of mare's milk, for they think that it makes men fat and strong: they use many herbs for food, especially those which grow near the river Don: very few use salt. Their kings, on occasions when they distribute food to their people, are accustomed to give one cow or one horse amongst forty men; and when these are killed, the chief men take only the intestines and divide them amongst themselves, warming them first at the fire to cleanse them before eating them: they not only complacently lick and suck their fingers, greasy with the fat, but also both the knife and its handle which have been used for the cleansing process. They consider horses' heads as great a luxury as we do boars' heads, and they are only served at the tables of men of rank. They have abundance of horses, low in the neck and small, but strong, alike able to endure labour and want of food, and to support themselves on the boughs and bark of trees, or on the roots of herbs, which they scratch out of the earth with their feet. These horses, thus inured to labour, are used with great effect by the Tartars; and the Russians say they are far swifter when ridden by Tartars than by other men. This breed of horses is called Pachmat. Their saddles and stirrups are of wood, unless they happen to seize or purchase any from the Christians. To save their horses' backs from being rubbed, they protect them with grass or the leaves of trees. They swim across rivers; and if they happen to be fleeing from an enemy whose force they greatly dread, they throw away saddles and dresses, and all their baggage, and escape in the greatest confusion. Their arms are bows and arrows; a sword is rarely found amongst them. They enter into a contest with the enemy with the greatest boldness from a distance; they do not, however, continue this mode of warfare long, but pretending flight, take an opportunity while their enemies are pursuing them to discharge their arrows backwards, and then, when the ranks of the enemy are broken, turn their horses suddenly round and attack them. When a battle is to be fought upon their native plains, and they have the enemy within arrows' flight, they do not enter into the engagement in regular battle-array, but draw out their forces into a winding circle, so as to afford themselves a freer and more certain opportunity of discharging their weapons at the enemy. They observe a wonderful degree of order, both in advancing and retreating; for performing which manœuvres they have leaders, who are very skilful in these matters; but if these should happen to fall under the enemy's weapons, or through fear should make an error in generalship, the confusion of the entire army becomes so great that they cannot again be restored to order, nor be prevailed upon to turn their shafts against the enemy. This kind of contest, they themselves, from the resemblance, call a dance; but if threatened with an engagement in a narrow defile, this stratagem cannot be used, and in that case they betake themselves to flight, because they are not armed either with shield, lance, or helmet, so as to be able to meet the enemy in an engagement hand to hand. Their style of riding is such, that they sit with the feet drawn up towards the saddle, so as to be able to turn round easily to either side; and if anything should happen to fall which they wish to pick up, they can lean upon their stirrups and easily lift it; and they are so skilful in this manœuvre, that they can perform it while their horses are galloping. When attacked with spears, they avoid the adversary's blow by suddenly lowering themselves on the opposite side, only holding on to their horses with one hand and foot. When they go out on ravaging expeditions to the neighbouring provinces, each man takes with him two or three horses as a supply, so that when one is tired out he may use one of the others: they lead the weary horses meanwhile by the hand. Their bridles are very light, and they use whips instead of spurs; they only use geldings in warfare, because they consider them more capable of sustaining fatigue and abstinence. The men use a similar dress to that of the women, except that the latter cover the head with a linen veil, and wear linen breeches like those of sailors. When their queens go into public they are accustomed to cover their faces; but the rest of the people, who live a roving life in the fields, wear dresses made of sheeps' skins, which they never change until they are entirely worn out and ragged with long use. They never stay for any length of time in one spot, for they consider it a great calamity to be obliged to remain long in the same place; hence, when they are angry with their children, and wish to utter a heavy imprecation against them, they are accustomed to say, "may you abide in one place continually like a Christian, and inhale your own stink!" So that when they have consumed the pasture which they may find on one spot, they migrate elsewhere, together with their cattle, wives, and children, which they always lead about with them in marshy places. Those, however, who live in towns and cities follow another course of life; when they are engaged in a war at all of a serious character, they place their wives, children, and old men, in the safest spots they can find.

They have no justice among them. When a man stands in need of anything, he can with impunity plunder another of it; and if any one is complained of before a judge for an act of violence, or for having inflicted any injury, the accused does not deny the fact, but simply says that he could not dispense with the article in question; upon which the judge usually gives his judgment [by addressing the plaintiff] in the following manner:—" If you in your turn stand in need of anything, seize it from other people." There are some who say that they are not plunderers: I leave it to others to decide whether they are plunderers or not. For a certainty, the men are most rapacious, because very poor, and are always coveting what is not their own,—taking away other men's cattle, plundering, and even kidnapping men, whom they sell to the Turks and others; or else surrendering them upon ransom, reserving the maidens only for their own use. They seldom besiege cities and fortified places; but take great pleasure in burning and plundering small towns and villages, thinking that the greater number of provinces they thus desolate, the larger is the dominion that they have gained to themselves. If in any quarrel among themselves a man be killed, and the perpetrators of the crime be taken, they are simply deprived of their horses, arms, and clothing, and are then set free. Even a murderer, after giving up his horse and his bow, is dismissed by the judge, merely with the charge to go and mind his own business.

Gold and silver is scarcely ever used amongst them, except by merchants, and that only in the way of commerce. Once, when a fat Tartar was taken by the Russians, a Russian asked him: " How, you dog, did you, who have nothing to eat, become so fat?" To which, the Tartar replied: " Why should not I have something to eat who own so vast a territory from east to west? can I not derive therefrom food enough in all conscience to satisfy me? I should rather think it is you who have not enough to eat, possessing so small a portion of the globe as you do, and having daily to contend for it."

The kingdom of Kazan, with the city and fortress of the same name, is situated on the further bank of the river Volga, nearly seventy miles below Lower Novogorod. The king of this province can raise an army of thirty thousand men, principally foot soldiers, amongst whom the Czeremissi and Czubaschi are the most skilful archers. They say that the Czubaschi excel in the art of navigation. The city of Kazan is sixty German miles distant from the principal fortress of Viatka. These Tartars are more civilized than the rest, in as much as they cultivate their lands, live in houses, and carry on various branches of merchandize. But Vasiley, Prince of Moscow, has so subjugated them, as to bring their kings entirely under his sway; which undertaking was the less difficult, not only from the convenient position of the rivers, which flow from Moscow into the Volga, but also from the commercial intercourse, which they could not dispense with. The people of Kazan formerly had a king named Chelealeck, who died, leaving a wife named Nursulta, without children, and she was taken to wife by one Abrahemin, who by this means gained possession of the kingdom. Abrahemin had by her two sons, named Machmedemin and Abdelatiw; by a former wife, named Batmassasolta, however, he had had a son named Alega, who, upon the death of his father, succeeded as the first-born to the throne. But as he was not entirely obedient to the commands of the Prince of Moscow, he was on a certain occasion made drunk at a festival by some of the councillors of the Prince of Moscow, whom he had sent thither to watch the disposition of the king, and who in that state placed him in a carriage, as if with the intention of conveying him home; but on that same night he was driven towards Moscow, and after being confined for a considerable time, was finally sent by the prince to Vologda, where he ended his days. His mother, together with his brothers Abdelatiw and Machmedemin, had been already removed to Bieloiesero. One of the brothers of Alega, named Codaiculu, was baptized, and received the name of Peter, and the present Prince Vasiley gave him his sister in marriage. Another of Alega's brothers, named Meniktair, continued in his own creed as long as he lived, but had many sons, all of whom, after their father's death, except one Theodore (who lived at Moscow when I was there), were baptized together with their mother, and died [in the Christian faith]. After Alega's abduction into Moscow, Abdelatiw succeeded him, but was removed from the sovereignty for a similar reason to that which had caused the removal of Alega, and Machmedemin was released by the prince from Bieloiesero, and placed on the throne in his stead. He continued to reign until the year of our Lord 1518. Nursulta, whom I have described as the wife of the kings Chalealeck and Abrahemin, after the death of Alega, married Mendliger, King of Precop. Having no offspring by Mendliger, she, from love of her first children, went to Moscow to Abdelatiw, and subsequently, A.D. 1504, to her other son Machmedemin, who ruled over Kazan.

The people of Kazan have now rebelled against the Prince of Moscow; and as this rebellion has given rise to many wars, and daily conflicts among the various princes who have united in the cause of each contending party, and as the war remains unterminated up to the present day, I have thought it right to describe its reason below. Upon the rebellion becoming known to Vasiley, Prince of Moscow, his indignation and thirst for revenge was such, that he sent an immense army with artillery against the people of Kazan. When the latter, who had to fight for life and liberty, heard of the terrible preparations made by the prince against them, and saw that they were unequal to contend with the enemy in an engagement hand to hand, they reasoned how they might circumvent them by stratagem. After having, therefore, first openly pitched their camp in front of the enemy, they placed the flower of their forces in ambush in convenient spots, and then assuming the appearance of being struck by panic, suddenly deserted their camp and betook themselves to flight. The Russians, who were at no great distance, becoming aware of the flight of the Tartars, broke their ranks, and rushed precipitately upon the camp of the enemy, and while they were engaged in plunder, and trusting in their own security, the Tartars came forth from their ambush, together with the Czeremissian archers, and carried such slaughter amongst them, that the Russians were compelled to leave their artillery and flee.

In that flight, two bombardiers left their guns and fled, but were kindly received by the prince upon their return to Moscow. One of them, named Bartholomew, who was an Italian by birth, afterwards conformed to the Russian ritual, and received large presents, together with great authority and favour, from the prince. A third bombadier returned from the slaughter, with the gun under his charge, and hoped that he should receive great and substantial favour from the prince, for the care with which he had preserved and brought back his piece. But the prince addressing him with reproaches, said: " In thus exposing me and thyself to so great danger, thou hast shewn a wish either readily to take to flight, or else to surrender both thyself and thy gun to the enemy. To what purpose is this preposterous diligence in preserving thy gun? I make no account of thy boasting. I have still men remaining who know not only how to found artillery, but also how to use them."

Upon the death of King Machmedemin, under whom the people of Kazan had revolted, Scheale, who married his widow, attained possession of the kingdom of Kazan by the assistance of the prince of Moscow and his wife's brother. He reigned only four years, greatly hated and despised by his subjects. These feelings were increased by his effeminate and degraded constitution of body, for he was a corpulent man, with a small beard, and an almost feminine face, which showed that he was by no means fit for a warrior. In addition to this, he despised and slighted the good will of his own subjects, showed an unreasonable spirit of conciliation to the Prince of Moscow, and trusted foreigners rather than his own people. The people of Kazan were induced, by these circumstances, to offer the kingdom to Sapgirei [Sahib Girei], son of Mendliger, one of the kings of Taurida; upon which Scheale [Schich Alei], being ordered to give up the kingdom, and finding himself inferior in forces, and that the minds of his own subjects were set against him, thought it best to yield to his fate, and returned with his wives, concubines, and all his chattels, to Moscow, whence he had come. This took place A.D. 1521. After this flight of Scheale from the kingdom, Machmetgirei, King of Taurida, conducted his brother Sapgirei into Kazan with a great army, and after confirming the good will of the people of Kazan towards his brother, on his road back to Taurida crossed the Don, and bent his steps towards Moscow. Vasiley, feeling at that time tolerably secure, and not apprehending an occurrence of the kind, when he heard of the approach of the Tartars, hastily collected an army, which he placed under the command of the General Dimitry Bielski, and sent it towards the river Occa, to check the advance of the Tartars. Machmetgirei speedily crossed the Occa, and pitched his tent near certain fish ponds thirteen versts from Moscow itself: sallying thence he spread fire and plunder over all the country; at the same time Sapgirei, who had also left Kazan with an army, laid waste Vladimir and Lower Novogorod. After these transactions, the two brother kings met at the city of Columna and united their forces. Vasiley, finding himself unequal to engage with so powerful an enemy, fled from Moscow, leaving his half brother Peter, a descendant of the kings of Tartary, together with some other noblemen, with a garrison to defend the fortress. So great was his fright, that he is said in his despair to have hidden himself for some time under a hay stack. On the 29th of July the Tartars made a farther advance, and devastated the country with fire in all directions; and such was the terror which they inspired amongst the people of Moscow, that they had little confidence in their security even in the city and the fortress. Such was the tumult which arose at the gates from the thronging of women, children, and other helpless people, who in their intrepidation fled into the fortress with carriages and vehicles of all kinds, that in their haste they checked each other's progress, and many were trampled under foot. This immense concourse of persons caused the air to become so pestilential in the fortress, that if the enemy had remained three or four days under the walls of the city, they must have been seized by the plague and died, for in so great a crowd huddled together, they was obliged to satisfy nature wherever they could find place. There were at that time at Moscow some Livonian ambassadors, who mounted their horses and betook themselves to flight, and seeing nothing around them but fire and smoke, and supposing themselves to be surrounded by the Tartars, made such speed, that in one day they reached Tver, which is thirty-six German miles distant from Moscow. The German bombardiers deserved great praise on that occasion, especially one Nicholas, born not far from Spier, an imperial city of Germany, near the Rhine, to whom was committed in very flattering terms the task of defending the city by the governor and all the counsellors, who were almost stupified with excess of fear, and who begged him to bring up the larger guns which were used for breaching walls, under the gate of the fortress, in order to drive away the Tartars. The size of these guns, however, was such, that three days would scarcely be sufficient to convey them to that spot, and they had not enough gunpowder even to load the largest gun with one charge. For it is constantly the custom with the Russians to be behindhand in everything, and never to have anything ready; but when necessity presses, they are anxious to finish everything rapidly. Nicholas, therefore, considered it advisable to have the smaller guns, which were kept hidden at a distance from the fortress, quickly fetched into the interior on men's shoulders; but during the delay a cry suddenly arose that the Tartars were at hand, which caused so much fear amongst the towns-folk, that the guns were left scattered about the streets, and even the defence of the walls was neglected. If a hundred of the enemy's cavalry had at that time attacked the city, they might easily have rased it to the ground with fire. In the midst of their fear, the governor and the garrison thought it best to appease King Machmetgirei by sending him a great number of presents, principally consisting of mead, in order to induce him to raise the siege. Machmetgirei accepted the gifts, and promised that he would not only raise the siege, but would also quit the province, if Vasiley would bind himself in writing to pay him a perpetual tribute as his father and ancestors had done. Letters to this effect having been willingly written and accepted, Machmetgirei withdrew his army to Rezan, and after granting the Russians permission to redeem and exchange prisoners, he sold the rest of his booty by auction. There was at that time in the camp of the Tartars one Eustace, surnamed Taskowich, a subject of the King of Poland, who had brought forces to the assistance of Machmetgirei, for hostilities were at that time pending between the King of Poland and the Grand Duke of Muscovy. This man brought up to the fortress some of the spoils for sale, with the intention that when opportunity offered he should rush into the gates, together with the Russians, who had come out to make purchases, and beating down the sentinels, thus take possession of the fortress. The king was willing to aid the attempt with corresponding subtlety.

He sent one of his people, in whom he could place confidence, to demand of the governor of the fortress, as the servant of his tributary, to supply him with whatever he required, and to come himself to him. The governor, however, Ivan Kovar, who was well acquainted with warlike matters and with the stratagems employed therein, could not be induced on any account to leave the fortress, but simply replied, that he had not yet learned that his prince had become the tributary and servant of the Tartars, but that when he should be officially informed on that point, it would be necessary that he should receive instructions as to what he should do. Whereupon the prince's letters, in which he had bound himself to the king, were produced and exhibited. While the governor was thus perplexed by the exhibition of these letters, Eustace, in pursuance of his own plan, approached nearer and nearer to the fortress, and in order the more perfectly to conceal his plan, the Knes Feodor Lopata, a man of distinction, with several other Russians who had fallen into the enemy's hands, in the taking of Moscow, were restored upon payment of a certain ransom. In addition to this, several of the prisoners who had been too negligently guarded, or who had in any manner been relieved from labour, had escaped into the fortress, and as the Tartars approached the fortress in great multitudes to demand them back again, and did not withdraw from the fortress, although the Russians in their fright gave up the refugees, this accession of new comers greatly increased the number of the Tartar assailants, so that the terror and despair of the Russians on account of the danger which threatened them was so complete that they were quite at a loss what to do. At this juncture one Johann Jordan, an artillery-man, a German, who came from the Innthal, estimating more clearly than the Russians the magnitude of the danger, of his own accord discharged the guns which had been ranged in order against the Tartars and Lithuanians, and so terrified them that they all left the fortress and fled. The king sent Eustace, the contriver of the above plan, to remonstrate with the governor on account of the injury thus inflicted; but the latter declared that the bombardier had fired the guns without his consent or knowledge, and laid all the blame of the offence upon him; upon which the king demanded that the bombardier should be delivered up to him, and, as often occurs in desperate cases, the greatest number decided that the man by whom they had been delivered from the fear of their enemies should be given up. The governor, Ivan Kovar, alone refused, and by his extreme goodness that German was on that occasion saved; for it so happened that the king, either from impatience of further delay, or because he considered his soldiers already sufficiently encumbered with booty, and that his own interests required it, raised his camp, and departed for Taurida, leaving behind him in the fortress those letters of the Prince of Moscow by which he had bound himself to pay him a perpetual tribute. But he took with him from Moscow so great a multitude of prisoners as would scarcely be considered credible; they say that the number exceeded eight hundred thousand, part of whom he sold in Kaffa to the Turks, and part he slew.

The old and infirm men, who will not fetch much at a sale, are given up to the Tartar youths (much as hares are given to whelps by way of their first lesson in hunting), either to be stoned, or to be thrown into the sea, or to be killed by any sort of death they might please. Those who are sold are compelled to serve for full six years; after that they are set free, but dare not leave the province. Sapgirei, king of Kazan, sold all the captives which he took from Moscow to the Tartars in the mercantile city of Astrachan, which is situated not far from the mouths of the Volga.

After the departure of the Tartar kings from Moscow, the

Prince Vasiley returned again to Moscow, and as he entered he saw standing, at the very gate of the fortress, where a great number had assembled to receive the prince, Nicholas, the German, by whose shrewdness and forethought the fortress, as I have said, had been saved, and said to him in a loud voice: "Thy fidelity towards me, and the zeal which thou hast shown in preserving the fortress, are known to me, and I will abundantly repay the obligation under which this act of duty has laid me." Upon the approach of the other German, Johann, who had suddenly routed the Tartars from the fortress of Rezan by discharging his guns, he said: "Art thou well? God has granted us life, but thou, in preserving it, hast given it to us a second time: great shall be our favour towards thee." Each of them therefore confidently hoped that they should receive liberal rewards from the prince; but nothing was given them, although they often wearied the prince on the subject, and reminded him of his promises. Disgusted at length with the prince's ingratitude, they begged their discharge, that they might visit their country and kinsfolk, from whom they had been long absent; which was allowed them, with a grant from the prince of ten florins to each, in addition to their former stipend.

Meanwhile a contention arose at the court of the prince as to the originator of the flight of the Russians at the Occa. The elder courtiers threw all the blame upon the Knes Dimitry Bielski, the commander-in-chief in the army, a young man, who had slighted their counsels, and through whose want of prudence they said that the Tartars had crossed the Occa. He, in rebutting the charge, declared that Andreas, a younger brother of the prince, was the first to take to flight, and that the rest followed him. Vasiley, in order that he might not appear too severe against his brother, who was evidently the author of the flight, imprisoned one of the governors who had fled together with his brother, caused him to be put in irons, and deprived him of his rank and his principality.

Afterward, as summer came on, Vasiley, resolving to revenge the slaughter inflicted by the Tartars, and to wipe out the shame which he himself had incurred from his flight and his concealment under the haystack, levied a large army, and providing himself with great store of guns and various kinds of offensive contrivances, such as had never been used in battle before by the Russians, and marching out of Moscow with all his army as far as the river Occa, took up his quarters before the city of Columna. Thence he dispatched heralds into Taurida, to Machmetgerei, to provoke him to a conflict, saying, that in the previous year he had been insidiously attacked, without a proclamation of war, after the fashion of thieves and plunderers. To this the king replied, that, in warfare opportunities were of as much importance as arms, and that consequently he made it his custom to choose his own time for fighting, in preference to allowing others to choose for him. Vasiley, being irritated by this language, and burning with the thirst of revenge, moved his camp, A.D. 1523, to Lower Novogorod, with the view of laying waste and taking possession of the kingdom of Kazan. Thence marching as far as the river Sura, on the confines of Kazan, he built a fortress, which he called after his own name: beyond this point he made no advance, but led his army back. In the following year, however, he sent out Michael Georgiovich, one of his chief counsellors, with greater forces than before, to subjugate the kingdom of Kazan. Sapgerai, king of Kazan, being alarmed at so formidable an array, sent for his nephew, the son of his brother the king of Taurida, a youth of thirteen years of age, to preside over the kingdom in the interim, and himself fled to the emperor of the Turks to beg his assistance and cooperation. As the youth, in obedience to his uncle's suggestion, arrived on his road at Gostinovosero,—that is, the island of merchants, lying amidst the waters of the Volga, not far from the fortress of Kazan,—he was received with honour and liberality by the princes of the kingdom. For the chief priest in that district was one Seyd, who was held in such great authority and veneration amongst them, that even kings in meeting him would stand, and bowing the head, take his hand as he sat on horseback, an honour otherwise granted only to kings. Dukes did not salute even his hand, but his knees, simple nobles merely saluted his feet, while plebeians were content if they could only touch his garments or his horse with their hand. As this Seyd secretly favoured the cause of Vasiley, he took diligent measures to seize the youth, in order that he might send him bound to Moscow; but when the lad was at length captured, he was publicly put to death by the knife.

Meanwhile Michael, the commander-in-chief of the Russian forces, hastened with his army to Kazan, and for that purpose despatched so great a number of vessels to Lower Novogorod, for the purpose of transporting away his guns and provisions, that the river, otherwise large, seemed to be absolutely covered all over with the crowd upon it; and on arriving at Gostinovosero, the island of merchants, he pitched his camp on the 7th of July, and remained there twenty days awaiting the arrival of his cavalry. In the meanwhile the fortress of Kazan, which was built of wood, was set on fire by some of the Russians who had been bribed for that purpose, and was burnt to the ground under the eyes of the Russian army. Even this favourable opportunity of taking the fortress was so completely neglected through the cowardice and indolence of the Grand Duke, that not only did he not lead out his soldiers to attack the castle hill, but he took no measures to prevent the Tartars building it again. But on the 28th day of the same month he crossed the Volga, at that point where the fortress lay, and encamped with his army on the river Kazanca, and waited twenty days for a favourable opportunity of accomplishing his object. While stationed there, the *Regulus* of the Kazan army pitched his tent not far from him, and often annoyed the Russians, though fruitlessly, with skirmishes of Czeremissian infantry. Upon this, King Scheale, who had come with his vessels to engage in that way, sent letters to him to demand his surrender to his hereditary sovereign. To which the latter briefly replied : " If you wish to have my kingdom, take it by the sword ; let us settle it between ourselves, and let him to whom fortune gives it, hold it."

While the Russians thus uselessly delayed, they began to suffer hunger from having sent away the provisions which they had brought with them ; for as the Czeremissi had laid waste all the surrounding territory, and diligently watched the track of the enemy, there was nothing left to be seized upon ; so that the prince was unable to gain information respecting the scarcity which oppressed his army, nor could they make any communication to him. Two governors had been appointed by Vasiley to attend to this business, one of whom, the Knes Ivan Palitzki, after loading the vessels with provisions from Novogorod, had to descend the river to join the army ; but he, after depositing the provisions, returned home rather precipitately, considering the existing state of affairs. The other had been sent for the same purpose with five hundred soldiers over land, but was slaughtered with his men by the Czeremissi, into whose hands he fell, scarcely nine of them escaping by flight amidst the confusion. The governor himself, being severely wounded, fell three days after into the hands of the enemy and died. When the rumour of this slaughter reached the army, so great a consternation arose in the camp, increased by a groundless report that the whole of the cavalry were slain to a man, that nothing was thought of but flight ; and though all were agreed upon this point, the only subject of doubt was whether they should return against the tide, which was very difficult, or wait to descend the river when time served, so as to enable them to reach other rivers, from which they might afterwards return home by a circuitous land journey.

During these consultations, the army meanwhile suffering under extreme famine, the nine men whom I have described as escaping from the slaughter of the five hundred, happened to arrive, and announced that Ivan Palitzki was come with provisions; but although the latter had hastened his journey, he had had the misfortune to lose the greater part of his vessels, and had but few remaining when he reached the camp. For, being weary with his daily labour, he had laid up one night to rest himself on the shore of the Volga, but was hailed by the Czeremissi, who came upon him with great clamour, inquiring who sailed by that way; they were answered by the servants of Palitzki, who took them for servants a-shipboard, and with much abuse threatened them with stripes on the following day for disturbing their master's sleep with their unseasonable vociferations. The Czeremissi replied: "You and we shall have other business to attend to to-morrow, for we will take you all bound to Kazan." In the morning, accordingly, before the sun was up, and while the entire bank of the river was covered with a thick fog, the Czeremissi made a sudden attack upon the ships, and threw such terror amongst the Russians, that Palitzki, the commander of the fleet, left ninety of his largest vessels, each containing thirty men, in the hands of the enemy, and loosing his vessel from the shore, and taking the Volga in midstream, escaped under cover of the mist, and reached the army almost in a state of nudity. A similar misfortune afterwards occurred to him in returning with several vessels in his train, when he again fell into the snares of the Czeremissi, and not only lost his vessels, but himself escaped only with great difficulty, and with very few of his men.

While the Russians were thus oppressed on all sides by hunger and the enemy's force, a troop of horse, dispatched by

Vasiley to join the army, was twice surprised by the Tartars and Czeremissi in crossing the river Viega, which flows northward into the Volga. The engagement was keen on both sides, but the Tartars at length gave way, and the Russians were enabled to join the rest of the army, which being thus reinforced with cavalry, commenced the siege of the fortress of Kazan on the 15th of August. On learning this, the governor pitched his own camp also on the other side of the town in sight of the enemy; and as the enemy sent out from time to time detachments of cavalry to ride about the fortress and challenge them to fight, many skirmishes took place between the opposing armies. We were informed by men worthy of credit, who were engaged in that war, that sometimes six Tartars had advanced into the plain to the Russian camp, and when King Scheale would have attacked them with one hundred and fifty Tartar horsemen, he was forbidden by the general of the army; and with two thousand horsemen drawn up before him in battle array, he was thus deprived of the opportunity of achieving his object. When the Russians attempted to surround the Tartars, and, as it were, to preclude their taking to flight, the latter would elude the attempt by gradually retreating before the Russians, and after gaining a little distance, would halt; but as the Russians would then do the same, the Tartars observing their timidity, would presently take to their bows, and send a flight of arrows amongst them, and thus putting them to the route, would pursue and would kill a great number. When the Russians a second time turned upon them, they would give way for a little space, again come to a halt, and thus baffled the enemy by pretending flight. While these manœuvres were going on, two of the Tartar horses were struck with cannon balls, but their wounded riders were carried off by their four remaining comrades, who were safe and sound in the sight of the two thousand Russian cavalry. During this by-play of the horse soldiers, a great force was brought up against the fortress with artillery, to besiege it; but the besieged defended themselves with no less activity, and also discharged their artillery against the enemy; but in the engagement they lost the only artilleryman that they had in the fortress, who fell struck by a cannon shot from the Russian station. On discovering this, some of the German and Lithuanian mercenaries conceived the hope of taking the fortress, which would unquestionably have been taken that day had the inclination of the general responded to their wish; but as he, observing the daily increasing famine under which his men were suffering, had already privately treated by messengers for a truce with the Tartars, he so strongly disapproved of this attempt of his soldiers, that he angrily reprimanded them, and threatened them with stripes for daring to attack the fortress without his knowledge or sanction. For he considered that he should best consult his prince's interests in so great a strait if he could enter into any kind of truce with the enemy, and could only carry back his artillery and army in safety. The Tartars also, on learning the wish of the commander, regarded it as a hopeful circumstance, and willingly fell in with the conditions proposed, that they should make peace with the prince by sending ambassadors to Moscow; which being thus settled, the General Palitzki raised the siege, and marched to Moscow with his army. There was a report that the general had been bribed with presents from the Tartars to raise the siege; and this report was strengthened by the fact, that a certain Savoyard had been caught in the attempt to decamp to the enemy with the gun which had been intrusted to him, and acknowledged, upon close examination, that he had received from the enemy silver money and Tartar goblets, that he might induce many to desert with him; but although taken in so manifest a crime, the general did not inflict a very heavy punishment upon him.

After this withdrawal of the army, which was said to have

consisted of a hundred and eighty thousand men, ambassadors came from the King of Kazan to Vasiley, to ratify the peace, and were still at Moscow at the time that I was there; and even at that time no permanent hope of peace was yet established, for Vasiley had, to the great prejudice of the people of Kazan, transferred to Novogorod the fairs which it had been the custom to hold near Kazan, in the Island of Merchants, and had proclaimed a heavy penalty upon any of his subjects who should in future go to the island for purposes of merchandize, in the hope that this removal of the fair might prove a great inconvenience to the people of Kazan; and that being prevented from buying salt, which they received in large quantities from the Russians at that fair alone, they might be induced to surrender. It happened, however, that by the removal of a fair of this sort, the Russians suffered as much inconvenience as the people of Kazan; for it produced a scarcity and dearness in many articles, which it had been the custom to import through the Caspian Sea from Persia and Armenia by the Volga from the emporium of Astrachan, and especially of the finer kinds of fish, amongst which was the beluga, which is taken in the Volga, both on this side and the other of Kazan.

Thus far I have been treating of the war which the Prince of Moscow waged against the Tartars of Kazan. I now return a second time to the general description of the Tartars, from which I had digressed.

Next to the Tartars of Kazan, we come to the Tartars known by the name of Nagai, who are located beyond the Volga, in the neighbourhood of the Caspian Sea, and dwell mainly by the shores of the river Jaick, which flows down from the province of Siberia. These people have no kings, but are governed by chiefs, or dukes. At the time that I was in Russia, three brothers gained possession of those duchies, and divided the provinces equally between them. The first of them, Schidack, had allotted to him the city of

Scharaitzick, lying eastward beyond the Volga, together with the district immediately adjacent to the river Jaick; the second, named Cossum, had the territory lying between the rivers Kama, Jaick, and Volga; while the possessions of Schichmamai, the third brother, included a part of the province of Siberia, with the country immediately surrounding it. The meaning of the name Schichmamai, is holy or powerful. Nearly all these countries are covered with wood, except that which borders upon Scharaitzick, which is all champaign country.

Between the Volga and Jaick, in the neighbourhood of the Caspian Sea, formerly dwelt the kings of Savolha, of whom we shall say more hereafter. In connexion with these Tartars, I heard a wonderful and almost incredible story from one Dimitry Danielovich, a man who, considering that he was a barbarian, was of remarkable dignity and truthfulness. He stated that his father had been on a former occasion sent by the Prince of Moscow to the King of Savolha, and that in that embassy he had seen in the island a certain seed, somewhat larger and rounder, but not unlike the seed of a melon, from which, when planted, grew up something very like a lamb, of the height of five palms, and that it was called in their language "boranetz", which signifies a lambkin, for it had a head, eyes, ears, and everything else in the form of a lamb. He also stated, that it bore a very fine wool, which was used by many people in those countries for making caps; and, indeed, I was assured by many people, that they had seen wool of that kind. He said, moreover, that the plant,—if plant it could be called,—had blood in it, but no flesh; but in lieu of flesh, there was a kind of matter very like the flesh of crabs; it also had hoofs, not horny like those of a lamb, but covered with a hairy substance resembling horn. Its stem came to the navel, or middle of the belly; it continued alive until the grass around it was eaten away, so that the root dried up for want of nourishment.

The sweetness of this plant was said to be remarkable, so that it was very much sought after by wolves and other ravenous beasts.[1]

Although I received this account about the seed and the plant as a passing observation, yet I have related it, as described to me by men by no means given to vain talking; and I repeat it with the less hesitation, because I was told by William Postel, a man of great learning, that he had heard from one Michael, who was public interpreter of Turkish and Arabic in the Venetian republic, that he had seen certain very delicate furs from a plant growing in those countries, which were used by the Mussulmauns to keep their heads warm after shaving them, and were applied also to their naked breasts, and which were brought from the neighbourhood of the Tartar city of Samarcand, and the countries lying north-east of the Caspian Sea, to Chalibontis. He said, moreover, that it was from an animal fixed on the ground like a plant, but that he had not seen the plant, nor knew its name, except that it was called "Samarcandeos". "As these details are not incompatible, they almost lead me to think," says Postel, "that this statement is not altogether fabulous, but rather that it is a fact, redounding to the glory of the Creator, to whom all things are possible."

Twenty days' journey eastward from the territory of Prince Schidack, we come to a people whom the Russians call Jurgenci, whose sovereign is the Sultan Barack, brother to the Great Khan or King of Cathaia. Ten days' journey from the dominions of Sultan Barack we come to those of the Khan Bebeid, this is that same Great Khan of Cathaia.

---

[1] The stems and leaf-stalks of ferns are often covered with scales, and with woolly-like false leaves. The Polypodium baromez is one of these. This plant is cut artificially to represent a lamb, and as such used to be regarded as a great curiosity in museums. For a representation of it, see Rymsdyk's *Museum Britannicum*, p. 38, tab. 15, fig. 2.

Astrachan is a wealthy city, and the great emporium of the Tartars, which gives its name to all the surrounding country. It lies on this side of the Volga, near to its mouth, ten days' journey below Kazan. Some say that it is not situated on the mouths of the Volga, but some days' journey thence. I think that the position of Astrachan is at that point where the Volga divides itself into many branches, described by some as seventy in number, and after making many islands, falls into the Caspian by the same number of mouths, with so great an abundance of water, that to people looking from a distance it has the appearance of a sea. There are some who call the city Citrahan.

Between Viatka and Kazan, in the neighbourhood of Permia, dwell the Tartars, who are severally named Tamenskii, Schibanskii, and Cosatzskii; of these the Tamenskii are said to dwell in the woods, and not to exceed ten thousand in number. There are, moreover, other Tartars beyond the Volga, called Calmucks, because they alone let their hair grow; and on the Caspian Sea is Schamachia, which gives its name to the country around it, and whose inhabitants excel in weaving silk dresses. The city is six days' journey distant from Astrachan, and was not long since, they tell me, subject, together with its district, to the King of Persia.

The city of Azov, of which I have already spoken, is situated on the Don, and is seven days' journey distant from Astrachan. It is five days' journey from the Taurica Chersonesus, reckoned principally from the city of Precop. Between Kazan and Astrachan, in an extensive tract along the Volga as far as the Dneiper, lie desert plains, which are inhabited by Tartars, having no fixed abodes, with the exception of Azov and the city of Achas, which lies on the Don twelve miles above Azov, excepting also those Tartars who live in the neighbourhood of the lesser Don, and who cultivate the soil and have settled habitations. The distance from Azov to Schamachia is twelve days' journey.

Returning in a south-west direction towards the neighbourhood of the Palus Mæotis and the Black Sea, we come to the people of the Aphgasi, who dwell on the river Cupa, which flows into the said marshes [the Palus Mæotis] at the point where the mountains, inhabited by the Circassians or Ciki, meet the river Merula, which flows into the Black Sea. These people, relying on their mountain fastnesses, yield no obedience either to the Turks or the Tartars. The Russians assert that they are Christians, that they live under their own independent laws, conform to the Greek ceremonials and ritual, and perform their sacred service in the Sclavonic language, which, indeed, they use in general. They are most audacious pirates, and sail down to the sea by the rivers which flow from their mountains, and plunder whomsoever they can, especially those merchants who take the route from Caffa to Constantinople. Beyond the river Cupa is Mengarlia, which is washed by the river Eraclea, and after it comes Cotatis, which some think to be Colchis. After it we come to Phasis, which, before it meets the sea, but not far from its mouth, forms the island of Satabellum, where report states that the fleet of Jason once anchored. Beyond Phasis is Trapezus.

The marshes of the Taurica Chersonesus, which are said to extend three hundred Italian miles in length, from the mouths of the Don up to St. John's Headland, measure in the narrowest part only two Italian miles. There stands the city of Krim, formerly the seat of the kings of Taurida, from which they received the name of Krimskii. The whole isthmus being hollowed out in the form of an island, to the extent of a mile and a fifth, the kings took the name of Precopskii instead of Krimskii, deriving the term from that hollowing out; for *precop* in the Sclavonic language signifies " dug through", whence it is evident that a certain writer was in error, when he said that one Procopius had reigned there.[1] Moreover the whole Chersonesus is divided in two by a wood, and that part which looks towards the Black Sea, in which is situated the celebrated city of Caffa, and which was peopled by a colony from Genoa, formerly called Theodosia, is entirely in the possession of the Turks. The Turkish sultan, however, after the seige of Constantinople and the overthrow of the Greek sovereignty, bought Caffa from the Genoese. The other part of the island is possessed by the Tartars. All the Tartar kings of Taurida, however, derive their origin from the kings of Savolha, and after some of them were driven out from the kingdom by internal sedition, being unable to find any fixed abode in the neighbourhood, they took possession of that part of Europe, and still mindful of the ancient grievance, continually carried on war with the people of Savolha. At length, within the memory of the last generation, Scheachmet, King of Savolha, came into Lithuania at the time that Alexander, the Grand Duke of Lithuania, held sway in Poland, and entering into a treaty with him, with their united forces drove out Machmetgerei King of Taurida. Both of the princes agreed in this movement, but afterwards, when the Lithuanians, according to their custom, delayed the war to an unreasonable period, the wife of the king of Savolha, together with the army which was then kept in the field, becoming impatient both of the delay and the cold, begged of their king, who was busying himself in some of the towns, to get rid of the King of Poland, in order that they might provide for their own interests in good time. As, however, they could not prevail upon him, the wife deserted her husband, and went over with part of the army to Mach-

---

[1] The editor has not succeeded in discovering the writer here alluded to; but Herberstein's explanation is borne out by the following passages in Botero's *Relationi Universali* (Ven. 1608, 4°, parte I, lib. i, fol. 118):—"Il Prencipe de' Tartari habita in Precopi, terra, onde prendono nomi i Tartari chi si dicono Precopiti. . . . Il Precopo, che essi chiamano Zar, che vuol dir Cesare," etc.

metgerei, king of Precop, who at her instigation dispatched the army of Precop to disperse the remainder of the forces of Savolha.

After the rout of these forces, Scheachmet, king of Savolha, seeing the miserable plight in which he was, fled, accompanied by nearly six hundred horsemen, to Alba, which is situated on the river Thyra, in the hope of obtaining assistance from the Turks; but learning that a plot was laid in that city to take him he turned back, and arrived with scarcely half of his cavalry at Kiev. In that city he was surrounded by Lithuanians and taken, and on being conducted to Vilna by order of the king of Poland, the king came forward to meet him, and after giving him an honourable reception, escorted him in his own company to a convention of the Poles, at which the desirableness of a war against Mendligerei was decided upon. But as the Poles took an unreasonable time in mustering their army, the Tartar took grievous offence, and began a second time to contemplate flight, but was apprehended in the attempt and taken back to the castle of Troky, four miles from Vilna, where I saw him and dined with him. This was the termination of the reign of the kings of Savolha, and together with them ended the race of 'the kings of Astrachan, who derived their origin from the same royal line.

After their extinction the power of the kings of Taurida received a great accession, and they became so formidable to the neighbouring nations, that they compelled the king of Poland to pay a certain stipend on condition that he should have their assistance in any case of pressing necessity. The prince of Muscovy also used from time to time to conciliate him [the king of Taurida] by sending presents, which he did because, as they [the prince of Muscovy and the king of Poland] were constantly embroiled in mutual wars, each strove to overwhelm the other by engaging the cooperation of the Tartar forces. He being aware of this, deluded both with vain hopes while he accepted presents from each, a course of conduct which became very apparent at the time that I was treating with the prince of Muscovy, in the name of the Emperor Maximilian, upon the subject of concluding a treaty of peace with the king of Poland. For as the prince of Muscovy could not be induced to enter upon equitable terms of peace, the king of Poland gained over the king of Precop by a bribe to attack Moscow with an army on one side, while he on the other should make an onset on the Russian territory in the direction of Opotzka. By this contrivance the king of Poland hoped to be able to compel the prince of Muscovy to reasonable terms of peace. The prince of Muscovy perceiving this, on his part sent ambassadors to negotiate with the Tartar prince, for the purpose of persuading him to turn his forces against Lithuania, which he stated to be entirely off its guard and unprotected by garrisons. The Tartar, consulting only his own advantage, followed his advice. As his power thus increased by the quarrels of these princes, and as he was occupied solely with the restless desire of increasing his own domain, his ambition enlarged itself in proportion, and having gained the alliance of Mamai, prince of Nahaica, he marched from Taurida with an army in the month of January, A.D. 1524, and attacked the king of Astrachan; and as the latter deserted the city and took to flight in great trepidation, he besieged and took it, and remained housed within the walls as conqueror.

Meantime Agis, one of the princes of Nahaica, rebuked his brother Mamai for having lent the aid of his forces to so powerful a neighbour; he at the same time warned him to keep a suspicious eye upon the daily increasing power of King Machmetgerei, for that it was possible from his intractable disposition that he might turn his arms both against himself and his brother, and not only expel both from the kingdom, but perhaps slay them or reduce them to slavery. Mamai, under the influence of these suggestions, sent a messenger to his brother, to exhort him to hasten to him with all the forces that he could muster, for that it was possible that Machmetgerei might, from the elation naturally consequent upon his great successes, be resting in comparative security, and that thus they might both be relieved from the fears which they entertained. Agis, yielding to his brother's advice, promised implicitly to be on the spot at the appointed time with an army which he had already levied for the purpose of defending the outposts of his kingdom in the midst of so many wars. Upon this understanding, Mamai immediately sent to King Machmetgerei, advising him not to corrupt his soldiery, and neglect their discipline, by keeping them constantly housed, but rather to leave the city and dwell in the open field, according to the custom of the Tartars. The king, in accordance with his advice, brought out his troops and encamped in the open country, upon which Agis advanced with his army and joined his brother. A short time after, they made a sudden onslaught upon King Machmetgerie, while he was dining with the son of the Sultan Bathir and far from having any apprehension of such an attack, and slew him; and overwhelming the greater part of his army, put the rest to flight. They pursued their conquest with great slaughter beyond the Don, even to Taurida. They laid siege to the city of Precop, which, as I have said, lies at the entrance of the Chersonese; but finding that they could not reduce it to surrender by force or any kind of effort, they raised the siege and returned home.

The King of Astrachan having thus by the agency of these princes regained his kingdom, the strength of the kingdom of Taurida gave way under the loss of their valiant and successful King Machmetgerei, who had reigned over them for a considerable time with great power.

After the murder of Machmetgerei, his brother Sadachgerei gained possession of the kingdom of Precop by the aid of the sultan of the Turks, in whose service he was at the time ; but being accustomed to Turkish habits, he offended the prejudices of the Tartars, by not appearing much in public, and did not allow himself to be seen by his subjects. The result of this was, that the Tartars, who could not endure so unusual a mode of conduct in their prince, expelled him, and put his brother's son in his place. Sadachgerei, being taken prisoner by his nephew, implored him suppliantly not to pursue him to the death, and from pity to his old age not to shed his blood, begging to be allowed to spend the remainder of his life in private in some fortress, and to retain only the name of king, while his nephew held the entire administration of the kingdom. His request was granted.

The titles of dignity amongst the Tartars are nearly as follows : — *khan*, as I have said above, signifies a king ; *sultan*, the son of a king ; *bü*, a duke ; *mursa*, the son of a duke ; *olbond*, a noble or councillor ; *olboadula*, the son of a nobleman ; *said*, a chief priest. A private man is called *ksi*. The post of rank next to that of the king is called *ulan*. The Tartar kings have four councillors, whose advice they mainly take in matters of importance. The first of these is called *schirni* ; the second, *barni* ; the third, *gargni* ; the fourth, *tziptzan*. Thus much about the Tartars. I must now speak of Lithuania, which is the country next bordering upon Muscovy.

Of Lithuania.

Lithuania is the province which lies nearest to Muscovy; but it is not of the province alone that I now mean to speak, but also of such districts immediately adjacent to it as are comprehended under the name of Lithuania. This country extends in a long tract from the town of Circass on the

Dnieper as far as Livonia. I may here remark, that the Circassians who dwell upon the Dnieper are Russians, and are distinct from those whom I have described above as dwelling in the mountains near the Black Sea. At the time that I was at Moscow, these people were governed by one Eustace Tascovitz, whom I have before spoken of as going with King Machmetgerei to Moscow; he was a man of great skill in military matters, and remarkable for his shrewdness, and from the frequent intercourse he had had with the Tartars, was able the more repeatedly to conquer them. He often even drew the Prince of Moscow himself, whose captive he had for some time been, into great dangers. In the same year that I was at Moscow, he showed remarkable skill in routing the Russians, a circumstance which I have thought worthy of description here. He led certain Tartars dressed in the Lithuanian costume into Russia, knowing that the Russians, taking them for Lithuanians, would fearlessly rush out upon them without hesitation. After having set an ambush in a suitable position, he awaited the arrival of the vengeful Russians. The Tartars, meanwhile, after depopulating the province of Severa, directed their march towards Lithuania; upon which the Russians, supposing them to be Lithuanians, changed their route, and, inspired with a thirst of vengeance, marched impetuously with a great force upon Lithuania. After laying waste the country, as they were returning laden with spoil, they were surrounded by Eustace, who came forth from his ambuscade, and were all of them slaughtered, to a man. When the Prince of Muscovy heard of this, he sent ambassadors to the King of Poland to complain of the injury which had been done to him. To which complaint the king replied: "That his people had not inflicted an injury, but had simply revenged one done to themselves." The Prince of Muscovy having been thus deceived on both sides, was ignominiously compelled to put up with his loss.

Beyond the country of the Circassians, there are no habitations of Christian men. At the mouth of the Dnieper stands the fortress and city of Otchakov, forty miles from Circass. It was not since in the possession of the King of Taurida, who took it from the King of Poland. It is now held by the Turks. From Otchakov to Alba (anciently called Moncastro), near the mouths of the Thira, is fourteen miles. From Otchakov to Precop is also fourteen miles. Seven miles beyond Circass, going up the Dnieper, lies the town of Cainov; eighteen miles from which is Kiev, the ancient metropolis of Russia, whose magnificence and evidently royal condition are shown by the ruins of the city, and the monuments, which are still seen lying in heaps. There may still be traced to this day on the hills in the neighbourhood the remains of churches and deserted monasteries, as well as numerous caverns, in which may be seen very ancient tombs, with the bodies in them not yet decayed. I have heard from men worthy of credit, that the maidens there seldom preserve their chastity beyond seven years of age. I have heard various arguments, none of which are satisfactory to me, to show the lawfulness of merchants abusing these maidens, although they are on no account allowed to carry them away. For if any one should be detected in the act of abducting a maiden, both his life and goods are forfeited, unless he be spared through the prince's clemency. There is also a law, that the property of foreign merchants who happen to die there, is confiscated to the king or his viceroy; and the same rule, which is observed among the Tartars and Turks with respect to the natives of Kiev, is also observed by the people of Kiev with respect to the Tartars and Turks after their death. There is a certain hill at Kiev, over which the merchants have to pass by a road which is none of the easiest; if any part of the carriage should happen to be broken in the ascent, all the articles in it are confiscated to the treasury. All these details were related to me by the Lord Palatine, Albert Gastol, who was the King of Vilna's viceroy in Lithuania.

Thirty miles from Kiev, going up the Dnieper, we come to Mosier, on the river Prepetz, which flows into the Dnieper twelve miles above Kiev. The Prepetz itself receives the waters of the river Thur, which abound in fish. The distance of Mosier from Bobranzko is thirty miles. Twenty miles above the latter place is Mohilev, which is six miles distant from Orsa. Such of the above-mentioned towns upon the Dnieper as lie upon its western shores are subject to the King of Poland, and those on the eastern to the Prince of Muscovy, except Dobrovna and Mistislav, which appertain to the dominions of Lithuania. After crossing the Dnieper, four miles bring us to Dobrovna, and twenty more to Smolenzko. Our route lay from Orsa to Smolenzko, and thence to Moscow.

The town of Borisov lies twenty-two miles west of Orsa, and is washed by the river Beresina, which flows into the Dnieper below Bobranzko. The Beresina, as I have seen with my own eyes, is even broader than the Dnieper at Smolenzko. I certainly am of opinion, that this Beresina, judging from the sound of the word, was what the ancients call the Borysthenes; for if we look to the description of Ptolemy, the sources of the Beresina agree more [with his account?] than those of that Borysthenes which they call Dnieper.

I have already, at the commencement of my work, spoken at sufficient length of the princes who ruled over Lithuania at the time when Christianity was first introduced into the country. The affairs of this nation were always prosperous up to the time of Vitold. If a foreign war threatened them, and they had to defend themselves against the forces of an enemy, when summoned they came forth with a great appearance of warlike demeanour, but more from ostentation than from any readiness to go to war; and when the selection was made, they soon began to fall off. And even those who remained would send back their best horses and clothing, with their names attached to them, and followed their general with a small outfit, as if acting under compulsion. The nobles also, who are compelled to supply a certain number of soldiers for the war at their own expense, would buy themselves off with a sum of money paid to the general, and remain at home; and this thing was thought so little disgrace, that the captains of militia and commanders made a public proclamation, both at the councils and throughout the fortresses, that any who wished it, might exonerate themselves by the payment of a sum of money, and remain at home. Indeed, so great was the licence which prevailed amongst them to do whatever they pleased, that they seem not only to have used, but to have abused, this unreasonable state of liberty, so as even to hold the property of their princes in pawn; so that princes who came into Lithuania could not live upon their own revenues, unless they were relieved by the assistance of their subjects. The people wear a long dress, and carry bows like the Tartars; but they have also a spear and shield, like the Hungarians. They have excellent geldings, which they ride unshod, and with soft bits.

Vilna is the capital of the country. It is a large city, lying embosomed among the hills, at the confluence of the rivers Velia and Vilna. The river Vilna flows into the Cronon some miles below Vilna. The Cronon washes the town of Grodno, the name of which is not very unlike the name of the river; and at the point where it falls into the German Ocean, separates the people of the Pruten (formerly subject to the Teutonic order, but now governed by Albert, hereditary Marquis of Brandenburg, who, since his submission to the King of Poland, has laid aside the cross and order) from the Samogithians. At the point I have described stands the city of Memel, for the Germans call Cronon, Memel, or in the country idiom Nemen. Vilna is surrounded by a wall, and contains many temples and houses built of stone; there is an episcopal palace there, in which on our return we were kindly received by Ivan, the natural son of King Sigismund, who was a man of great kind-heartedness and lived in the palace at that time. It has also a parish church and several monasteries, with a convent of Franciscans, which was constructed at immense expense, and remarkable for the strictness of its discipline. The Russian churches in it are much more numerous than those which have been built for the observance of the Roman ritual. There are three Roman bishoprics in the principality of Lithuania, namely, those of Vilna, Samogithia, and Kiev. The Russian bishoprics in the kingdom of Poland and Lithuania and their incorporated principalities, are the archbishopric of Vilna and the bishoprics of Plotzk, Vladimir, Lutsk, Pinski, Kholm, and Premisl. The Lithuanians traffic in horns, wax, and cinders, in which they principally abound, and great quantities of which are exported to Dantzic, and thence into Holland. Lithuania gives an abundant supply of pitch and timber for ship-building, and also wheat. At the time that Christian was ejected from the throne of Denmark, and when the sea was infested with pirates, salt was not imported from Britain but from Russia, and the same is now used among the Lithuanians.

At the time that I was in Lithuania, there were two men principally distinguished for warlike renown, namely, the Knes Constantine Ostroski and the Knes Michael Linzki. Constantine had routed the Tartars very frequently. It was his custom not to attack the horde while out on their predatory excursions, but to pursue them when returning laden with booty; for as they retired to a spot where they thought they might have an opportunity of resting and refreshing themselves without fear of disturbance, but which spot was known to him and fixed upon as the point of attack, he would give notice to his own soldiers to cook their food for that night beforehand, for that he would not be able to allow them much fire the following night. On the following day, therefore, the Tartars would continue their journey, and when night came, seeing no flame or smoke, would suppose that the enemy had either retreated or dispersed themselves, and would then let their horses loose upon the pasture, take their meal, and go to sleep. Constantine would then make his onset at break of day, and thus overwhelm them with a terrific slaughter. The Knes Michael Linzki, who had gone into Germany while yet a youth, and had demeaned himself valiantly under Albert, Duke of Saxony, in his war with Friesland, and had gained himself great renown amongst all ranks of soldiers, returned to his own country imbued with the manners of the Germans, among whom he had grown up, and had high rank and authority given to him at the court of the King Alexander; so much so, indeed, that the king took his advice and decision in every question of difficulty. It happened, however, that he fell into a quarrel with Ivan Saversinski, palatine of Troca, on account of the king, but the quarrel being at length arranged, everything remained quiet between them during the life of the king; but after the king's death, the hatred which had been buried in the mind of Ivan, on account of having been deprived of his palatinate through his antagonist's influence, again awoke. The consequence was, that the latter, with his accomplices and friends, was charged with treason to King Sigismund, who had succeeded Alexander, was slandered by certain of his rivals, and declared to be a traitor to his country. The Knes Michael, smarting under such an injury, often appealed to the king, and demanded that the cause should be equitably judged between himself and Saversinski, declaring that he would then be able to clear himself from so heavy a charge; but finding that the king would not listen to his petition, he went over to Hungary to Vladislav, the king's brother. Thence he sent both letters and messengers to the king, imploring him to recognize his plea; but when he found that all his efforts were of no avail, incensed at the indignity offered him, he told the king that he should resent such infamous conduct, and that he himself would one day live to repent it. Then betaking himself to his home in anger, he dispatched a confidential servant to the Prince of Muscovy, with letters and instructions. He wrote, that if the king would promise him a safe and independent livelihood, granted him in writing and under his oath, that it should be to the prince's honour and profit, and that he would go over to him with the fortresses which he possessed in Lithuania, and all the other places which he had taken either by force or surrender. The Prince of Muscovy knowing the valour and skill of the man, was overjoyed at receiving this message, and promised that he would do all which Michael demanded of him, and gave the letters and the oath which he desired.

When every thing had been done by the Prince of Muscovy according to agreement, Michael, burning with revenge against Ivan Saversinski, who was staying at that time in his villa near Grodno (in which I afterwards spent a night), fell upon him with all his forces, and, to prevent his escape, set a guard of soldiers round his house, and sent in a Mahomedan assassin, who attacked him while asleep in his bed, and cut his head off. This done, he advanced with his army against the fortress of Miensko, and strove to take it either by force or surrender. Frustrated in his attempt on Miensko, he laid siege to other fortified towns; but learning that the forces of the king were advancing against him, and that they were far superior to his own, he gave up the siege of these fortresses, and betook himself to Moscow, where he was honourably received by the prince, who was well aware that there was no man in Lithuania equal to him. The prince entertained the hope, that by his counsels, operations, and industry, he might be able to gain possession of the whole of Lithuania;

and in this hope he was not altogether mistaken, for after taking counsel with him, he a second time laid siege to Smolensko, one of the chief principalities of Lithuania, not so much by the strength of his forces, as by the perseverance of this one man, for the very presence of Michael alone took away from the soldiers who formed the garrison all hope of defending the city; and he prevailed on them, through the combined agency of their fears and his promises, to surrender the fortress. He did this the more boldly, and with greater zeal, because Vasiley had promised him that if, by any means, he could succeed in taking Smolensko, he would make a grant to him in perpetuity of the fortress, together with the adjacent province. These promises, however, he afterwards broke; and when Michael appealed to him on the score of his covenant, he did nothing but delude and cajole him with vain hopes. Michael becoming seriously offended at this conduct, and not having yet forgotten King Sigismund, whose favour he hoped he might easily gain through the medium of some friends of his who dwelt at the court of that sovereign, sent one of his confidential servants to the king, promising that if he would pardon any offence that he might have committed against him, he would return into his service. This message was very acceptable to the king, and he ordered that the letters of safeguard which Michael requested, should be immediately sent to him by a messenger. As, however, Michael did not place implicit confidence in the king's letters, and in order that he might return with the greater security, he petitioned that similar letters should be sent him from Georg Pisbeck and Johann von Rechenberg, who were German knights and councillors of the king, and whom Michael knew to have such authority over him, that they could compel the king against his will to keep his promise. This request was granted him; but as it happened that the messenger who was sent upon this business fell into the hands of the sentinels of the prince of Muscovy, and was taken, the whole affair became known, and was speedily communicated to the prince, by whose order Michael was seized. At the same time, a certain Polish youth, of the noble family of Trepko, had been despatched to Moscow by King Sigismund to communicate with Michael, and in order to execute the king's commands with the greater success, he pretended to be a refugee; but he also fell into a similar misfortune, and was seized by the Russians; and when he stated that he was a refugee, he was not believed, but he kept his secret so faithfully, that though he was put to severe torture, he would not reveal it.

After the capture of Michael, he was brought into the prince's presence at Smolensko, who said to him, "Traitor, I will inflict on thee a punishment worthy of thy deserts!" To which he replied: "I do not acknowledge the crime of treason which thou layest to my charge, for if thou hadst kept faith towards me with respect to thine own promises, thou wouldst have found me a most faithful servant to thee in every respect; but when I saw that thou madest light of them, and madest it thy chief aim to evade me, it became a heavy grievance to me that I had not been able to accomplish those things which I had conceived in my mind respecting thee. I have always despised death, and will therefore willingly undergo it; but never more let me see thy face, O tyrant." Upon this he was led away, by the prince's command, through a great concourse of people to Viesma, where the commander-in chief of the army, after having caused the heavy chains with which he was to be bound to be thrown before him, thus addressed him: "The prince, as thou knowest, O Michael, honoured thee with the greatest favour whilst thou faithfully servedst him, but since thou hast thought fit to carry on thy treasonable practices with a high hand, he presents thee with this reward as suitable to thy merits;" saying which, he ordered the fetters to be fastened on him. While Michael was thus being bound with chains, he turned to the surrounding populace, and thus addressed them: "Lest a false rumour should be spread amongst you as to the cause of my imprisonment, I will briefly unfold to you what I have done, and why I have been taken prisoner, and that you may learn from my example what kind of prince you have over you, and what every one of you can or ought to expect from him." With this commencement, he related to them the entire reason of his coming into Muscovy, as well as the promises which the prince had made, under the confirmation of written documents, and with the addition of his oath, and shewed how he had, in no respect, adhered to those promises. He then proceeded to state, that as he had been deceived in his expectations from the prince, he had wished to return to his own country, and for that reason he had been taken prisoner; since this injury was unjustly inflicted upon him, he should take no great pains to escape death, especially as he knew that it was alike the lot of all to die by the common law of nature. As he was a man of strong frame, and of an intellect which could turn itself to any subject, and whose judgment in council had great weight, and of ready wit, alike in matters of humour as in those of more serious moment, and evidently a man for all occasions, as the saying is, he had, by this versatility of genius, won for himself great favour and authority with all men, especially with the Germans amongst whom he had been brought up. He had routed the Tartars in the reign of King Alexander with a signal slaughter, nor since the death of Vithold had the Lithuanians ever gained so renowned a victory over the Tartars. The Germans designated Michael, in the Bohemian language, "Pan"; but as he, in the first instance, had followed the ritual of the Greeks, as a Russian, but afterwards left it to follow the Roman ritual, when in chains he again adopted the Russian form of worship, in order to soothe and mitigate the wrath and indignation of the prince against him. Many men of rank, at the time that

I was in Moscow, pleaded with the prince for his liberation, and above all the prince's wife, who was Michael's niece, being his brother's daughter; the Emperor Maximilian also interceded for him, and sent special letters to the prince, in his own name, in my first embassy; but so little effect had all these intercessions, that permission was not granted me to see him: indeed, no great opportunity of seeing him was allowed to any body; but in my second embassy, his liberation being accidently spoken of, I had the question rather frequently put to me by the Russians, whether I knew him, to which I replied, that I had only occasionally heard his name mentioned, and I believed that was all I was ever likely to know of him. At length Michael was liberated and discharged: the reason of which was, that the prince, who had married his niece during the lifetime of his former wife, put such reliance in his valour, that he thought his children would, through his means, be kept safe in possession of the kingdom, from interference on the part of his brothers; and he finally appointed him, by his will, tutor to his sons. Subsequently, after the death of the prince, Michael having reproached the prince's widow with wantonness, was charged by her with treason, and died an unhappy death in prison. Not long after the perpetration of this crime, she is said to have been carried off by poison in the midst of her recklessness, and her paramour, Ovczina, was butchered and torn to pieces.

Volonia contains the most warlike people amongst the principalities of Lithuania.

Lithuania is extremely woody, and has in it extensive marshes and numerous rivers; some of which latter, namely, the Bog, the Prepetz, the Thur, and the Berisina, flow eastwards into the Dnieper; others, namely, the Boh, the Cronon, and the Nareo, flow towards the north. The climate is severe, and the animals of all kinds small. Corn is very abundant, but the crop rarely comes to maturity. The people are miserable, and oppressed with heavy servitude ; for when any man who is attended by a host of servants, enters the house of any husbandman, he is at liberty to do with impunity whatever he thinks fit, to seize and consume any of the necessaries of life, and even cruelly to beat the husbandman himself. The husbandmen are not allowed access to their masters on any account without bringing presents, and when they are admitted, they are referred to the stewards and officials, who, unless they receive presents, will make no arrangement, nor give any decision to the advantage of the applicant. Nor was this the case only with the poor, but also with the nobles, whenever they wished to obtain any favour from their official superiors. I once heard a certain youthful minister, of high rank about the king, say that the only word in Lithuania was " gold". The king has an annual tax paid to him for defending the boundaries of the kingdom. Beyond the ordinary assessment, the people have to work for their masters six days out of the week. When a serf marries, or when his wife dies, or when his children are born, and also when they die, he is compelled to pay a certain sum at the time of the event being acknowledged. So heavy is the servitude in which they have been kept up to the present day, that if any man happen to be condemned to death, he is compelled, if his master order it, to take the infliction of the punishment upon himself, and to hang himself with his own hands ; and if he should refuse to do so, he is first cruelly beaten, and then hanged, nevertheless, and brutally cut to pieces. With such severity is this process carried out, that if the judge or governor appointed to decide upon the case, should see any attempt at delay on the part of the culprit, and use a threat, or only say " make haste", the man's master becomes angry, upon which the wretch, in his dread of the extremity of punishment, puts an end to his own life with the noose.

Of their Wild Beasts.

Lithuania possesses other wild beasts, besides such as are found in Germany, namely, bisons, buffaloes, and alces, which are wild horses, called by some onagri [wild asses]. The Lithuanians call the bison, in their own language, "suber". The Germans improperly call it "aurox" or "urox", which name better suits the buffalo, which manifestly has the form of an ox, while the bison is a very dissimilar kind of animal; for the bisons have manes, and are hairy about the neck and shoulders, with a kind of beard hanging from their chins, their hair smelling of musk, their heads short, their eyes large and fierce, as if they were on fire, and their foreheads broad, with horns generally so wide apart and stretched out, that the space would take in three tolerably stout men; a fact which was shown by Sigismund, King of Poland, father of the present King Sigismund Augustus, whom we know to have been a man of well-built and strong frame, who tried the dangerous experiment with two others of no less bulk than himself. The back of the bison is raised as with a kind of hump, the anterior and posterior parts of the body being more depressed.

Those who hunt the bison had need be men of great strength, agility, and cunning. A suitable spot for the hunt is selected, where there are trees growing at equal distances from each other, with trunks of moderate thickness, so that it may be easy to run round them, and yet sufficiently large to protect the body of a man. Each of the hunters places himself at one of these trees, and when the bison has been roused by the dogs that are set upon him, and is driven towards the spot, he rushes with great ferocity upon the first hunter who presents himself. The latter, however, protects himself by placing the tree between them, and strikes the beast with his hunting-spear, wherever he can; the animal does not often fall under the blow, but, exasperated with fury, not only tosses with his horns, but also darts out his tongue, which is so rough and strong, that if it only touch the garment of the hunter, it will lay hold of it and draw him, and the beast will never leave him until he has killed him. But if the huntsman should become weary with chasing about and striking, he presents to the beast his red cap, against which he will rage both with feet and horns. If, however, another of the hunters wishes to join the contest before the beast is slain, which must be done if the men wish to get away with a whole skin, it is easy to call off the beast against himself by once shouting the barbarous cry of "lululu!"

Masovia, which borders on Lithuania, is the only province which has in it the kind of buffalo which in the language of the country is called thur, but which we Germans may with propriety call urox. They are a sort of wild oxen, not unlike tame oxen, except that they are entirely black, with a line down the back having white blended with it. They are not very plentiful, and there are certain districts which are charged with the care of them; and it is only in some few preserves that they are kept. They are allowed to herd with tame cows, but have a mark set upon them to distinguish them. This is done because they are afterwards looked upon as degraded by the other buffaloes, and are not admitted into their herd; and the calves which are produced by the cross breed are not long lived. The King Sigismund Augustus, at the time I was ambassador at his court, made me a present of one which was just dropped, and which the hunters had taken, driven half-lifeless from the herd. It had the skin which covers the forehead cut away, which I suppose was done for some purpose, but from thoughtlessness I neglected to enquire why it was done. This is certain, that girdles made of the hide of the urox are much esteemed, and it is a vulgar opinion that parturition is assisted by wearing them.

Queen Bona, the mother of Sigismund Augustus, presented to me two girdles of this kind, one of which my most serene mistress, the Queen of the Romans, graciously accepted as a present from me.

There is an animal in Lithuania, named in their language "loss", which the Germans call "ellem", and to which others give the Latin name "alce".[1] The Poles maintain that it is the "onager", which means wild ass; but it does not correspond in form to that animal, for it has cloven hoofs, although it is true that some are found with the hoof solid, but this is of rare occurrence. The animal is taller than a stag, with rather prominent ears and nostrils, with horns somewhat differing from those of a stag, and of a colour more tending to white. It is very swift of foot; it does not run like other animals, but rather with an ambling gait. Their hoofs are worn as amulets against the falling sickness.

In the desert plains about the Dnieper, the Don, and the Volga, is a wild sheep, called by the Poles "solhac", by the Russians "seigack", of the size of a doe, but with shorter hoofs, with high stretching horns, marked with rings, of which the Russians make transparent knife-handles. They are swift of foot, and take very lofty leaps.[2]

Samogithia is a province which lies to the north of the Baltic sea, and is next to Lithuania. It divides Prussia from Livonia by the space of four German miles. It is not remarkable for any fortress or fortified town. It is governed by a prince from Lithuania, who is designated in their language Starosta, which signifies an elder: this governor is not easily removed from his office, except upon very serious charges, but holds it in perpetuity as long as he lives.

The province has a bishop, who is subject to the Pope of Rome.

---

[1] The elk.
[2] This is either the capra ibex, or capra ægagrus, two allied species belonging to the genus *ægoceros* of Pallas.

This one thing is principally worthy of notice in Samogithia, that while the men of the country are remarkably tall in stature, some of their children will also prove of great height, but others, by a sort of freak of nature, are extremely small, and decided dwarfs.

The people of Samogithia wear a mean-looking dress, mostly of an ash colour: they dwell in low, long-shaped cottages, in the middle of which they make their fires, and when the father of the family is seated at his fire-side, he sees all his cattle and household stuff around him, for it is their custom to have their flocks under the same roof with themselves, without any separation. The elders use buffalo horns for goblets.

The men are courageous and warlike: in battle they make use of coats of mail and various other kinds of armour, but their principal weapon is a rather short lance, like a hunting-spear. They have such small horses, that it is scarcely credible that they should prove equal to the great exertions which they undergo. Abroad they are used in battle, and at home in agriculture.

In ploughing the land, they do not use iron, but wood, which is the more remarkable, that the soil is not sandy, but so stiff that a fir tree will never grow in it. It is the custom of the ploughmen to carry out with them several pieces of wood to work the ground with, instead of a ploughshare, so that when one is broken they may have another at hand, that no time may be lost. One of the governors of the province, in order to relieve the peasants from the severity of their labour, introduced a considerable number of iron ploughshares; but as it happened, from the unfavourableness of the season in that and a few following years, that the crops did not answer the expectations of the husbandmen, the barrenness of their fields was ascribed by the common people to the iron ploughshare, for they could think of no other cause: and the governor, fearing an insurrection, took away the iron shares, and allowed them to till their fields in their own fashion.

This province abounds in woods and forests, in which horrible sights may occasionally be witnessed; for in them there dwell a considerable number of idolators, who cherish, as a kind of household gods, a species of reptile, which has four short feet like a lizard, with a black fat body, not exceeding three palms in length. These animals are called "givoites",[1] and on certain days are allowed to crawl about the house in search of the food which is placed for them. They are looked upon with great superstition by the whole family, until the time when, having satisfied their hunger, they return to their own place. But if any accident should occur to them, they believe that their household god, the reptile, has been ill-received and ill-fed. On my return from my first journey to Moscow, I came to Troki, and was informed by the landlord of the house at which I happened to put up, that he had in that same year purchased some bee-hives of one of these reptile-worshippers, and had by his reasoning won him over to the true faith of Christ, and persuaded him to kill the reptile which he worshipped: but some time after when he returned to look at his bees, he found the man with his face deformed, and with his mouth drawn in a hideous manner up to his ears. On inquiring the cause of so fearful a disaster, he replied, that he was punished with this calamity by way of expiation and penance for having laid guilty hands upon the reptile his god, and that he should have to suffer many more grievous penalties, unless he returned to his former mode of worship. Although this did not take place in Samogithia, but in Lithuania, I have quoted it as a specimen of their customs.

They say that there is no better or finer honey found than in Samogithia; that it is white, and has but little wax with it.

[1] This seems to be a species of *scincus*, or rather perhaps *gecko*.

The sea which washes Samogithia, and which is called by some the Baltic, by some the German, by others the Prussian, and by others the Venetic sea, and which the Germans call Pelts, in allusion to the Baltic, is properly named a gulf; for it flows within the Cimbrian Chersonese, which is now called by the Germans, Yuchtland and Sunder Yuchtland, but in Latin, Jucia,—a word derived from the same source. It washes also that part of Germany which is called by the Germans Low, beginning at Holstein, which lies next to the Cimbrian Chersonese, then flows by the country of Lubeck, then by Vismar, Rostock, the cities of the dukes of Mecklenburg, and the whole region of Pomerania, which country derives its name from the circumstance of which we are speaking; for in the Sclavonic language, Pomorüae, signifies near the sea, or maritime. After that it flows by Prussia, the capital of which is Gdanum, which is also called Gedanum and Dantiscum. The Duke of Prussia, however, has a seat which is called Mons Regius [Konigsberg]. In that locality they fish, at a certain time of the year, for the amber which floats upon the sea. This fishery is carried on at great risk by persons engaged in it, on account of the sudden ebb and flow of the sea.

The sea skirts Samogithia only by the space of about four miles, after which it flows along an extensive tract comprising Livonia and the country called Khurland, doubtless so named from the Cureti, as well as some districts which are subject to the Russians; it then flows round Finland, which belongs to the Swedes, whence also the name of the Venedi is supposed to have derived its origin. On the other side it flows by Sweden.

The whole of the kingdom of Denmark, which principally consists of islands, is comprised in this gulf, with the exception of Jucia and Scandia, which are attached to the continent. The island of Gothland also, which is subject to the King of Denmark, lies in this gulf. Some have thought that the Goths came thence; but it is too small to have been able to hold such a multitude of men; besides, if the Goths had come from Scandia, they must have returned from Gothland into Sweden, and again bent their course backwards by Scandia, which is not at all consistent with reason. In the island of Gothland there are still remaining the ruins of the city of Wisby, in which the quarrels and disagreements of the sailors who passed by that way used to be judged and settled, and questions of business concerning distant maritime places were brought to that city and argued.

The province of Livonia extends a long distance by the sea shore; its metropolis is Riga, which is under the government of the master of the Teutonic order. The province comprises two bishoprics, namely that of Revel and Oesel, besides the archbishopric of Riga. It contains several towns, the chief of which is Riga, which is situated on the Dwina, not far from its mouth, as well as Revel and Derbt. The Russians call Revel, Bolivar; and Derbt, Turgovgorod: Riga retains its name in both languages. It has in it the navigable rivers, the Rubo and the Nerva.

The prince of this province, as well as the brothers of the order, the principal of whom are styled commanders, as also the nobles and citizens, are nearly all German.

As three languages are used by the common people, so they are divided into three orders or tribes. Every year a fresh supply of labourers and soldiers are brought into Livonia out of the German principalities of Juliers, Gelderlund, and Munster, to replace those who have died, or those who, after fulfilling their yearly duty, return in freedom to their own country.

They possess so great a quantity of horses of a remarkably fine strong breed, that hitherto they have been able to endure, and vigorously to withstand, the repeated hostile inroads made upon their territory both by the King of Poland and the Grand Duke of Muscovy.

In the year of our Lord 1502, in the month of September, Alexander, King of Poland and Grand Duke of Lithuania, prevailed upon Walter von Pletenberg, the lord of Livonia, under certain stipulations, to lead an army against the provinces of the Grand Duke of Muscovy, promising that by the time he reached the enemy's country, he himself would be present with a large force. But as the king did not come at the appointed time, and as the Russians, when they heard of the approach of an enemy, came forth to meet the master with a vast multitude; the master finding that he was deserted, and that he could not retreat without extreme disgrace as well as peril, first addressed his soldiers in a few words, as time was pressing, and then discharged his artillery and vigorously attacked the enemy, and at the first onslaught routed the Russians, and put them completely to flight. But as the conquerors were few in number in comparison with the enemy, and loaded with heavier furniture, they were unable to pursue the enemy very far; the Russians perceiving this, took fresh courage, and again returning to the ranks, made a vigorous attack upon Pletenberg's infantry, who could only present to the enemy a force of about one thousand five hundred. In that battle, the general, Matthew Pernauer, with his brother Henry, and the standard-bearer Conrad Schwartz, perished. A glorious action is related of this standard-bearer; for when overwhelmed with the darts of the enemy, and unable to stand any longer from exhaustion, before he fell, he called out with a loud voice for some brave man near him to take the flag from him: on hearing which, Lucas Hamerstete, who boasted of being sprung, although illegitimately, from the dukes of Brunswick, ran to the spot, and endeavoured to take the standard from the hands of the dying man; but Conrad, either from suspicion of his fidelity, or thinking him unworthy of so great an honour, refused to deliver it up to him. Indignant at this affront, Lucas drew his sword and cut off Conrad's hand, which held the standard; Conrad, however, grasped the standard with his other hand and with his teeth, and held it till it tore; Lucas then snatching up the fragments of the flag, betrayed the infantry, and deserted to the Russians. The result of this treachery was, that nearly four hundred foot soldiers were horribly slaughtered by the enemy; the remainder, who kept the ranks, returned safe with the cavalry. Lucas was the cause of this slaughter. Being subsequently taken prisoner by the Russians, and sent to Moscow, he held for some time an honourable position at the prince's court; but writhing under the injury he had sustained from the Russians, he subsequently escaped secretly from Moscow, and went over to Christjern, King of Denmark, who made him his captain of artillery; but as some of the foot soldiers who had escaped from the above slaughter, and had fled into Denmark, informed the king of his treachery, and declared that they would not fight in his company, King Christjern sent him to Stockholm, and changes afterwards taking place in the state of the kingdom, Josterick *alias* Gustavus, King of Sweden, on recovering Stockholm, admitted Lucas, whom he found there, into the number of his intimates, and made him governor of the town of Viburg; but finding himself accused of I know not what crime, and fearing somewhat serious consequences, he again betook himself to Moscow, where I saw him honourably enrolled among the stipendiaries of the prince.

Sweden, which adjoins the Russians' dominions, is united to Norway and Scandia, much as Italy is united to the kingdom of Naples and Piedmont. It is washed on nearly all sides: first, by the Baltic Sea, and then by the ocean which we now call the Frozen Ocean. Sweden, whose royal city is Holmia,—called by the inhabitants Stockholm, and by the Russians Stecolna,—is a very extensive kingdom, comprising many different nations. Amongst these, the Goths are remarkable for their valour in war. They are divided into Ostrogoths and Westrogoths; the former meaning eastern, and the latter western Goths, from the situation of the countries which they inhabit. Marching out of this country, they became in former times a terror to the whole world, as several authors have recorded.

Norway, called by some Nortwagia, lies in a long range contiguous to Sweden, and is washed by the sea; and as the latter took its name from *sud*, that is, south, so the former derives its name from *nort*, that is, the north, in which direction it lies. For the Germans have used their own vernacular names for the four cardinal points, to designate provinces lying in those respective directions; for *ost* signifies east, whence the name of Austria, which the Germans properly call Osterreich. *West* is the German word for the Occident, whence comes the name of Westphalia; and in the same manner as I have above said, from *sud* and *nort*, come Swetia and Nortwagia.

Scandia is not an island, but a continent, forming part of the kingdoms of Sweden, and skirting the country of the Goths in a long tract. A great part of it now belongs to the King of Denmark; but as writers on these matters have described it as larger than Sweden itself, and have stated that the Goths and Lombards proceeded thence, these three kingdoms seem, according to my opinion, to have been comprehended as one great body, under the single name of Scandia; for at that time that part of the land between the Frozen Ocean and the Baltic Sea, which washes Finland, was unknown, and is indeed but little known to this day, on account of the great number of marshes and innumerable rivers, together with the inclemency of the climate; this has been the cause that many have described the whole of this immense island [peninsula] under the single name of Scandia.

With respect to Corela, we have already said that it is tributary both to the King of Sweden and the Prince of Russia, and lies between the dominions of both of these princes; hence each claims it as his own. Its boundaries extend as far as the Frozen Ocean. As, however, many various accounts have been given of the Frozen Ocean by different writers, I have thought it not inappropriate to subjoin a brief description of the navigation of that sea.

The Navigation of the Frozen Ocean.

At the time that I was at the court of the Grand Duke of Muscovy, as the ambassador of the Most Serene Prince my master, there happened to be there Gregory Istoma, the interpreter of that prince, an industrious man, who had learned the Latin language at the court of John, King of Denmark; and as he had been sent by his prince in the year 1496 to the King of Denmark, in company with one Master David (a Scotchman by birth, and at that time the King of Denmark's ambassador, with whom also I became acquainted in my first embassy), he gave me a short account of his journey; and as from the great difficulties of the road, this journey seemed to be an extremely laborious one, I have conceived the wish briefly to describe it just as I received it from him. In the first place, he said that being dispatched by his prince, in company with the aforesaid ambassador David, he had reached Great Novogorod; but as at that time the kingdom of Sweden had revolted from the King of Denmark, and the Grand Prince of Muscovy was on that account at issue with the Swedes, so that the travellers could not follow the ordinary road in consequence of the disorders occasioned by the war, they were obliged to take a route which, though safer, was much longer. The first portion of it, which was difficult enough, was from Novogorod to the mouths of the Dwina and Potivlo; he stated that there could not be a more abominable road than this for the trouble and difficulties which it exposed them to, and that it was three hundred miles long. The party then embarked in four boats at the mouths of the Dwina, and sailed along the right-hand shore of the ocean, and there saw some lofty and bluff mountains, and after accomplishing sixteen miles, and crossing a certain gulf, they sailed along the left shore, and leaving the open sea to their right, which, like the adjacent mountains, takes its name from the river Petchora, they came to the people of Finlapeia. Although these people dwell in low cottages, scattered here and there along the sea coast, and lead an almost savage life, they are yet more gentle in their manners than the wild Laplanders. He stated that they were tributary to the Prince of Muscovy.

A voyage of eighty miles, after leaving the land of the Laplanders, brought them to the country of Nortpoden, which is subject to the King of Sweden. The Russians call the country Kaienska Semla, and the people, Kaiemai. Then coasting along a winding shore which stretched out to the right, he said that they came to a certain headland called Holynose [Sviatoi Nos]. Holynose is a huge rock, in the shape of a nose, protruding into the sea, under which is seen a cave which every six hours receives the waters of the ocean, and forms a whirlpool, and alternately discharges them with great uproar, causing a similar whirlpool. Some have called it the navel of the sea. He stated that the force of this vortex was so great, that it would draw into it ships and other things in the neighbourhood, and swallow them up; and that he himself was never in greater danger, for finding that the whirlpool began suddenly and violently to draw the ship in which they sailed towards itself, they escaped with great difficulty by laboriously plying their oars. Having passed the Holynose, they came to a certain rocky mountain, which they were obliged to sail round. Here they were detained several days by contrary winds, upon which a sailor said, " This rock which you see is called Semes, and unless we appease it with a gift we shall not easily pass it." Istoma, however, reproached him with his vain superstition. The sailor, upon this rebuke, held his peace; and, after being detained there four days by the tempest, the wind abated, and they weighed anchor. When a favourable wind arose for carrying them on, the pilot said, " You laughed at my warning about appeasing the rock Semes, as though it were an empty superstition; but if I had not secretly climbed the rock in the night, and propitiated Semes, you would on no account have had a passage granted to you." Upon being questioned as to the offering which he had made to Semes, he said that he had poured out upon the projecting rock which we had seen some oatmeal mixed with butter.

He further stated that, in sailing onwards, they came to another huge promontory, forming a peninsula, named Motka, at the point of which was the fortress of Barthus, which signifies a garrison house, for the kings of Norway maintain a military garrison there for the defence of their borders. He stated that this promontory jutted so far into the sea that it would take nearly eight days to sail round it, so that to prevent the delay which this would occasion, at the expense of great exertion they carried over their boats and baggage on their shoulders, a distance of half a mile across the isthmus. They afterwards sailed up to the country of the Ditciloppi, who are wild Laplanders, to a place named Dront [Drontheim], two hundred miles north of the Dwina; and they say that the Prince of Muscovy exacts tribute even as far as this place. They then left their boats and performed the rest of their journey by land, in sledges. He further related that there are herds of deer there, as plentiful as oxen are with us, which are called in the Norwegian language, " rhen". They are somewhat larger than our stags, and are used by the Laplanders instead of oxen, and in the following manner: they yoke the deer to a carriage made in the form of a fishing boat, in which the man is bound by his feet lest he should fall out while the deer is at full speed; in his left hand he holds a bridle, to guide the course of the deer, and in his right a staff, with which to prevent the upsetting of the carriage, if it should happen to lean too much on either side. He stated that, by this mode of travelling, he himself had accomplished twenty [German] miles in one day, and had then let loose the deer, which returned of its own accord to its own master and its accustomed home. Having at length accomplished this journey, they came to Berges [Bergen], a city of Norway, quite in the north, amongst the mountains, and then reached Denmark on horseback.[1] At Dront and Berges the day is said to be twenty-two hours long in the summer solstice.

Blazius, another of the prince's interpreters, who a few years before had been sent by his prince into Spain to the emperor, gave me another and more compendious account of his journey; for he said, that when he had been dispatched from Moscow to John, King of Denmark, he had travelled as far as Rostov on foot; that he took boat at Pereaslav, and sailed thence by the Volga to Castromos; thence he travelled by a land journey of seven versts up to a certain small river, along which he sailed first to Vologda, thence to Suchana and Dwina, and so on, as far as Berges, a city of Norway; that in his passage he overcame all the dangers and toils related above by Istoma; and at length came straight to Hafnia, the metropolis of Denmark, which is called by the Germans, Kopenhagen. Both of them stated that they returned to Moscow through Livonia, and each accomplished the journey in the space of one year; though Gregory Istoma said, that in the middle portion of that time he had been detained in many places by storms, and suffered great delays. Each distinctly affirmed, that he had traversed seventeen

---

[1] He must of course mean the nearest point to Denmark.

hundred versts, that is, three hundred and forty [German] miles in this journey.

The said accounts are confirmed by that Demetrius, who recently went to Rome as ambassador to the Pope, and from whose relation Paulus Jovius drew up his description of Russia, and who took this same route in his embassy to Norway and Denmark. But all of these, upon my questioning them respecting the Frozen or Icy Ocean, gave me no other reply, than that on the sea-coasts they had seen several very large rivers flowing into the sea with such force and abundance as to drive back the very waters of the sea for a considerable space from the shore, and that the rivers themselves were frozen together with the sea to a certain distance from the shore. This takes place in Livonia and other parts of Sweden; for although in the sea the ice may be broken by the force of opposing winds, yet in the rivers the ice is seldom raised or broken, unless an inundation occur, for the blocks of ice which are carried down by the rivers into the sea float about upon it for nearly a whole year, and afterwards, through the intensity of the frost, become united together, so that sometimes the ice of many seasons may be seen combined in one mass. This may be easily understood from the blocks of ice which are driven on shore by the winds. Indeed, I have heard from persons of good authority, that the Baltic Sea is often frozen over in many places.

The persons above-mentioned stated that in that country, which is inhabited by the wild Laplanders, the sun does not set during the summer solstice for forty days, but that during three hours of the night the body of the sun seemed to be obscured by a kind of dimness, so that its rays were not visible; but nevertheless it afforded so much light that no one was prevented by darkness from doing his work. The Russians boast that they receive tribute from these wild Laplanders, which, although a thing not to be expected, need not create surprise, as they have no other neighbours who demand tribute from them. In lieu of tribute-money, they pay skins and fish, for they have no other possessions. When they have paid their annual tribute, they boast that they owe no one anything, and that they are their own masters.

Although the Laplanders have no bread or salt, or other provocatives of the palate, and only live upon fish and game, they seem to be very prone to sensuality.

They are all very skilful bowmen; so that if they meet with any of the nobler kinds of game in the chase, they will kill it, by discharging their arrows at the snout, so that they may procure the skins entire and uninjured. When going out to hunt, they leave merchants and other foreigners, who are their guests, at home with their wives; and if upon their return they find the wife cheerful and more joyous than usual from the company of the guest, they make him some present; but if otherwise, they expel him with disgrace. Already they begin to lay aside their innate ferocity, and to show more courtesy in the company of foreigners, who travel thither for the sake of merchandize. They give free admission to merchants, who bring them clothes made of thick cloth, hatchets, needles, spoons, knives, cups, pottery, meal, and a variety of other things; so that now through feeding on cooked victuals they have become more civilized in their manners. The garments which they wear consist of the skins of various animals sewn together, and sometimes they come to Moscow in this kind of dress; a very few wear leggings and hats made of deer-skin. They use no gold or silver money, but confine themselves to simple barter; and as they know no other language than their own, they appear like dumb men amongst foreigners. They cover their huts with the bark of trees, but nowhere do they keep to any fixed habitation; but after they have taken what game and fish they can find in any one spot, they migrate elsewhere.

The above-mentioned ambassadors of the Prince of Moscow declared that they had seen very lofty mountains in those parts, always vomiting flames like Etna; and that in Norway itself there were many mountains, which had become exhausted by constant burning. This has led some to assert that the fires of purgatory were situated there; and when I went on my embassy to the court of Christian, King of Denmark, I heard nearly the same story concerning these mountains from those who happened at the time to be governors of Norway.

The ocean which lies about the mouths of the river Petchora, to the right of the mouths of the Dwina, is said to contain animals of great size. Amongst others, there is one animal of the size of an ox, which the people of the country call *mors*. It has short feet, like those of a beaver; a chest rather broad and deep compared to the rest of its body; and two tusks in the upper jaw protruding to a considerable length. This animal, together with other animals of its kind, on account of its offspring and for the sake of rest, leaves the ocean and goes in herds to the mountains, and before yielding itself to the very deep sleep which naturally comes over it, sets, like the crane, one of its number to keep watch; and if this one should slumber or happen to be killed by a hunter, the others may easily be taken; but if he give the customary sign, by lowing, the rest of the herd immediately take the alarm. They precipitate themselves into the ocean with great rapidity, as if they were carried down the mountain in a carriage, and there they rest for a time upon the surface of the floating blocks of ice. The hunters pursue these animals only for the tusks, of which the Russians, the Tartars, and especially the Turks, skilfully make handles for their swords and daggers, rather for ornament than for inflicting a heavier blow, as has been incorrectly stated. These tusks are sold by weight, and are described as fishes' teeth.

The Frozen Ocean extends far and wide beyond the Dwina to Petchora, and as far as the mouths of the Obi, beyond which is said to lie the country of Engroneland.[1] I am given to understand that this country is separated from intercourse with our people by lofty mountains covered with eternal snow, as well as by the ice, which is constantly floating upon the sea, throwing danger and impediments in the way of navigation; and hence the country is as yet unknown.

On their Manner of receiving and treating Ambassadors.

When a person going to Russia as ambassador approaches the frontiers of that country, he dispatches a messenger to the nearest city, to intimate to the governor of such city, that he is about to enter the territory of the prince as ambassador from such and such a sovereign. Upon which the governor makes careful inquiry not only as to the prince by whom he is sent, but also as to the condition and dignity of the ambassador himself, and with what retinue he comes; and having informed himself upon these points, he sends some one with a company to receive and escort the ambassador, taking into consideration the dignity of the prince by whom the ambassador is sent, and the rank of the ambassador himself. At the same time also he signifies to the grand-duke whence and from whom the ambassador comes. The person dispatched by the governor to meet the ambassador in the same manner

---

[1] It is difficult to imagine by what blunder Herberstein assigns this locality to Engroneland, a country whose name is first found mentioned in the account of the reputed voyage of the two Zeni, and appears in the map accompanying that account to represent Greenland.

sends one of his people in advance to intimate to him that a great man is coming, who intends receiving him at a certain place, which he specifies. They use the expression " great man", because it is given to all persons of superior rank, for that is the title which they bestow upon every powerful or noble personage, or baron, or other illustrious or distinguished man. But at the point of meeting the said delegate is so jealous of giving place, that in winter time he orders the snow to be swept away wherever it may lie, so that the ambassador may pass, but he himself will not give way on the public beaten road. This further custom also they observe at the meeting: they send a messenger to the ambassador to desire him to alight from his horse or carriage, and if the latter should excuse himself on the plea of weariness or sickness, the servant makes answer, that the message of his master is not allowed either to be delivered or heard, unless the parties are standing. The delegate takes watchful heed not to alight first from his horse or carriage, lest by so doing he should seem to derogate from his master's dignity, and will not himself alight till he has first seen the ambassador dismount from his horse.

In my first embassy, I told the person who came to meet me from Moscow, that I was weary with travelling, and that we could transact our business on horseback; but for the reason I have mentioned, he did not think fit to go through the ceremony in this fashion. The interpreters and the rest had already alighted, and advised me to do the same; to which I replied, " That as soon as the Russian alighted, I would alight". The fact was, that when I found they laid so much stress upon the matter, I was equally unwilling to fail in my duty to my own master, or to compromise his dignity. But as he refused to descend first, and as this question of pride was causing some little delay, in order to put a stop to the business I moved my foot from the stirrup as if I were about to alight, and the delegate seeing this, immediately dismounted; I, however, got down from my horse very slowly, which made him greatly vexed that he had been cheated by me.

After this, he approached me, and with uncovered head, said, "The Captain N., of the province, etc., representative of the great lord Vasiley, by the grace of God, king and lord of all Russia, and grand-duke, etc. (repeating the names of the chief principalities), hath ordered me to inform thee, that having understood thou wert come as ambassador of so great a prince to our great master, he hath sent us to meet thee, and to conduct thee to him (repeating the title of the prince and governor). He also desired us to inquire whether you had ridden well?" (for this is their fashion in receiving you, to inquire, have you travelled well). The delegate then holds out his right hand to the ambassador; but after this, he no more takes the lead in showing respect, unless he sees the ambassador also uncover his head. After this, perhaps actuated by the duty of courtesy, he of his own accord presses upon the ambassador the inquiry as to whether he has travelled in comfort; he finally gives a signal with his hand, as much as to say, "mount, and proceed". When all have mounted their horses, or entered the carriages, he remains together with his people in the same spot, nor does he give place even to the ambassador, but follows a long way behind, and is particularly careful that no one shall go backward or ride behind him. As the ambassador proceeds, he soon begins to make inquiries, first as to the name of the ambassador and each of his servants, then as to the names of his parents, and from what province such an one comes, what language such an one knows, and what is his condition in life, and whether he is the servant of any prince, or a relative or kinsman of the ambassador, or whether he had ever been before in that province; all which points are immediately reported by letter to the grand-duke. After the ambassador has proceeded a little distance, a man meets him saying, that he has an order from the governor to provide him with everything that he requires.

The consequence was, that after leaving Dobrovna, a little town of Lithuania, situated on the Dnieper, and having that day accomplished eight [German] miles, when we reached the frontiers of Russia, we had to pass the night in the open air. We threw a bridge across a little river which had overflowed its banks, so as to enable ourselves when midnight was passed to proceed, in order to reach Smolensko; for the city of Smolensko is only twelve German miles distant from the frontier or entrance into the principality of Russia. On the morrow, when we had advanced nearly one German mile, we were entertained with every mark of distinction; but after proceeding half a mile further, we found that we had patiently to pass the night in a place appointed for us in the open air. Having again made an advance of two miles on the following day, a spot was again allotted to us for passing the night, where we were sumptuously and gaily received by our attendant.

But on the following day, which was Palm Sunday, although we had ordered our servants to make no stoppages whatever, but to proceed straight on to Smolensko with our luggage; yet, after advancing two German miles, we found that they had been detained in a place allotted to them for passing the night. When they found that we were proceeding further, they begged us at least to take dinner there, to which request we were obliged to yield, for on that day our conductor had also invited some of his master's ambassadors, the Knes Ivan Posetzen Jaroslavski, and Simeon Trophimov, his secretary, who were returning from the emperor with us on their road from Spain.

I, who knew the reason of their detaining us so long in these deserts (for they had sent on a messenger from Smolensko to the grand-duke announcing our arrival, and waited for an answer as to whether they should conduct us to the fortress or not), wished to put their intentions to the test, and started on my road towards Smolensko. When the other caterers observed this, they immediately ran to our conductor to inform him of our departure, and soon returned and besought us, mingling even threats with their prayers, that we would remain. But while they were running backwards and forwards, and as we had nearly reached the third station for passing the night, my caterer said, "What art thou doing, Sigismund? why, in pursuance of thine own will, dost thou venture to advance in a strange country against the command of its sovereign?" To which I replied: "I am not accustomed to live in woods like the wild beasts, but under shelter and amongst men. The ambassadors of your sovereign have passed through my master's kingdom at their own pleasure, and have been conducted through cities, towns, and villages; let the same privilege be granted to me. Nor, indeed, is it the command of your master; nor do I see any cause or necessity for such delay." They afterwards said that they intended to make a little digression from the main road, giving as a reason that night was already drawing on; and that, moreover, it was by no means expedient to enter the fortress at a late hour. We, however, despising the arguments which they advanced, bent our steps direct to Smolensko, where we were received at a distance from the fortress in such narrow sheds, that we could not have led our horses in without first breaking down the doors. On the following day, we again sailed along the Dnieper, and passed the night upon that river, nearly opposite the fortress. The lieutenant-governor at length sent his people to receive us, and honoured us with almost a quintuple quantity of drink,—namely, Malmsey and Greek wines, —and also with different kinds of mead, bread, and various dishes of meat.

We remained ten days in Smolensko awaiting the reply of the grand-duke; two nobles came from the grand-duke to take charge of us, and to conduct us to Moscow, but on entering either of our houses, dressed as they were, in suitable apparel, they by no means thought of uncovering their heads, and considered that it was our place to do so first; but this we neglected to do. When, however, the message of each prince had, in its turn, to be delivered and received, at the mention of the prince's name we made our obeisance. In the same manner, however, as our arrival at Smolensko had been delayed through our detention at various places, so were we also detained longer than was seemly in that city. But to prevent our being too seriously offended by the extension of the delay, and that they themselves might not seem in any way to slight our wish, they came to us more than once to say that we should depart tomorrow morning; we consequently rapidly prepared ourselves for departure in the morning, and waited in readiness the whole of the day. At length in the evening they came with a considerable amount of ceremony; but the reply was, that they could by no means start on that day. A promise, however, was again given, as before, that they would enter on the journey in the morning; but a similar delay occurred, for with difficulty we made our departure on the third day after, and the whole of that day we were kept fasting.

On the day following they made arrangements for a longer journey than we could accomplish by our means of conveyance. Meanwhile all the rivers had overflowed, through the quantity of water occasioned by the melting of the winter snows; the smaller streams also, which were not confined by any banks, poured down so great a force of water as to render them impassable without the greatest exertion; even the bridges were set afloat, by the superabundance of the water, within one, two, or three hours of their construction. Count Leonhard Nugaroli, the emperor's ambassador, very narrowly escaped drowning on the second day after our departure from Smolensko. In fact, while I was standing upon the floating-bridge, and looking after the transportation of our luggage, his horse fell under him, and left him on the bank. The two caterers, who were then close to the count, could not stir a foot to render him any assistance, so that, had not others, who were at a good distance, run forward to help him, it would have been all over with him. We came that day to a certain bridge, which the count and his people had already crossed with extreme risk, when I, who knew that the carriages could not follow, remained on this side of the bridge, and entered the house of a certain peasant; and, as I observed that the caterer showed great negligence in providing food for us, telling us, in answer to our questions on the subject, that he had sent on the provisions beforehand, I commenced purchasing some food from the housewife, with which she readily supplied us at a fair price; but when the caterer became aware of this, he forthwith laid his commands upon the good woman not to sell me anything. On perceiving this, I sent back his messenger, and ordered him to tell the caterer that he must either himself immediately provide food for us, or give his permission for me to purchase a stock, for if he did not, I would make him shorter by the head. "I know," said I, "your plans; ye are put in possession of considerable supplies by the command of your sovereign, and that in our name; but you do not afford us the advantage of them, and this is the reason why you do not allow us to live at our own expense." I then threatened him that I would report all these matters to the prince. By this language I lowered his dignity to such a degree, that he afterwards not only shewed me attention, but a certain amount of respect.

After this, we came to the confluence of the rivers Voppi and Dnieper, and thence sent on our baggage, in boats, by the Dnieper, which were carried against the stream as far as Mosaisko; we, however, crossed the Dnieper, and passed the night in a certain monastery. On the following day our horses were obliged, at considerable risk, to swim, for the space of half a German mile, across three rivers, and several other smaller streams, which were overflowing with water. We overtook them by a circuitous route, being conveyed in fishing-boats along the Dnieper, by a certain mark; and at length we reached Moscow on the 26th of April. When we were half a German mile distant from that city, there met us that old secretary, who had been ambassador in Spain, full of haste, and covered with perspiration, to announce that some grandees had been despatched by his master to receive us on the road, mentioning the names of those who had been appointed to await our coming, and to give us an honourable reception; at the same time he remarked that it behoved us, at the meeting, to alight from our horses, and to hear the words of his master standing. We afterwards shook hands and talked together; among other things, I asked him the cause of his being in such a violent perspiration, upon which, raising his voice, he replied, " Sigismund, our mode of serving our sovereign is different from thine." As we proceeded, we saw a number of men drawn up in long array, like a regiment, and as we drew near they alighted from their horses, upon which we did the same; and, at the moment of our meeting, one of them took the initiative, and commenced his communication in the following manner : " The great Lord Vasiley, by the grace of God, King and Lord of all Russia, etc. (repeating every title), has understood that ye are come as ambassadors from his brother Charles, chosen Emperor and supreme King of the Romans, and his brother Ferdinand; and hath sent us, his councillors, with an injunction to inquire of you with respect to the health of his brother Charles, Emperor and supreme King of the Romans." Then followed the same respecting Ferdinand. The second speaker, addressing the count, said: " Count Leonhard, my great master (repeating every title) hath ordered me to come forth to meet thee, and to escort thee to thy residence, and to see that thou art provided with every necessary." The third speaker said the same to me.

While these various intercommunications were made we all kept our heads uncovered, after which the foremost spokesman again addressed us, saying, "Our great master (repeating the title) has ordered me to inquire of thee, Count Leonhard, whether thou hast been well on thy journey." He then put the same question to me. We replied to these questions agreeably with the etiquette customary amongst them: "God give health to the grand-prince, by the mercy of God and the favour of the grand-duke we have been well on our journey." The same person again spoke as follows: "The grand-duke, etc. (repeating the title at length), has sent thee, Leonhard, an ambling nag with a saddle, together with another horse from his own stable." He then made a similar address to me. On our expressing our thanks for these presents, they held out their hands to us, and inquired of each of our party in turn whether we had been well on our journey.

At length they said that it was fitting that we should do their master the honour to mount the horses which he had presented to us, which we accordingly did; and having sent on our people crossed the river Mosque, and followed in the rear. On the bank of that river there is a monastery, whence we journeyed across a plain, and were conducted into the city through crowds of people, who assembled around us from all quarters; and in this fashion we reached our hotels, which were situated at the further side of the city. The houses were empty, both of inmates and furniture; but each of the caterers signified to his respective ambassador that he, as well as those ambassadors who had travelled with us from Smolensko, had orders from their sovereign to provide us with every necessary. They also appointed us a scribe, stating that it would be his duty to bring us daily food and other necessaries, and concluded by begging us, if there was anything which we wanted, to intimate it to them. They afterwards paid us a visit nearly every day, always making inquiry respecting our necessities. They have one fixed allowance of provisions appointed for German ambassadors, another for Lithuanian ambassadors, and another for the ambassadors from other countries. The appointed caterers, I say, have a certain number attached to each person, with instructions as to how much bread, drink, meat, straw, hay, and other things they shall give to each according to his number. They know how much wood they have to allow for the kitchen, and also how much for heating the stoves, as well as how much salt, pepper, oil, onions, and other minor things they have to supply for each day. The same calculation is to be observed by the caterers who accompany ambassadors into and out of Moscow; but although they used to provide us with a superfluity both of meat and drink, they would give us in exchange nearly everything which we desired. They always brought us five different kinds of drink, namely, three sorts of mead, and two of beer. I had sometimes sent to the market to purchase certain articles with my own money, especially live fish, but this they took as a great affront, stating that their master would be greatly offended at it. I also intimated to the caterer, that I wished to provide beds for the noblemen whom I had with me, five in number; but he immediately replied, that it was not the custom to provide beds for anybody: to which I answered, that I did not ask for them, but wished to buy them, and that I made the remark to him that I might not again offend him as I had previously done. On the following day he returned to me, and said, " I have made a report to the councillors of my master respecting the subjects upon which we were conversing yesterday. They have ordered me to tell you not to spend your money for beds, for they promise that they will treat you in the same manner as you have treated our people who have visited your country."

After we had remained in the hotel two days, we inquired of our caterers on what day the prince would summon us to an audience. " Whenever you wish," was their reply, " we will refer the question to our sovereign's councillors." We requested that it should be done immediately. A period was then appointed, which was put off to another day. On the day before that day the caterer himself came to say, " My lord's councillors have commanded me to announce to thee that thou must appear before our prince to-morrow." Moreover, on every occasion that they summoned us, they had interpreters with them. On that same evening the interpreter returned, and said : " Be in readiness, for you will be summoned into the presence of our master." Again in the morning he returned, repeating the same piece of warning : " To-day you will be in the presence of our master." Then within a quarter of an hour one or other of our caterers would come to say: "Some grandees will shortly come for you, so that it behoves you to be assembled together under the same roof." As soon therefore as I had gone to the house of the imperial ambassador, an interpreter came immediately to say that the grandees and chief men about the prince's court, who were to conduct us to the palace, were already arrived. One of these was the Knes Vasiley Taroslovski, allied by blood to the grand-duke, another was one of those who had previously received us in the name of the prince, and these were accompanied by a considerable number of noblemen.

Meanwhile our caterers endeavoured to persuade us to show honour to these grandees, and to go forth to meet them; to which we replied, " That we knew our duty and should do it." But as they had already alighted from their horses and were entering the count's hotel, the caterers forthwith urged us to advance to meet them, and thus, by a deferential expression of respect, in some degree give precedence to their prince over our own masters. But we, while they were coming up stairs, made various pretences of delay, so as to retard the meeting; and we encountered them right in the middle of the staircase, and invited them to enter the house so as to rest a little, but that they refused to do. The knes himself said: "Our great sovereign (repeating the whole title) has given orders that you should come to him."

We then mounted our horses, and went on our way accompanied by a great escort; but on approaching the Kremlin fell into so great a crowd, that in spite of the exertions of our attendants, we had much difficulty in passing through. For it is a custom amongst these people, that on all occasions when distinguished ambassadors from foreign kings and princes are to be conducted to the court, the lower class of nobles, stipendiaries, and soldiers, assemble together by command of the prince, from the neighbouring and surrounding districts. All the taverns and shops of the city are on such occasions shut up, all buyers and sellers are expelled from the market-place, and the citizens gather together to the scene of display from all quarters. The result of this is, that the power of the prince appears very great in the eyes of foreigners, from such an immense concourse of men as his subjects; while, on the other hand, his dignity is made apparent to all his subjects, when they see such embassies sent to him by foreign princes.

On entering the Kremlin, we saw men of different ranks arranged in different parts or divisions of the building. Near the gate stood the citizens, the soldiers and stipendiaries occupied the fore-court, accompanying and preceding us on foot, and prevented us, by halting, from approaching or alighting from our horses near the steps; for no one is permitted, except the prince, to alight from his horse near the steps. This is done by way of showing greater honour to the prince. Then first, as we come to the middle of the steps, certain of the prince's councillors came forward to meet us, presenting us their hands and lips, and led us a little further on our way. Then, having passed the steps, other councillors of higher rank came forward to meet us, offering their right hands, by way of salutation, their predecessors meanwhile retiring; for it is the custom, that those who advance first, should make way for those who follow, and these again for the next in rotation, and so take their place in order, according to previous arrangement. Then, upon our entering the palace, where the lower order of nobles stood ranged around, the chief councillors in like manner came forward to meet us, and saluted us in the same order, and after the same fashion. At length we were conducted into another hall, which was crowded with the knesi and other persons of high rank, from whose number and of whose rank the councillors are chosen, and thence to the prince's chamber, before which stood the gentlemen who attend daily upon the prince. During this time, not a single one of those who stood around showed the least mark of respect to us; but on the contrary, if we happened in passing to salute or speak to any one with whom we were familiarly acquainted, he would make no reply, just as if he had never known any of us, or had never received a salute from us before. At length, on our entering the presence of the prince, the councillors immediately arose (the prince's brethren, if any happen to be present on these occasions, do not rise, but remain seated, with their heads uncovered), and one of the chief councillors addressed the prince in their manner, without being required to do so, in our name, in the following words: "My great lord, the Count Leonhard strikes his forehead before thee, for thy great favour." He then says the same for Sigismund. The first is as much as to say he bows and pays thee honour; the second, he offers thee thanks for the favour received: for they regard striking the forehead as expressive of salutation, rendering of thanks, and everything of that kind. For whenever any one makes a petition, or offers thanks, it is the custom to bow the head; if he wishes to do so in a very marked manner, he bends himself so low as to touch the ground with his hand; but if he desires to offer his thanks to the grandduke for any great favour, or to beg anything of him, he then bows himself so low as to touch the ground with his forehead. The prince sat with his head uncovered in a place of distinction higher than the rest, against a wall decorated with a picture of a certain saint, with his hat, called *kopack*, on a stand at his right hand; and on his left, his staff, with a cross on it, called *possoch*, and a washhand basin and two ewers, with a towel placed by them. They say that the prince believes that in giving his hand to an ambassador of the Roman creed, he gives it to an unclean and impure person; and that, therefore, after their departure, he immediately washes his hands. Opposite the prince, but in a less elevated position, was placed a decorated seat for the ambassadors.

After we had offered our salutation, as above described, the prince himself pointing to the seat with his hand, directed us to it, both by word and gesture. When we had duly saluted the prince from this spot, an interpreter came forward, who translated our communication, word by word. When, among other things, the names of Charles and Ferdinand transpired, he arose, and descended from his seat; and after hearing the salutation to the end, said, " Is our brother Charles, elect emperor and supreme king of the Romans, well?" To which the count replied: " He is well." He then ascended the steps, and sat down. Afterwards, when my salutation was completed, he put the same question to me respecting Ferdinand. He then called each of us in turn to him, and said: " Give me thy hand ;" with the addition of the question, " Hast thou been well on thy journey?" To which each of us replied after their fashion: " God grant that thou mayst live in health many years. By the grace of God and thy favour, I have been well." Thereupon he ordered us to be seated; before doing so, however, we offered thanks, according to their custom,—first to the prince, then to the councillors and knesi, who remained standing, in compliment to us, and bowed our heads in each direction. Sometimes it is the custom for ambassadors from foreign princes,—especially those from Lithuania, Livonia, Sweden, etc.,—when admitted into the prince's presence, each, together with his retinue and servants, to distribute their respective gifts.

The mode of offering gifts is after this wise. When the embassy has been heard and explained, the councillor who has introduced the ambassadors to the prince, rises, and addresses all the audience in a clear and distinct voice: My great Lord N., the ambassador M. strikes his forehead to thee with such and such a gift; and this he repeats a second and a third time. He then announces, in the same manner, the names of each of the nobles and attendants, and their respective gifts. Meanwhile a secretary is appointed to stand by his side, to note down the names, not only of the ambassadors, but also of each person who brings an offering, according to their rotation, and of the presents attached to each name. They call such presents "pominki", which is a kind of remembrance. They gave a hint to our people respecting these presents, to which they replied that it was not our custom. But I return to my subject.

After the salutation had been gone through, and we had been some time seated, the prince invited each of us in rotation, with these words, "You will dine with me." I may here add that, in my first embassy, he had, according to their custom, invited me in this manner, "Sigismund, thou wilt eat our salt and bread with us." Presently after, he called our caterers to him, and spoke to them in a low voice, but I know not what he said, but each of them in his turn gave instruction to the interpreters, who said to us, "Arise, let us retire to another house;" where, while we explained the remainder of the embassy, and our commissions, to certain councillors and secretaries appointed by the prince, the tables were set in order. When the preparations for dinner were made, and the prince, his brothers, and the councillors, already seated, upon our being shown into the banqueting-room, the councillors and all the others immediately arose in deference to us; and we, in our turn, having been informed of their habits, before they sat down, offered our thanks to them by bowing on all sides, and took a place at the table which the prince himself indicated to us with his hand. The tables were arranged around the banqueting-room. In the middle stood a table laden with a variety of gold and silver goblets. At the table at which the prince sat, a space was left at each side of him, as wide as he could reach with his hands extended, beyond which it is the custom for his brothers to sit, if any are present, the elder on his right hand, and the younger on his left; at a somewhat greater distance from the brother, is the seat of the elder knesi and councillors, who take precedence according to the place which each holds in the prince's favour. We sat at another table opposite the prince, with our friends and attendants at a small distance from us; opposite whom, on the other side, sat those who conducted us from our hotel to the palace. At the lower tables, on both sides, sat those whom the prince had invited as a special favour, in which number the stipendiaries are occasionally included. On the tables were placed vessels, some filled with vinegar, some with pepper, and others with salt, which were all arranged along the length of the table, so that every fourth guest had each of these three articles before him. Then came in the servers, dressed in magnificent robes, and walking round the centre table, stood opposite the prince.

Meantime, when all were seated, the prince called one of his servants to him, and giving him two long pieces of bread, said: "Give this to Count Leonhard, and this to Sigismund." The servant taking the interpreter with him accordingly

presented the bread to each of us in rotation, accompanied by
the following speech : " O Count Leonhard, the Grand Duke
Vasiley, by the grace of God, King and Lord of all Russia,
and Grand Duke, extends his favour to thee, and sends thee
bread from his own table." These words the interpreter
delivered to us in a loud voice. We received this expression
of the prince's favour standing. The other guests also, with
the exception of the prince's brothers, rose up in compliment
to us. For such an expression of honour and favour as this,
it is not necessary that any answer should be given, except
in so far as that you accept the offered bread, place it upon the
table, and express your thanks by an inclination of the head,
first to the prince himself, and then to the councillors and the
rest of the guests, turning the head round in every direction
and bowing. Bread is used by the prince to express his
favour towards anybody, but when he sends salt, it is intended to express his affection—indeed it is not possible for
him to show greater honour to any one at an entertainment
given by himself, than by sending him salt from his own
table. I may, moreover, state that the loaves, which are
made in the form of a horse's collar, seem in my opinion to
serve as emblems of the hard yoke and perpetual servitude of
those who eat them. At length the servers going out for
food, again without showing any honour to the prince, first
brought in brandy, which they always drink at the commencement of the dinner; then they brought in roasted
swans, which it is almost always their custom to lay before
their guests for the first dish whenever they eat meat.
Three of these being placed before the prince, he pierced
them with his knife to try which was the best, and which he
would choose in preference to the rest, and immediately
ordered them to be taken away. The sewers going out in
the same order in which they had entered, placed the swans,
after they had been cut up and divided into parts, in smaller
dishes, laying four pieces of a swan upon each dish. Then

coming in again they placed five dishes before the prince, and distributed the remainder among the prince's brothers, the councillors, the ambassadors, and the rest of the guests in rotation. A certain person stands by the prince to present him his cup, and it is he by whom bread and various dishes are sent by the prince to different individuals. The prince generally gives a small portion of the swan to his sewer to taste, and then cuts off portions from different parts and tastes them; after which he sends one of his brothers, or one of the councillors or ambassadors, a dish of which he has tasted. Viands of this kind are always offered with especial solemnity to ambassadors, in the same manner as has been related respecting the bread, and in receiving them it is not only the duty of him to whom they are sent, but of all the rest, to rise; so that one is put to no slight fatigue in rising, standing, offering thanks, and then bowing one's head in all directions as often as the prince's favour is shown to any of the company. In my first embassy, when I served as ambassador from the Emperor Maximilian, I had to rise several times in honour of the prince's brothers; but as I saw that they offered me no thanks in return, and made no response whatever, every time afterwards when I perceived that they were about to receive a favour from the prince, I began immediately to talk with somebody and to pretend to know nothing about it; and although somebody opposite would beckon to me and call to me while the prince's brothers were standing, I pretended so long to know nothing about it, that it was not till after the third admonition from them that I would inquire what they wanted, and while they were telling me in reply that the prince's brothers were standing, the ceremonies would in some sort be over before I looked and rose up. Then, as sometimes I rose too late and sat down again immediately, they who sat opposite would laugh, and I, pretending to be otherwise engaged, asked them what they were laughing at; but as no one liked to tell the reason, at length appearing to understand the case, I put on a grave countenance and said: "I am not here now as a private person, I shall certainly show disrespect to him who shows disrespect to my master." Moreover, when the prince sent food to any of the younger people, and an observation was made upon my not rising, I answered: "Whoever honours my master, him also I will honour." When we began to eat the roast swans, they placed vinegar on the table with salt and pepper mixed in it, which they used instead of sauce or gravy. Sour milk was also placed on the table for the same purpose, with pickled cucumbers, and prunes cooked with the same object, which are not removed during dinner time. The same fashion is observed in bringing in the other dishes, unless they be again taken away to be cooked. Various kinds of drink are placed on the table, namely, malmsey, Greek wine, and different kinds of mead. The prince generally orders his goblet to be presented to him once or twice, and after drinking from it, he calls the ambassadors to him in rotation, and says, "Leonhard," or "Sigismund," as the case may be, "thou hast come from a great sovereign to a great sovereign, thou hast made a great journey; after thou hast experienced our favour it shall be well with thee; drink, and drink well, and eat well even to thy heart's content, and then take thy rest, that thou mayst at length return to thy master."

They say that each and every vessel which we looked upon, in which were placed meat, the drinks, the vinegar, the pepper, the salt, and all the other things which were set upon the table, were of pure gold; and from their weight this would seem to be true. Four persons stood on each side of the centre table, each holding his goblet, out of which the prince often drank, very frequently addressing the ambassadors, inviting them to eat. Sometimes he put questions to them, and showed great courtesy and kindness. He asked me among other things, whether I had shaved my beard, which is expressed in one word, namely, "brill". When I answered in the affirmative, he said: "The same thing has occurred to ourselves;" which is as if he were to say, "We also have shaved." For when he married his second wife he shaved off the whole of his beard, which I was told had never been done by any other prince.

The sewers used to be dressed in dalmatics, similar to those worn by the Levites when performing their sacred functions; but they also wore girdles. Now, however, they wear a different kind of robe, called in their language "terlick", which is loaded with gems and pearls.

The grand-prince sometimes spends three or four hours over dinner. During my first embassy, our dinner was prolonged till one o'clock in the morning; for just in the same manner as they often spend the whole day in deliberating over matters involving doubt and difficulty, and do not leave it till it has been maturely discussed and decided upon, so also they will sometimes consume a whole day over their banquets and convivial meetings, and only retire when darkness overtakes them.

The prince often honours his guests by sending them dishes and drink. He never meddles with matters of serious moment during dinner; but when the dinner is over, it is his custom to say to the ambassadors, "Now you may depart." When thus dismissed, they are escorted back to their hotels by the same persons who had conducted them to the palace, who state that they have orders to remain with them in the hotel, to make merry with them. Silver goblets, and various other vessels containing liquor, are then produced, and all strive to make each other drunk; and very clever they are in finding excuses for inviting men to drink, and when they are at a loss for a toast to propose, they begin at last to drink to the health of the emperor and the prince his brother, and after that to the welfare of any others whom they believe to hold any position of dignity and honour.

They think that no one ought or can refuse the cup, when these names are proposed. The drinking is done in this fashion. He who proposes the toast takes his cup, and goes into the middle of the room, and standing with his head uncovered, pronounces, in a festive speech, the name of him whose health he wishes to drink, and what he has to say in his behalf. Then after emptying the cup, he turns it upside down over his head, so that all may see that he has emptied it, and that he sincerely gave the health of the person in honour of whom the toast was drunk. He then goes to the top of the table and orders many cups to be filled, and then hands each man his cup, pronouncing the name of the party whose health is to be drunk, on which each is obliged to go into the middle of the room, and, after emptying his cup, to return to his place. He who wishes to escape too long a drinking-bout, must pretend that he is drunk or sleepy, or at least declare that, having already emptied many cups, he cannot drink any more; for they do not think that their guests are well received, or hospitably treated, unless they are sent home drunk. It is the common practice for the nobles and those who are permitted to drink mead and beer, to observe this fashion.

In my first embassy, when I had brought my business to a conclusion, and had received my dismissal, at the close of the dinner to which I was invited (for it is the custom to invite ambassadors to dinner on their departure, as well as on their arrival), the prince rose, and standing up at the table, ordered his cup to be given him, and said: "Sigismund, I wish to drink this goblet to the affection that I bear to our brother Maximilian, elect Emperor and supreme King of the Romans, and to his health; which toast thou also shalt drink, and all the others in rotation, that thou mayest witness our love towards our brother Maximilian, and report to him what thou seest." He then handed me the cup, and said, "Drink to the health of our brother Maximilian, elect Emperor and supreme King of the Romans." He then handed it to all the other guests, as well as to those who were otherwise present, using the same words to each. Having received the cups, we drew back a small space, and, bowing our heads towards the prince, drank. When all this was finished, he called me to him, held out his hand, and said, "Now depart."

It is, moreover, the common custom for the prince to invite ambassadors, after their business is concluded, to join him in the amusement of hunting. There is, near Moscow, a place planted with thickets, forming an excellent preserve for hares, in which a very great number of hares are preserved, as in a warren, and no one dare catch them, or cut the plantations, under a very heavy penalty. He also has a great number of chaces and other places for preserving game, and whenever he wishes to enjoy this amusement, he orders hares to be brought from different places; for the more hares he takes, the greater amusement does he think it, and the greater is the honour that he thinks he has gained to himself. Also, when he comes into the field, he sends some of his councillors, together with some of the courtiers or knights, to summon the ambassadors to his presence. When they are brought to him, and approach the prince's presence, they are required, at the suggestion of the councillors, to alight from their horses, and to advance some steps towards the prince. When we were brought to him in this manner, during the hunt, he was sitting on a richly-caparisoned horse, and covered with a splendid robe, and taking off his gloves, but keeping his head covered, he received us condescendingly; and, holding out his bare hand, said, through an interpreter, "We have come out for our amusement; we have summoned you to take part in it, hoping that you may derive pleasure therefrom: mount your horses, therefore, and follow us." He had on his head a cap called a "kolpack", with jewelled ornaments hanging on each side, from back to front, from which rose plates of gold in the form of feathers, moving up and down with

his motion. His robe was like the terlick, and made of cloth
of gold. From his girdle hung small knives, after the fashion
of the country, as well as a dagger; behind him hung, below
his girdle, a kind of weapon like a cæstus, such as they commonly use in war. The handle is somewhat more than a
cubit long, with a thong of two palms' length attached to it;
at the end of which is a knob, or kind of block, of brass or
iron, which is gilt all over. At the right side of the prince
was the banished Tartar King of Kasan, named Scheale, and
on the left two young knesi, one of whom carried an ivory
hatchet, which they call "topar", very like what we see stamped
on Hungarian coins. The other carried a club, also like an
Hungarian club, which they call " schestpero", which means
six-winged. King Scheale carried two quivers at his girdle,
one of which contained his arrows and the other his bow.
There were more than three hundred horsemen in the field.
As we rode along, the prince would order us from time to
time to stop at this or the other place, and occasionally to come
nearer to him. When we reached the hunting ground, he
spoke to us and said, that it was the custom whenever he
amused himself with hunting, for himself and other gentlemen of rank to lead the hounds with their own hands, and
recommended us to do the same. He then appointed two
men to each of us, each of whom led a dog for our own
especial amusement. To which we replied, that we grate-
fully accepted this favour; and told him that such was the
custom also in our own country: but he made this remark
by way of excuse, because a dog is regarded among them
as an unclean animal, and it is a defilement to touch a dog
with the naked hand. Moreover, about an hundred men
stood in long array, one half of whom were dressed in black,
and the other in yellow; not far from them stood all the
other horsemen, to prevent the hares from running through
and escaping. Nor was any one permitted from the commencement to let a hound slip, except King Scheale and

ourselves. The prince first cried out to the huntsman, ordering him to commence the sport, and he immediately galloped at full speed to the other huntsmen, who were there in great number, and who all of them at once gave the halloo, and let loose both the mastiffs and grey-hounds, and a merry thing it was to hear the cry of so many different kinds of dogs, for they have a great many kinds of most excellent hounds. Some of them, called "kurtzi", are only intended for hunting hares; they are very handsome, with hairy tails and ears; generally bold dogs, but not adapted for going over much ground. When the hare shows herself, three, four, five, or more dogs are slipped, and set after her on all sides; and when she is taken, there is loud hallooing, as if they had taken a large wild beast. If the hares happen to run out somewhat slowly, the prince immediately calls to any one whom he may see in the thickets, holding a hare in a bag, and cries out to him, "hui! hui!" which means that he is to let the hare loose. Thus the hares sometimes come out as if they were asleep, and leap about amongst the dogs, just as goats or lambs do in the midst of the flocks. He is thought to have done the cleverest day's work whose dog catches the greatest number of hares. The prince himself openly praised the ambassador whose dog caught the greatest number.

When the chase was over, all mustered together, and brought the hares they had caught into one place; and when they were counted, the number amounted to about three hundred. The prince's horses which were used on that occasion were not so numerous or so handsome as I should have expected; for on my first embassy, when I was present at a similar entertainment, I saw a far greater number of beautiful horses, especially of that race which we call Turkish, but which they call "argamak". There were also a great number of falcons, some white and some purple, and remarkable for their size, such as we call gyr-falcons, and they "kretzet", which they use for taking swans, and cranes, and other birds of that kind.

The kretzet are very bold birds, but not so fierce or so formidable in their attack, that other birds, even birds of prey, should fall down and die at the sight of them flying in the air, as a certain person, in writing of the two Sarmatias,[1] has fabulously related. It is, indeed, consistent with experience, that if any one is hunting with a hawk or nisus, or any other falcon, and a kretzet, which they immediately detect by its flight from a long distance, should fly towards them, they dare not pursue their prey any further, but become frightened, and stop in their career.

Trustworthy, and indeed distinguished, gentlemen have told me, that the kretzet, when they are taken from the places where they make their nest, are sometimes shut up, four, five, or six together, in a kind of carriage prepared for that purpose, and that they observe a certain order of seniority in taking the food which is offered them,—whether it is by reason, or instinct, or by what process this is done, is uncertain. Moreover, in the same degree as they are fiercer and rapacious in their attack upon other birds, they are very gentle amongst themselves, and never use their beaks against each other. They never wash themselves in water like other birds, but only use the sand, with which they clear themselves of lice. They take so much pleasure in the cold, that they make a practice of standing either upon ice or upon stone.

I return to my subject. The prince, after the hunt, proceeded to a certain tower constructed of wood, at five miles distance from Moscow, where certain tents were stretched. The first, which was like a house, was for himself; the second for King Scheale; the third for us; then others for different persons and purposes: and after we had arranged ourselves in them, the prince also entered his tent, and

[1] Miechov.

changing his dress, immediately sent for us; and when we had entered, seated himself on a chair of ivory. On his right sat King Scheale [Scheik Ali], and we opposite, on a seat allotted to ambassadors at times when an audience is given to them, or when they have matters of business to treat about. Below the king sat certain knesi and councillors, and on the left side such of the younger knesi as were honoured with the prince's especial favour and regard. When all were seated, there were first brought some confections (as they call them) of coriander, aniseed, and almonds; then nuts, almonds, and a whole pyramid of sugar, which the servants presented on their knees to the prince, the king, and ourselves. The drink was presented in a similar manner; and the prince showed his favours in the same way as he does at dinners. In my first embassy we had dinner at that place; and it happened, that through the tent being shaken, the bread, which they call the "Blessed Virgin's bread", and which they worship and eat as consecrated bread, and keep with great reverence deposited in some distinguished part of the house, fell on the ground, and the prince and all the rest were so thunderstruck at the accident, that they stood trembling until a priest was sent for, who picked it up from the grass with the greatest care and reverence. When the collation was finished, and we had taken the cup sent to us by the prince and drunk, he dismissed us, saying, "Now depart". After our dismissal, we were escorted with all honour to our hotels.

There is another kind of amusement at which, as I have heard, he entertains other ambassadors. Bears are kept confined in a very large house used for that purpose, in which the prince is accustomed to exhibit games for the amusement of ambassadors. He has some men of the lowest condition, who, by the command and under the observation of the prince, attack the bears with pitchforks, and provoke them to fight; and if in the encounter they happen to be wounded by the irritated and maddened bears, they run to the prince, crying, " See, my lord, we are wounded". To which the prince replies, " Go, I will show you favour", and then he orders them to be taken care of, and clothes and certain measures of corn to be given them.

Moreover, when the time was come for us to receive our discharge and to be dismissed, we were honourably invited, as before, to dinner, and conducted to the palace. Each of us also was presented with a robe of honour, trimmed with sables. Upon our being ushered, dressed in these robes, into the prince's council-room, the marshal immediately announcing the name of each of us in rotation, said, " My great lord, Leonhard and Sigismund, by thy great favour, strike their foreheads to thee"; *i. e.*, they return thanks for the presents they have received. He added to the robe of honour eighty sables, three hundred ermine, and fifteen hundred squirrel skins. In my first embassy, he gave me in addition, a carriage or sledge, with a beautiful horse, with white bear-skin trappings, and all the necessary appendages. Lastly, he presented me with a great quantity of fish, belugæ, ozetri, and sterled,[1] enclosed in copper vessels, but unsalted, and dismissed me with extreme kindness. I have already described at large, in speaking of the dismissal of the Lithuanian ambassadors, the remainder of the ceremonies adopted by the prince in dismissing ambassadors, as well as in receiving them, when they enter the frontiers of his territory, and how they maintained and treated them until their return to the same point. On this occasion, however, as we had been sent by the Emperor Charles and his brother Ferdinand, the Archduke of Austria, for the purpose of bringing about a lasting peace, or at the least a truce, between the Prince of Muscovy and the King of Poland, I have thought right to subjoin an account of the ceremonies adopted by the Prince

---

[1] The first is a kind of porpoise, the two others are sturgeon, see pages 13 and 14.

of Muscovy in signing the articles of truce. When, therefore, the truce with Sigismund, king of Poland, was agreed upon, and the articles drawn up, we were summoned to the prince's palace, and being conducted into a certain apartment, found the Lithuanian ambassadors already there. Those councillors of the prince also who had concluded the treaty with us came into the room, and turning to the Lithuanian ambassadors, addressed them to the following effect:—" Our prince was willing, out of especial regard to the request of certain great princes, to enter into a lasting peace with your King Sigismund, but though it was impossible on any terms to do that at present, he has willingly consented, at the instance of the said princes, to enter into a truce. Which truce being arranged and lawfully signed, the prince has ordered you to be sent for, and requested your presence." Moreover, they held letters made out by the prince to be given to the King of Poland, sealed with a small red seal, which was attached to them. On the obverse was the figure of a naked man, sitting on a horse without a saddle, and transfixing a dragon with a spear.[1] On the reverse, an eagle with two heads, with a crown on each head. They had also the letters of truce drawn up in a certain form, with corresponding letters, only with the names and titles changed, which were to be sent back to the prince in return, in which there was no difference of expression, except in this clause, which was added at the end of the letters: "We, Peter Giska, palatine of Polotsk, and captain of Drogieczin, and Michael

[1] The St. George on the seal attached to the letter sent by the Grand Duke of Muscovy to Edward VI. by the hands of Richard Chancelor, is described by Hakluyt (vol. i, fo. 255, ed. 1598-9), as "the image of a man on horseback, *in complete harnesse*, fighting with a dragon." The Greeks, from whom the Russians in all probability derived their reverence for this saint, always represented St. George clad in armour. The naked figure, as above described, is represented in the corner of the frontispiece to the present volume, and shows a coarseness of design, betraying more of the uncultivated Tartar than the civilized Greek.

Bohusch Bohutinovich, treasurer of the grand duchy of Lithuania, and captain of Schlovin and Kamenetz, ambassadors of the King of Poland and Grand Duke of Lithuania, declare, and have thereto kissed the sign of the cross, and have bound ourselves that our king will also confirm the same letters in the same manner by kissing the cross; and for the better confirmation of this engagement, have sealed these letters with our seals." After these letters had been heard and witnessed, we were all summoned together into the presence of the prince. On entering his presence, he ordered us to be seated, and addressed us in the following words:— "John Francis, Count Leonhard, and Sigismund, ye have besought us in the name of Pope Clement VII, and of our brother Charles and his brother Ferdinand, to enter into a lasting peace with Sigismund, king of Poland. As we have not been able to effect this on terms convenient to both, ye have requested that at least we should enter into a truce, which truce we now make and accept, out of our love to your respective princes; and while in so doing we show our justice to the king, and confirm these letters of truce, we desire you to be present, and to report to your respective masters that you were present at the completion and lawful signing of this truce, and that you have seen that we have done all this for love of them."

At the conclusion of this speech he called his councillor, Michael Georgeovich, and ordered him to take the gilt cross which hung by a silken cord on the opposite wall. The councillor then took a clean napkin, which was placed on a ewer in a basin, and laying hold of the cross with great reverence, held it in his right hand. At the same time the secretary held the letters of truce in both hands, in such a manner that the letter of the Lithuanians, which lay at the bottom, protruded far enough for the clause by which the Lithuanians bound themselves to be distinctly seen. At the same moment as Michael placed his right hand holding the cross upon these letters, the prince arose, and addressing the Lithuanian ambassadors, explained in a long speech that he should not have refused peace, recommended by the special request and instigation of the great princes, whose ambassadors they saw then present, if that peace could have been brought about upon any suitable terms; but as it was impossible to enter upon a lasting peace with their king, he had, out of consideration to those princes, entered into a truce of five years by virtue of those letters (pointing to the letters with his finger). "Which truce," said he, "we shall observe as God will, and show our justice to our brother King Sigismund—on this condition, however, that the king give us letters corresponding in every respect, and written in the same tenor; and confirm them in the presence of our ambassadors; and do justice by us; and see that they be at length conveyed to us through our ambassadors. In the meantime you will also bind yourselves with an oath, that your king will perform and observe each and all of these articles." He then looked upon the cross, and signed himself three times with the sign of the cross, bowing his head each time so that his hands nearly touched the ground; then advancing nearer, and moving his lips as if in prayer, he wiped his mouth with the napkin, and spitting upon the ground he kissed the cross, and then first touched it with his forehead and afterwards with each eye; then receding, he again bowed his head and signed himself with the cross. After this he desired the Lithuanians to advance and do the same. Before the ambassadors did so, the one named Bohusch, who was of the Russian creed, repeated the formula by which they had bound themselves, and which was drawn up at great length, although containing little or nothing more than was contained in the sentence above given. Peter, the colleague of Bohusch, who was of the Roman Church, also repeated each word of it, and the prince's interpreter likewise translated it to us word for word. After the formula had been repeated and interpreted, Peter and Bohusch, each in his turn, kissed the same cross in the presence of the prince. This done, the prince sat down and spoke to the following effect. " Ye have seen that at the special request of Clement, Oharles, and Ferdinand, we have performed our part in justice to our brother, Sigismund, king of Poland: do thou therefore, John Francis, report to the pope ; and thou, Count Leonhard, to Charles ; and thou, Sigismund, to Ferdinand, that we have done these things for love of them, and to prevent the effusion of Christian blood by wars between the two nations."

After he had made these statements in a long speech, in which the usual titles were given at length, we in our turn promised that we would faithfully carry out his instructions. He then called to him two of his principal councillors and secretaries, and intimated to the Lithuanians that they had been already appointed ambassadors to the king of Poland: he finally ordered several goblets to be brought, and with his own hand presented them to us and to the Lithuanians, as well as to each of our own and the Lithuanian noblemen present. Finally, calling the Lithuanian ambassadors by name, he said: " You will explain to our brother, King Sigismund, what we have now done, and what otherwise you have understood from our councillors." Having said this, he arose and again said : "Peter and Bohusch, ye will in our name make obeisance (here he slightly bowed his head) to our brother, Sigismund, King of Poland and Grand Duke of Lithuania." He then sat down and called each one to him, and presenting his right hand to them and the noblemen of their company in rotation, he said: " Now depart." And so he dismissed them.

My Journeys into Russia.

In the year 1515 there came to Vienna, to the Emperor Maximilian, Vladislaus and his son Louis, kings of Hungary and Bohemia, and Sigismund, king of Poland; and after marriages had been contracted and solemnized in that city, between various members of their familes, and a mutual friendship established between them, the emperor, among other things, made a promise that he would send ambassadors to Vasiley, Grand Duke of Russia, who had brought about the peace between himself and the King of Poland. The persons appointed by the emperor to undertake the embassy, were Christopher, Bishop of Laybach, and Peter Mraxi; but as the bishop delayed the undertaking, although John Dantiscus, afterwards Bishop of Helsperg,[1] who was King Sigismund's secretary, growing impatient of the loss of time, continually urged him to start, the task of undertaking this embassy was allotted to me shortly after my return from Dantzig.

Immediately on my receiving the emperor's commands, at Hagenau, a town of Alsace, I departed; and first crossing the Rhine, passed through the territory of the marquises of Baden, touching at the towns of Rastadt, Erlingen, Pfortzach, and so into the duchy of Wirtemburg. I then came to the imperial city of Erlingen, situated on the Neckar, and thence to Gopingen and Geislingen.

Afterwards, crossing the Danube at Ulm, I passed through Gunsburg and the town of Purgow, from which the marquisate of Burgow takes its name, and so reached Augsburg,

[1] Johann Flachsbinder, named Dantiscus, from Dantzig, his birthplace, editor of the *Soteria*, a collection of panegyrics on Herberstein, of several of which he was also the author.

which is situated on the Lech; and there I was met by Gregory Sagrevski, the Russian ambassador, and Chrysostom Columnus [Colonna?], the secretary of Elizabeth, widow of John Sforza, of Milan and Bari, who became the companions of my journey. Leaving Augsburg in the beginning of the year 1516, we crossed the Lech, and passed through the following cities and towns of Bavaria,—Fridberg, Inderstorff, Freysingen, the seat of a bishopric on the river Ambor [Iser?], Landschuct, on the Iser, Gengkhofn, Pfarkhirchen, and Scharding, on the Inn. Crossing the Inn, and proceeding along the banks of the Danube, we reached Austria, above the Ens. We then entered Linz, a town on the banks of the Danube, and capital of that province; and crossing a bridge thrown across the Danube at that place, passed through the towns of Galneukirchen, Pregarta, Pierpach, Kunigsvisn, Arbaspach, Rapolstein, into the archduchy of Austria, and so through the towns of Claraval, commonly called Zvetl, Rastafeld, Horn, and Retz. We then proceeded direct to Snoima [Zneym], a town in Moravia, beyond the river Teya, which for the most part separates Austria from Moravia. At this place I heard of the death of my colleague, Peter Mraxi; and thus, agreeably with the emperor's wish, I took upon myself alone the task which had been assigned to us conjointly.

From Zneym to Wolfernitz [Wolframitz] and Brunn, then to Olmutz, the seat of a bishopric, on the river Moraw. These three cities, Zneym, Brunn, and Olmutz, are the principal cities in the marquisate. Thence to Lipnik.

Hranitza, in German, Weissenkirchen.

Itzin, in German, Tischen.

Ostrava, in German, the town of Ostra, where we crossed the river Ostravitza, which washes the town, and separates Silesia from Moravia.

Afterwards to Freistatt, a town of Silesia, belonging to the dukes of Tischen, and situated on the Elsa.

NOTES UPON RUSSIA.

Strumen, in German, Schwartzwasser.

Ptzni, in German the principality of Ples, at two miles from which is a bridge across the Istula [Vistula], the boundary of the Bohemian territory.

Beyond the bridge, over the Vistula, is the territory of Poland; and at one mile from that spot we enter the principality of Oschwentzin [Osvieczin], in German, Auschwitz, where the river Sola falls into the Vistula.

Beyond Oschwentzin, we crossed the Vistula by a bridge, and after completing eight miles, reached Cracow, the capital of the kingdom of Poland, and put our carriages on sledges.

Proceeding from Cracow
To Prostovitza, four miles.
Vislitza, six miles.
Schidlov, five miles.
Oppatov, six miles.
Savichost, four miles; where again crossing, and leaving the river Vistula to the left.
Ursendov, five miles.
To the palatinate of Lublin, seven miles; where, at a fixed time of the year, are held some celebrated fairs, at which assemble people from all parts of the world, Russians, Lithuanians, Tartars, Livonians, Prussians, Germans, Hungarians, Armenians, Walachians, and Jews.

Cotzko, eight miles; but before reaching it, we came to the river Viepers, which flows towards the north.

Meseriz, eight miles; a little beyond which is the frontier of Poland.

Melnik, a town of Lithuania, on the river Bug, six miles.
Bielsco, eight miles.
Narev, where a river of the same name flows out of a lake, and certain marshes, and takes a northward course, four miles.

From Narev, crossing a wood, eight miles; beyond which

is the town of Grinki, in which came royal messengers to meet us (called Pristavl), who supplied us with provisions, and escorted us to Vilna.

Thence to Grodna, six miles. This principality is comfortable enough, considering the nature of the climate. There is a fortified city, called by the Germans Mumel, situated on the river Nemen, which also flows by Prussia itself. This city was formerly governed by the grand-master of the Teutonic order, but is now held under the title of a duchy by Albert, hereditary marquis of Brandenburg. I think, from the name of the town, that this is the river Cronon. It was there, and in the same house or palace (as they call it) in which I was entertained, that Ivan Savorsinski was slain by Michael Linski. Here also I left the Russian ambassador, whom the king had forbidden to go to Vilna.

Prelai, two miles.
Wolronick, five miles.
Rudniki, four miles.
Vilna, also four miles.

Before arriving at Vilna, some persons of distinction were sent out in readiness to meet me, and to give me an honourable reception in the name of the king, and who escorted me to my hotel in a sledge, or wide carriage, spread with cushions, and with furniture of silk and gold, accompanied on each side by the servants of the king. Then came Peter Tomitzki, who was then Bishop of Premisl, and vice-chancellor of the King of Poland, a man whose distinguished virtue and integrity were acknowledged by all, and who received me most kindly in the name of the king. Shortly afterwards he conducted me, under escort of a great number of courtiers, to the presence of the king himself, who received me most kindly in the presence of a great number of the chief men and nobles of the grand duchy of Lithuania.

At that time, the marriage which the emperor had promoted through my medium as ambassador, between the king himself and Bona, the daughter of Giovanni Galeazzo Sforza, was contracted and solemnized.

There were there in close confinement three Russian generals, to whom, in the battle of Orsa in the year 1514, the chief command of the Russian army had been intrusted. By the king's permission I was allowed to pay my respects to them, and consoled them to the best of my ability.

Vilna, the capital of the grand duchy of Lithuania, stands at the point where the rivers Velia and Vilna meet; they flow into the Nemen or Cronon. I left Chrysostom Columna [Colonna?] there, and did not stay there any length of time.

I left Vilna on the 14th of March, but not by the public and usual road into Russia (one of which is by Smolensko, and the other by Livonia); but taking the road which lies between these two, four miles brought me to Nementschin, and eight miles further to Svintrawa, crossing the river Schamena.

On the following day to Disla, six miles, where is a lake bearing the same name; and four miles to Drismet, where the Russian ambassador, whom I had left at Grodno, returned to me.

Four miles to Braslaw, on the lake Nawer, which is a mile in length.

After five miles, we reached Dedina, and the river Dwina, which the Livonians, whose territory it runs through, call Duna. Some call it Turantum.

Seven miles thence to Drissa; and hastening on, we again came to the river Dwina, at the town of Betha; and as the river was frozen over, we were carried sixteen miles up it in sledges, after the fashion of these people, and then we came upon a point where two high roads met. While we were doubting which one we should take, I sent a servant into a peasant's house which stood on the bank to inquire; but as the ice was fast melting under the noonday sun, the messenger fell in amongst the melting and broken ice near the bank, and was only extricated with difficulty. It happened also that at a certain place the river was entirely melted on both sides, and the ice being removed, we had only that part of the ice which continual traffic had hardened, and which was comprised within the tracks of the carriage-wheels, to serve us by way of a bridge to cross over, which we did with great dread and risk. The general rumour increased our alarm; for we were told, that not long before, about a hundred Russian nobles, in crossing over the same river when it was frozen, had been all drowned to a man.

From Drissa to Doporoski, six miles; and thence to the principality of Polotzko, which they call Waiwodate, seated on the river Dwina, which some call the Rubo. At this place we were received with distinction in the midst of a large concourse of people, and were treated with magnificence and cordiality, and finally conducted to our residence.

Between Vilna and Polotzco are numerous lakes, and a considerable number of marshes, with woods of immense extent, stretching even as far as fifty German miles.

On proceeding further, we found the road on the frontiers of the kingdom by no means safe, on account of the frequent skirmishes made on each side, and there were either no inns, or they were deserted. But after passing through several marshes and woods, we came to the cottages of the shepherds Harbsle and Milenki, in which journey my Lithuanian guide deserted me. In addition to the discomforts of the inns, must be mentioned the extreme difficulty of the road, in as much as we had to travel amongst lakes and marshes slippery with snow and ice, until we came to the town of Nischa, seated on a lake of the same name.

Thence four miles to Quadassen; at which place we crossed with great fear and peril a certain lake, in which the waters stood above the ice, and reached the hut of a certain peasant, where, by the foresight of my companion George, we were supplied with provisions from the Russian territory. Indeed, at that place I was unable to distinguish or take any observation of the boundaries of each prince.

Corsula is, without dispute, in the Russian dominions. Having crossed the two rivers, Velicaricka and Dsternicza, at this place, after two miles we came to Opotzka, a fortified city on the Velicaricka, where is a floating-bridge, over which the horses passed for the most part up to their knees in water. The King of Poland besieged this fortress at the time that I was at Moscow treating for peace. Although in those places it would seem to be impossible to draw up an army, on account of the great number of marshes, woods, and innumerable rivers; nevertheless, they march straight on in whatever direction they please, for they send before them a great number of peasants, who cut down and remove the trees and every other impediment, and throw bridges over the marshes and rivers.

Thence eight miles to Voronecz, a town situated on the river Szoret, which, after receiving the waters of the river Voronecz, a little lower down, passes by the town of Velicaricka.

Fiburg, five miles.

Volodimeretz, a town with a fort, nearly three miles.

Brod, a house of a certain peasant, also three miles. Five miles from thence we crossed a bridge over the river Ussa, which flows into the Scholona.

The fortified city of Parcho, seated on the river Scholona.

A certain house, called Opoca, near which the river Vidocha falls into the Suchana, five miles.

Thence, after crossing seven rivers, to a house named Reisch, also five miles.

The house of Dverenbutig, five miles; half a mile below which, the river Pschega, after receiving the waters of the river Strupin, flows into the Scholona; into which flow four other rivers, which we crossed on that day.

Five miles to Sotoki, a little fellow's house, at four miles from which we at length reached Great Novogorod, on the fourth of April. But between Polotzko and Novogorod we crossed so many marshes and rivers, that even the inhabitants have no names for them; much less can any one record or describe them.

During a short stay of seven days for rest at Novogorod, I was received at a banquet by the governor himself, on Palm Sunday, and kindly recommended by him to leave my servants and horses there, and to travel to Moscow with post-horses, as they are commonly called. In compliance with which, I departed, and we first came to Brodnitz, a journey of four miles; after which, we made a whole day's journey along the Msta, a navigable river, which takes its rise in lake Samstin. It happened on that day, as we were riding with the said post-horses through a meadow where the snow was melting, the horse of my Lithuanian servant fell, and went quite over together with the servant, but rolling himself over a second time, like a wheel, he came upon his hind legs, and stood up again, without in the meanwhile touching the earth with his sides, or injuring the servant, who lay prostrate under him.

After this, straight to Seitskov, beyond the river Nischa, six miles.

To Harosczi, beyond the river Calacha, seven miles.

To Oreat Rechelvitza, which lies on the river Palamit, seven miles. On that day we crossed eight rivers, and one lake, frozen over indeed, but covered with water above the ice.

At length, on the sixth day before Easter, we came to the post-house, and crossed three lakes. The first, lake Voldai, which is one mile in breadth, and two in length; the second, lake Lutinitsch, of no very great size; and the third, lake Jhedra, on which stands a town of the same name, at eight miles distance from Oreat. In truth, on that day we had a most difficult and dangerous journey in following the beaten track through these lakes, which were still frozen, but inundated with a vast quantity of water from the melting snow; nor dared we turn aside from the public road, both on account of the depth of the snow, and because no sign of any path was visible. After completing this difficult and dangerous journey, we came to

Choitilova, seven miles; below which, after crossing two rivers, Schlingva and Snai, at the point of their confluence, and where they flow into the river Msta, we reached Voloschak, and there rested on Easter Day. Afterwards, having completed seven miles, and crossing the river Tverza, we came to

Wedrapusta, a town on its banks; and thence descending seven miles, came to the city of

Dverschak; two miles below which we crossed the river Schegima in fishing boats, and came to the town of

Ossoga, where we rested a day; and the day after, sailed seven miles along the river Tverza, and reached

Medina; and after dinner again took boat, and travelled seven miles on that most celebrated river, the Volga, and so came to the principality of

Tver. Here taking a larger vessel, we sailed along the Volga, but before long came to a part where the river was frozen over and blocked up with masses of ice, but by dint of great exertion and labour we managed to get to land at a certain point; but as the ice was frozen into a thick mass, it was with difficulty that we at length reached the bank. Thence we went on foot to the house of a certain peasant, and mounting some ponies that we happened to find there, came to the monastery of Saint Elias, where we changed our horses, and reached, at a distance of three miles in a straight line from that place, the town of

Gerodin, seated on the Volga.

Thence to Schossa, three miles.

To Dschorno, a post station, three miles.
To the town of Clin, on the river Januza, six miles.
To Prissack, a post station, three miles.
To Schorna, situated on a river of the same name, three miles.

At a distance of three miles from that place, we at length reached Moscow on the 18th of April. Of our reception and treatment in that city, I have already spoken at sufficient length, in describing the mode of treating and receiving ambassadors.

My Return.

I said at the outset that I was sent to Moscow by the Emperor Maximilian, to make peace between the princes of Poland and Muscovy, but that I returned without accomplishing my object; for while the ambassadors of the King of Poland were present at Moscow, and I was treating for peace and harmony, the king drew up his army before the fortress of Opotzka, but without effect. Upon which the prince refused to enter into a truce with the king; and my negotiation being thus put a stop to, I was honourably dismissed.

Leaving Moscow, therefore, I went straight to Mosaisko, eighteen miles.

Viesma, twenty-six miles.

Drogobusch, eighteen miles.

I then came to Smolensko, eighteen miles; after which we had to pass two nights in the open air in the midst of a deep snow; but I received much cheerful and respectful attention from my guides, who strewed hay to some depth upon the ground, and covered it with the bark of trees; we spread a table-cloth, and sitting down to the table cross-legged, after the fashion of the Turks or Tartars, we took our meal, and drinking somewhat freely, made a long supper of it. Next night we came to a certain river, not at all frozen at the time we came up to it; but after midnight the cold was so intense, and the river frozen so hard, that ten heavily laden waggons first crossed over it; but the horses were driven to a spot where the current of the river was stronger, and passed over amongst the broken ice.

At that point, which is twelve miles from Smolensko, my guides left me, and I proceeded for Lithuania; and at eight miles from the frontier, came to Dobrovna, where I received abundance of the necessaries of life, with Lithuanian hospitality.

To Orsa, four miles; between which and Viesma we had the Dnieper on our right, which river we had to cross twice at no long interval, both above and below Smolensko. Leaving it near Orsa, we came straight to

Druzek, eight miles.

Grodno, eleven miles.

Borisov, six miles, on the river Beresina, whose sources Ptolemy ascribes to the Dnieper.

Lohoschakh, eight miles.

Radochostye, nearly seven miles.

Crasno Sello, two miles.

Modolesch, two miles.

The town of Creva, with a deserted fortress, six miles.

Mednick, also a town with a deserted fortress, seven miles, and thence at length we came to

Vilna; and there stayed a few days, after the departure of the king for Poland, while my servants were returning with my horses from Novogorod through Livonia. On receiving my horses, I immediately made a diversion of four miles from the road into Troki, in order to see some bisons, called by some "uri", but in German, "auroxen", and which were there kept enclosed in a garden. The palatine, although somewhat offended by my sudden and unexpected arrival, nevertheless invited me to a banquet, at which Scheachmet, the Tartar king of Savolha, was present, who was kept there in honourable servitude, as if in free custody, in two castles surrounded with walls, and situated amongst the lakes. In the course of dinner, he conversed with me on many subjects, through an interpreter, calling the emperor his brother, and declaring that all princes and kings were brothers to each other.

Having dined, and, according to the custom of the Lithuanians, received a present from the palatine, I proceeded on my journey first to the town of Moroschei, and then to

Grodno, fifteen miles.

To Grinki, six miles; and after crossing a wood,

To Narev, eight miles; and thence to the town of

Bielsko; where I met with Nicolas Radovil, the palatine of Vilna, to whom I had already conveyed letters from the emperor, and who, although he had formerly presented me with an ambling nag and two carriage horses, now on this second occasion made me a present of a good gelding, and forced upon me also some Hungarian gold pieces, together with a ring, which he begged me to wear, in order that seeing it daily, I might the more easily remember him, especially in presence of the emperor.

From Bielsko, to the fortified wood-built town of Briesti, on the river Bug, into which flows the Muchavetz; and thence to the town of

Lamas; where leaving Lithuania, I entered the first Polish town, namely,

Partzov; at a short distance above which flows the small river Jasonica, which separates Lithuania from Poland.

Thence to Lublin, nine miles.

Rubin,

Orsindoff,

Savichost, on the other side of the Vistula.

The fortified city of Sandomir, situated on the Vistula, at the distance of eighteen miles from Lublin.

Poloniza, on the river Czerna, in which are taken very splendid fish, which are commonly called "lachs".[1]

The new city called Cortzin, with a walled fortress.

This place reminds me of a marvellous and almost incredible circumstance, which I have thought ought not by any means to be passed over. Once, in returning from Lithuania through this country, I fell in with a man who held a high place amongst the Poles, whose name was Martin Svorovski, who invited me very earnestly, and took me to his house, and received me with great cordiality. While we were talking familiarly on various subjects, he related to me that a certain nobleman named Pierstinski (at the time that King Sigismund was waging war beyond the Dnieper), being dressed in rather heavy cavalry armour, went into the river between Smolensko and Dobrovna up to his knees, and his horse suddenly becoming restive, he was thrown off into the middle of the stream, and as he did not appear for some time, was given up with certainty as a lost man; but that suddenly, in the presence of King Sigismund himself and his army, consisting of nearly three thousand men, he emerged from the water and came up to the bank. Now, although I was impressed with the authority of the man, yet he seemed to me to be telling a story of a very incredible character; nevertheless, it happened that on that same day we came, accompanied by Martin, to the new city of Cortzin, where lived a man of very high rank amongst the Poles, one Christopher Schidloveczki, castellan of Cracow, and captain of the same place. As I was received there by him at a very splendid entertainment, in company with many other most illustrious men, the recollection of this story of Pierstinski recurring to my mind, I could not refrain from making mention of it, which, in fact, happened very opportunely; for it was confirmed,

[1] A kind of salmon.

not only by the guests, who quoted the king as an eye-witness of the fact, but Pierstinski himself was also present at the entertainment, and so explained the matter, as to make it easy to believe it. For he said, that after being thrown from his horse, he three times raised himself above the water, and that by that time, as before stated, he had been considered as lost, and no assistance was brought to him, but at the third time he succeeded in extricating himself: that he then opened his eyes, and moved forward, holding his hand up by way of a sign to them to assist him. When he was asked if he had swallowed water, he answered, that he had done so twice. I wish to relate these things to others as I have heard them told to me: but now I return to the continuation of my journey.

Prostvitza, where the best beer is brewed.

Thence to Cracow, the capital of the kingdom, and seat of royalty, situated on the Vistula, eighteen miles from Sandomir, a city, I say, famous for the great number of its clergy, students, and merchants, at which place I received an honourable dismissal, accompanied by a present from the king, to whom my embassy was very acceptable.

Thence straight to Lipovetz, to which is attached a fortress, used as a prison for priests who are found guilty of more than ordinary crimes.

Thence three miles to Osventzin, situated on the Vistula, a town of Silesia, but under the dominion of Poland; at which place the river Sola, which flows down from the mountains which separate Silesia from Hungary, falls into the Vistula. Not far below the said town is the river Preyssa, which falls into the Vistula on the other side, separating Silesia from the territories of Poland and Bohemia.

To Ptzina (in German, Ples), a principality in Silesia, under the dominion of Bohemia, three miles.

To Strumen (in German, Schwartzwasser), two miles.

To Freystactl, a town belonging to the dukes of Teschin,

washed by the river Elsa, which empties itself into the Oder.

Thence to Ostrava, a town of Moravia, washed by the river Ostrava, which separates Silesia from Moravia.

The town of Itschin (in German, Titzein), four miles.

The town of Hranitza (in German, Weissenkirchen), washed by the river Betuna, one mile.

To Lipnik, one mile; whence, while we were bending our course straight to Wistricia, a distance of two miles, we happened to be seen from a hill by Nicholas Czaplitz, a nobleman of that province, as we were advancing towards him, and he immediately seized a weapon, and, together with his two companions, put himself in a position to attack us. As I regarded this as an act of drunkenness rather than of temerity on the part of the man, I immediately ordered my servants to make way for him in the middle of the road as he came to meet us. But he, disregarding this act of civility, threw himself into the midst of the snow, and looking fiercely at us as we passed by, tried to compel the servants who followed behind with the carriages to do the same as we had done in clearing the way for him; but this they could by no means manage to do, and thereupon he drew his sword and threatened them. As this produced a disturbance on both sides, and the servants who were behind mustered together, he presently received a wound from a cross-bow shot, and his horse being also wounded, fell under him.

Pursuing my intended journey afterwards, in company with the Russian ambassadors, I came to Olmutz, where this man also had arrived wounded; and as he was known as an inhabitant of that country, he hoped to avenge himself by means of a crowd of labourers who were met together, and employed in digging and embanking fish-ponds. By sober advice, however, I checked, and indeed foiled his attempts.

From Olmutz to the small town of Bischov, four miles.

To Niklspurg, a town with a splendid fortress, four miles; which, although situated one mile beyond the river Teya, which in many places separates Austria from Moravia, nevertheless, is adjacent to Moravia, and subject to its dominion.

Thence to Mistlbach, a small town of Austria, three miles. Ulrichskirchen, three miles.

After another three miles, we reached Vienna, a city on the Danube, celebrated by many writers; and had the good fortune to bring thither two carriages safe and sound all the way from Moscow.

From Vienna, I came to Neustadt, eight miles; and thence, beyond the mountain of Semring and between the mountains of Styria, to Salzburg. I afterwards overtook the emperor at Innspruck, a town in the country of Tyrol; and His Majesty was not only gratified by my report of what I had done in pursuance of his commands, but also was highly delighted with my description of the customs and ceremonies of the Russians. So much was this the case, that Matthæus, cardinal of Salzburg, who was a great favourite of the emperor, and an industrious and very experienced prince in all matters of business, jocosely protested, in the presence of the emperor, against his hearing or learning any more of these ceremonies from me, except in his presence.

The Russian ambassador being soon after dismissed, and receiving his discharge from the emperor, and as I was at the same time appointed ambassador to Hungary, to King Lewis, I conducted him to Vienna, by the route of the Inn and the Danube. In that city I left him, and without delay took my seat in a Hungarian carriage; in which, with three mares harnessed together, I was carried on at a very rapid rate, and in a few hours traversed thirty-two German miles, and reached Buda. This great speed was owing to the judicious resting and changing of the horses at convenient stages. The first of which was at Prukh [Bruck], a little town on the river Leytha, which divides Austria from Hungary, at a distance of six miles from Vienna. The second, at the small fortified town of Ovar (in German, Altenburg), a distance of five miles. The third, in the town of Jaurinum, which is the seat of a bishopric, and called by the Hungarians, Turr, and by the Germans, Rab, from the river Raba, which washes the town, and falls into the Danube. This place is distant from Ovar five miles. The fourth, which is six miles below Jaurinum, is situated in the district of Cotzi, from which the coachmen derive the name which they give to their vehicles, from whence the coaches are promiscuously called "cotzi".[1] The last was in the district of Vark, five miles from Cotzi, where the horses' feet were examined, to see whether the nails have fallen out or become bent, and the carriage and harness were mended; all these repairs having been attended to, five miles further on we reached Buda, which is the seat of royalty.

After explaining and completing my embassy in the royal town of Buda, and having finished my audiences, which are commonly called "rakhusch", from the place where they are held, and which is not far from the city, I was dismissed with great honour by the king, and returned to the emperor, whose death occurred in the following January, in the year of our Lord 1519.

I have thought proper to add this allusion to my expedition into Hungary, because it formed almost a continuation of my journey from Moscow.

But as I have thus fallen into an allusion to the kingdom of Hungary, I cannot refer to it without the deepest grief and lamentation, inasmuch as this kingdom, which was previously in a most flourishing and powerful condition, has now so suddenly become, in the sight of all men, subject to the greatest afflictions. Truly, there is a certain term allotted to kingdoms and empires, as to everything else; but the noble

[1] For a note on this subject, see page cxiv of the Introduction.

kingdom of Hungary certainly appears to me to have been reduced to its present condition, not by the treachery of the fates, but by wicked and unjust administration. King Matthias, who was neither sprung from royal blood, nor illustrious by birth from any ancient stock of dukes or princes, was, nevertheless, a king, not only in name, but in reality, and not only bravely resisted the prince of the Turks, but endured without yielding his severest attacks; he even harrassed the emperor of the Romans himself, as well as the kings of Bohemia and Poland, and finally became a terror to all his neighbours. In the same degree, however, as the kingdom of Hungary attained to the height of power in the life of this king, through his valour and illustrious deeds, so when he was removed did it begin to sink, as if labouring under the burden of its own prosperity. For his successor Vladislaus, King of Bohemia, the eldest son of Casimir, King of Poland, although a pious, religious, and unblameable prince, was utterly incompetent to govern so warlike a people, especially in the presence of so great an enemy. For the Hungarians having become more brutal and insolent under such prosperity, abused the kindness and clemency of the king, and fell into licentiousness, luxury, sloth, and arrogance, vices which grew in them to such an extent, that they even held the king himself in contempt. Moreover, after the death of Vladislaus, these vices prevailed still more under his son Louis, and what warlike discipline remained amongst them, utterly decayed; nor could the youthful king, on account of his age, remedy these evils; for, indeed, in other respects he was not brought up to that seriousness of character which became his position. The chief nobles of the kingdom, and especially the prelates, indulged in a degree of luxury, which would scarcely be credited, and carried on a kind of rivalry amongst themselves and the barons as to which should surpass the other in profusion and splendour. They kept the rest of the nobility in fealty to them, partly by rewards and presents, partly by their own power and intimidation, in order to retain the greater number of followers, and to engage their service and applause at public meetings. It would be wonderful to relate with what pomp and ceremony, and with what a crowd of armed horsemen, they entered Buda, preceded by trumpeters, as if it were a kind of triumph.

Moreover, when they went to, or returned from court, they proceeded with so large an escort of attendants and guards, that the streets and passages could scarcely contain the crowd. When a banquet was to be held, the trumpets sounded at each man's house throughout the city, the same as in a camp, and the dinners were protracted for many hours, to the prevention of all sleep and rest; while, by way of contrast, there was a kind of solitude about the king's palace, and the frontiers of the kingdom were the while left destitute of the necessary garrisons, and were laid waste by the enemy with impunity. Bishoprics and all the higher offices of the state were conferred promiscuously, without consideration of merit; and the greater the power that any man obtained, the greater was the right he was considered to have. Thus justice suffered, and the weak were oppressed; and everything like good order being removed and upset, a new plan was invented to bring a stain upon the commonwealth, with an injury to the people. This was the licence of bringing in a silver money, by which the former good money being melted down, an inferior coin began from time to time to be struck; and these again being withdrawn, another better kind was issued, which, nevertheless, could not retain its just value, but was sometimes considered worth more, and sometimes less, according to the cupidity of the wealthy; and was even almost openly adulterated with impunity by certain private persons. At length, the decline, or rather confusion, of all things throughout Hungary, was such, that any one who had the least experience could see that it must be ruined, even if it had had no enemy on its borders. For my own part, I did not hesitate at the time that I was acting as ambassador for my prince at Buda, to advise Mary the queen of Hungary (introducing the subject incidentally), to look to the future, and to get together and set aside some provision against any emergency; and not to trust too much to the power and youth of her husband, nor to the wealth of her brothers, points in which she was exposed to the liability of death and a variety of accidents. I reminded her of the old proverb which says, " It is a good thing to have friends ; but that they are unfortunate who are compelled to make use of them." I told her that the Hungarians were a fierce, restless, seditious, and turbulent people, who showed little justice or friendship to visitors and strangers. That Hungary was threatened by a most powerful enemy, who desired nothing better than to subject her to his dominion. Thus I brought her back to the question of her own interests, and advised her to make some provision, with which to assist herself and her relatives in case of any misfortune, and told her, moreover, that it was a more royal thing to help others than to need their assistance. Although, however, this admonition was taken in good part, considering the manner of royalty, and I was thanked, yet it turned out that good and faithful counsel was of no avail, but that which I had feared and foreboded in my mind, to our great misfortune, came to pass. Nor was this the end of the tragedy. The court, such as it was, remained ; and so little relaxation was there in pomp, arrogance, insolence, and luxury, that one of the courtiers not inappropriately remarked, that he had never seen or heard of any kingdom dying with greater joy or jollity than Hungary.

Although, however, the affairs of Hungary were in this desperate condition, such was the insolence of the Hungarians, that they made no scruple not only to throw

haughty contempt at their extremely powerful neighbour the
Turk, but even to provoke him against them by injuries and
insults. For when Soliman, the present emperor, on the
death of his father, proclaimed to the neighbouring countries,
according to their custom on such occasions, that he had
succeeded to his father's territories, and that the opportunity
was open to all to declare peace or war, and sent this proclamation more particularly to the Hungarians by his ambassadors; and as there were not wanting those who advised
them to seek peace with the Poles as they had previously done
with Soliman, the Hungarians not only rejected this wholesome advice, but even seized the ambassadors of the Turkish
emperor, and put them in confinement. Soliman, incensed at
this insult, invaded Hungary; and first taking Naudoralba,
which was not only the strongest fortress in Hungary but in all
Christendom, proceeded to take others also, and succeeded so
far as to gain possession of Buda, the seat of royalty, and all
the principal most fortified citadels, and in fact the best and
most flourishing part of the entire kingdom. And he now
threatens the remaining portions in such a manner, that they
may almost be regarded as subdued and conquered. It is true
the Hungarians thought they had some right to detain the
ambassadors of Solyman, inasmuch as his father had detained
Barnabas Bel, an ambassador from the Hungarians, who had
been sent to him, and had taken him with him in the expedition undertaken against the Sultan. But had the Hungarians
held their peace about this, since as, the saying is, wrath
without strength is a useless thing, they would have done
better than by the gratification of an impotent revenge to
provoke a more powerful enemy, and so to call down upon
themselves their own destruction, as well as draw their
neighbours into the same danger. At the time that Solyman
a second time took possession of Buda (for it had been taken
once before, but rendered up to John Zapolski, and now,
after his death, was a second time besieged and taken, and

our army routed), I went to him in the name of my prince as ambassador, in company with the illustrious Count Nicolas von Salm, and had to kiss the tyrant's right hand in the cause of peace, a proceeding which at that time seemed necessary not only for all Hungary but even for the neighbouring provinces.

Moreover, it is too notorious to need telling what unequal preparations were made for the conflict of King Louis with Solyman. A young king, unskilled in warfare, and never before engaged in war, was exposed with a few men, for the most part unfit for fight, to encounter a most crafty enemy, inflated with many recent victories, and leading with him the flower of an army with which he had subdued the East and a great part of Europe. Those troops which would have been the strength of the Hungarians were retained by John Zapolski, the Waywod of Transylvania; nor would he allow them to go to the assistance of the king. He also, after the death of the king, aimed at gaining the sceptre, which he had long coveted, and which indeed had been destined for him when a boy by his father, Stephen Zapolski. For I recollect to have heard from John Lazki, who was secretary to Casimir, King of Poland, and afterwards Archbishop of Gnesno, that this Stephen Zapolski, after the death of King Matthias, at whose court he held the highest degree of authority, when there was a talk about creating a new king, embraced his son John, who was yet an infant, and said: "If, my son, thou wert only as large as this," indicating only a little greater size than that of his child was, "thou shouldst now be king of Hungary." And this incident was constantly adduced by the said archbishop as a good omen, and as having the form of a prognostication whenever we talked together upon the subject of bringing about a peace between my prince and John Zapolski. And indeed it came to pass, that John, through Solyman, obtained the royal seal and dignity, together with a portion of Hungary; and the same is now, contrary to all law and treaties, looked forward to by his son, or rather by those in whose power he is,—they, meanwhile, never taking into consideration how treacherously they have already been treated by the tyrant and ejected from Buda. But souls which are blinded with the lust of reigning are borne on to their own destruction, and drag their neighbours with them.

If Christianity had not held a garrison (and that it has had a very strong one there has been shewn by daily experience, and by slaughters repeated upon slaughters), yet, were it but for the wealth alone with which the great and good God has most bountifully endowed it, and from which it has been able to supply the neighbouring nations, it would not only have been incumbent upon the Hungarians themselves, but upon all Christians to struggle for its welfare as for a common country. For what is there scarcely in the whole range of nature which is good and precious, which is not possessed by Hungary? If you seek metals,—what part of the world is more productive of gold, silver, copper, steel, and iron, than Hungary? It is true it is deficient in lead, and is said to have no tin, if it be right to say that it has not that which has not hitherto happened to be found. It has also metallic salts of the best and purest quality, which are cut in the quarries in large blocks. It has, moreover, in some places, and this is a fact which may justly cause surprise, a kind of water which alters the nature of metals, and turns iron into copper.

It produces wines, differing in character according to the different places in which they are made, and in several parts even beyond Sirmium [Simach], which is famous for the amount of produce and the excellence of its wines, which we lost; there are some wines so generous and excellent that they might be taken for Cretan wines. I say nothing of the vegetation and the boundless abundance of all kinds of the best fruits. Then as to game and everything which is taken in hunting or hawking, why should I not speak of them? For the abundance is so great in Hungary, that it is considered as a very offensive thing to forbid the peasantry either to hunt or hawk; and the common people have scarcely inferior banquets to those of the nobility, as regards hares, fallow deer, stags, wild boars, thrushes, partridges, pheasants, aurochsen, and everything of the same kind which elsewhere is coveted for more refined tables. Cattle indeed is so abundant, that you might well wonder whence came such numbers of large herds of oxen, and flocks of sheep, as are exported into foreign countries, such as Italy, Germany, and Bohemia. For while there are many roads lying open through Moravia, Austria, Styria, Sclavonia, and other provinces bordering upon Hungary, through which cattle can be driven in herds from this country, it has been noticed that by one of them alone, namely, the Vienna road, more than eighty thousand oxen have been driven in one year into Germany.

And now what shall I say as to the abundance of fish of all kinds? So great is it, not only in the Danube, the Drave, the Save, and all the smaller rivers, but also in the Theiss, which runs from the north-east nearly through the heart of Hungary, that fish is sold at the very lowest price, and is all but given away; and, indeed, is often not taken away unless given for nothing. Nor is the abundance alone of such wealth in Hungary a thing almost incredible; but their superiority is such, that provisions of the same kind produced in other countries cannot be placed in comparison with them. So much the more marked and melancholy will be the remembrance of this generation amongst posterity, that it did not devote all its energies to the preservation of a kingdom so wealthy, and so aptly placed for the subduing of the greatest enemy of the Christian name.

My Route on my Second Embassy.

After the death of the Emperor Maximilian, I was sent as ambassador of the Styrians to Charles, King of Spain, and Arch-duke of Austria, and at that time Emperor Elect; to whom afterwards the Prince of Muscovy also sent his ambassadors to confirm certain treaties which had already been entered into with the Emperor Maximilian. The emperor in his turn wishing to gratify the Prince of Muscovy, gave his brother, the Arch-duke Ferdinand, the task of advising Louis, King of Hungary, so to manage with his uncle Sigismund, King of Poland, that he should consent to equal terms of peace or of truce with the Prince of Muscovy. In consequence of which, the Count Leonhard Nugaroli, in the name of the Emperor Charles, and I, in the name of his imperial brother Ferdinand, Infant of Spain, Arch-duke of Austria, etc., started from Vienna for Hungary, and came to Buda in haste with our message to King Louis; and after explaining our commission, and transacting our business according to our instructions, returned to Vienna, and immediately afterwards travelled in company with the Russian ambassadors who had then returned from Spain, and passed through the towns of

Mistlbach, six miles.
Wistermitz, four miles.
Wischa, five miles.
Olmutz, four miles.
Sternberg, two miles.
Parn, where there are iron mines, two miles. At two miles from which we crossed a bridge thrown over the river Morau, and there quitting Moravia, entered the principality of Silesia.
Jagerndorf, three miles; then by

Lubschiz, two miles.

Little Glogow, two miles.

Crepitza, two miles; and after crossing the Oder to the fortified city of Opolia, situated on the river Oder, where the last Duke of Opolia held his seat, three miles.

Oleschno (in German Rosenberg), the other side of the river Malpont, which at that time overflowed its banks to a wonderful extent, seven miles.

At the distance of nearly two miles we reached Old Crepitza, where we learned that the King of Poland was at that time in the town of Pieterkov (in which the court is accustomed to hold its meetings), and thither accordingly we sent a servant. On his return, he reported that the king was about to depart direct from Cracow, for which place we accordingly started from Crepitza, and came first to

Clobutzko, two miles.

The monastery of Czestrchov, where an image of the blessed virgin is worshipped by a large assembly of people, principally Russians, three miles.

Scharki, five miles.

Cromolov, three miles.

Ilkusch, where there are famous lead mines, four miles.

At a distance of five miles from thence we reached Cracow, on the second day of February. At this place we had no respect paid us on that occasion; nor did any one come forward to meet us; nor were any hotels allotted to us; nor did any of the courtiers receive us with any act of civility, any more than if they had been perfectly ignorant of our arrival. When an audience was granted to us by the king, he slighted the cause of our embassy, and reproved the officiousness of our princes as inopportune, especially when he saw that the Russian ambassadors, who were returning from Spain from the emperor, were travelling in our company; so much did he suspect the Prince of Muscovy of some plot. What neighbourhood or relationship, he asked, is there between your princes and the Prince of Muscovy, that they should of their own accord constitute themselves mediators? Especially, he urged, as he himself had put no such request to our princes, and could easily compel his enemy to conform to equitable conditions of peace. In reply, we bore testimony to the pious and Christian objects and sincere intention of our princes, and assured the king that they were earnestly desirous to see, and use every effort to bring about mutual friendship and goodwill between Christian princes. We even said, "If it be objectionable to the king that we should prosecute our commission, we will return and leave it unaccomplished, or, at least, will report the matter to our royal masters, and await their reply thereon." After this reply we were received somewhat more courteously and liberally, and even had hotels assigned to us. On that occasion an opportunity was afforded me of asking payment of the thousand florins which had been promised me in writing by the mother of Queen Bona, because I had previously, by command of the Emperor Maximilian, treated for this very marriage of her daughter. The king received the deed of promise from me in a gracious manner, and kept it until my return, when he took care to have me paid in full.

Leaving Cracow on the fourteenth day of February, we travelled in sledges with tolerable comfort through the following towns of Poland:—

The new city of Cortzin,
Polonitza,
Ossek,
Pocrovitza,
Sandomeria,
Savichost,
Ursendoff,
Lublin,
Parczov.

Three miles from thence we reached Polovitza, a town of

Lithuania, and had in many places to make our road across bridges, which were thrown across the numerous marshes; thence to

Rostovsche, two miles.

Pessiczatez, three miles.

Briesti, a large fortified town on the Bug, into which flows the river Muchavetz, four miles.

The town of Kamenetz, where there is a wooden fortress with a stone tower, five miles; and five miles from thence, after crossing the two rivers, Oschna and Beseschna, we came to

Schereschova, a new town built in a large wood, on the river Lisna, which also flows by Kamenetz.

Novidvor, five miles.

Porossova, two miles.

Volkovitza, four miles. In no part of our journey did we have more comfortable accommodation than in this place.

Pieski, a town on the river Selva, which takes in Volhynia, a province of Russia, and flows into the Nemen.

One mile to Mostu, a town on the river Nemen, which takes its name from a bridge thrown over the Nemen; for the word "most" means a bridge.

Czutzma, three miles.

Basiliski, three miles.

Radomi, five miles.

Hestlitschkami, two miles.

Rudniki, five miles.

Vilna, four miles. On this occasion, however, we did not come to Vilna through the places which I have enumerated since mentioning Volkovitza, but turned our course eastward, towards the right, through

Solva,

Slonin,

Moschad,

Czernig,

Oberno,
Ottmut,
Cadayenov,
The town of Miensko, thirty-five miles distant from Volkovitza.

Beyond this, all the rivers flow into the Dnieper, whereas the others which we had passed fall into the Nemen.

Borissov, a town on the river Beresina, of which I have spoken above, eighteen miles.

Reschak, forty miles. In these places we refrained from taking a short road, on account of the immense deserts; but following the ordinary track, and leaving the town of Mohilev at a distance of four miles to the right, we passed through

Schklov, six miles.

Orsa, six miles.

Dobrovna, four miles; and passing through other places mentioned in my first journey, at length reached Moscow, where, after negotiating for a long while, we could obtain no other answer than this: "If the King of Poland desires peace with us, let him send his ambassadors to us, according to custom, and we will enter into peace with him if he ask it of us." At length, we sent some of our people to the King of Poland, who was then in Dantzig, and at our request he dispatched his own ambassadors, namely, Peter Gysca, Palatine of Plock, and Michael Bohusch, Treasurer of Lithuania.

When the prince heard that the Lithuanian ambassadors were not far from Moscow, he suddenly, under pretence of going to hunt and give relaxation to his mind (although the weather was by no means suited for hunting), set off for Mosaisko, where he keeps an immense number of hares. He then summoned us thither before the Lithuanians had entered the city, and then making out and confirming the treaty of truce, dismissed us on the 11th of November, on which occasion he inquired of us by what route we meant to return, intimating that he had understood that the Turks were at Buda, but that he did not know what success they had had. We returned to Dobrovna by the same road as that by which we had come, and there received our baggage, which we had sent on by the Dnieper from Viesma. There also we found our Lithuanian guide, who was awaiting our arrival; and from him we then first heard of the death of Louis, king of Hungary.

Four miles from Dobrovna brought us to Orsa; thence following the same road as I had taken in my return from my first embassy, we came to Vilna, and were there kindly received and treated with great cordiality, by John, Bishop of Vilna, a natural son of the king.

Thence to Rudnik, four miles.

Wolkonik, three miles.

Meretsch, a town which takes its name from the river so called, seven miles.

Osse, six miles.

Grodno, a principality, lying on the river Nemen, seven miles.

Grinki, six miles. On reaching this place on the 1st of January, a frost came on with such severity, the force of the wind meanwhile rolling up the snow like a whirlwind, that the horses' testicles and the bitches' teats were partly frozen, and fell off, withered with the cold; indeed, I had nearly lost my nose, but for the timely warning of my guide; for I went into a house, and only begun to get sensation in it by soaking and rubbing it with snow, as my guide advised me, which produced a kind of tingling, and then, as it gradually dryed, I recovered. There was a Russian cock also, who sat on the top of our carriage, after the German fashion, who was already dying of the cold, when my servant cut off his crest, which was frozen, and thus not only saved him, but put such life in him, that he immediately stretched out his neck and crowed, to our great admiration.

From Grinki, through a great wood, to

Narev, eight miles.
Bielsco, four miles.
Milenecz, four miles.
Mielnik, three miles.
Loschitzi, seven miles. Eight miles thence to

Lucov, a town of Poland, situated on the river Oxi. The governor of this place is called Starosta, which signifies Elder, who is said to have three thousand noblemen in his territory. In fact, it contains some villages, where the number of nobles has increased to such an extent, that there is not a peasant amongst them.

The town of Oxi, situated on the river of the same name, five miles.

The town of Steschicza, below which the river Viepers flows into the Vistula, five miles.

The town of Svolena, five miles, where we crossed the river Viepers, and came to

Senna, five miles.
Polki, six miles.
Schildlov, a town surrounded by a wall, six miles.
Wislicza, a walled town situated on a lake, five miles.

Prostvicza, six miles; and four miles from thence we at length returned to

Cracow, where I carried out various measures beyond my instructions; but which I knew would be acceptable and profitable to my royal master, who had been recently elected king of the Bohemians.

From Cracow, we directed our route towards Prague, passing through

Cobilagora, five miles.
Ilkusch, where are some lead mines, two miles.
The town of Bensin, at no great distance below which the river Pietza separates Poland from Silesia.

Pielscovicza, a town of Silesia, five miles.

Cosle, a walled town on the river Oder, which they call Viagra, four miles.

Biela, five miles.

The city of Nissa, the seat of the bishops of Breslaw, where we were most kindly welcomed and treated by James the bishop, six miles.

Othmachov, a fortress belonging to the bishop, one mile.

Baart, three miles.

Glacz, a town and county of Bohemia, two miles.

Ranericz, five miles.

Jeromiers, also nearly five miles.

Bretschaw, four miles.

Limburg, a city on the Elbe, four miles.

Six miles from whence I at length reached Prague, on the river Moldau, and there found my prince, now elected King of the Bohemians, and called thither to his coronation. At which coronation, on the 24th of February, I was present. I was moreover sent, as a mark of respect and honour, to receive the ambassadors from Moscow, who arrived soon after me; and when they saw the extent of the city and fortress, they declared that it was not a fortress or a city, but rather a kingdom, and that it was a very great thing to acquire such a kingdom without bloodshed.

My gracious and good sovereign, moreover, when he heard my report, and at the end of a consultation on the subjects which were at that time most important, expressed his satisfaction at what I had done, both as regards the diligent execution of his own commands, and what I had effected over and above his instructions. And as I represented myself to be out of health from the effect of going through all these great exertions, he with his own mouth promised me his favour; and since all these things have been acceptable to the king, they have been most gratifying to me.

THE END.

OF THE

NORTH-EAST FROSTIE SEAS

AND

KINGDOMES LYING THAT WAY,

ETC.

GATHERED IN PART AND DONE INTO
ENGLYSHE BY RICHARDE EDEN.

(*FIRST PRINTED IN* 1555.)

Of the Northeast Frostie Seas, and Kyngdomes lying

THAT WAY, DECLARED BY THE DUKE OF MOSCOUIA, HIS AMBASSADOUR, TO A LEARNED GENTLEMAN OF ITALIE, NAMED GALEATIUS BUTRIGARIUS: LIKEWISE THE VIAGES OF THAT WORTHYE OLD MAN, SEBASTIAN CABOTE, SOMETYMES GOVERNOUR OF THE COMPANIE OF THE MERCHANTES OF CATHAY, IN THE CITIE OF LONDON.

IT is doubtlesse a marueilous thyng to consyder what changes and alterations were caused in all the Romane Empyre by the Gothes and Vandales, and other Barbarians into Italy. For by their inuations were extinguyshed all artes and sciences, and all trades of Merchandies that were vsed in dyuers partes of the worlde. *The Romaine Empyre.*

The desolation and ignoraunce whiche insued hereof, continued as it were a cloude of perpetuall darknesse among men for the space of foure hundred yeeres and more, insomuche that none durst aduenture to goe any whyther out of theyr owne natiue countreys: wheras before the incursions of the sayde barbarians, when the Romane Empyre floryshed, they myght safely passe the seas to all partes of East India, whiche was at that tyme as well knowen and frequented, as it is nowe by the nauigations of the Portugales. And that this is true, it is manifest by that whiche Strabo wrytteth, who was in the tyme of Augustus and Tiberius. *Four hundred yeeres of ignoraunce. East India well knowen in olde time. Strabo.*

For speakyng of the greatnesse and ryches of the citie of Alexandria in Egypt (gouerned then as a prouince of the Romanes), he wrytteth thus:—This onely place of Egypt is apte to receyue all thynges that come by sea, by reason of the commoditie of the hauen, and lykewyse all suche thynges *The great rychesse of Egypt.*

as are brought by lande, by reason of the ryuer of Nilus, whereby they may bee easely conueyed to Alexandria, beyng by these commodities the rychest citie of merchauntes that is in the worlde. The reuenues of Egypt are so great, that Marcus Tullius sayth in one of his orations, that kyng Ptolomeus, surnamed Auleta, the father of queene Cleopatra, had of reuenues twelue thousande and fyue hundred talentes, whiche are seuen millions and a halfe of golde. If therefore this kyng had so great reuenues when Egypt was gouerned of so fewe and so negligently, what myght it then be woorth to the Romanes, by whom it was gouerned with great diligence, and theyr trade of merchaundies greatly increased by the trafficke of Trogloditica[1] and India: wheras in tyme past there coulde hardly be founde xx shyppes togeather that durst enter into the gulfe of Arabie, or shewe theyr prowesse without the mouth of the same. But at this present, great nauies sayle togeather into India, and to the furthest partes of Ethiope, from whence are brought many rich and pretious merchandies into Egypt, and are carried from thence into other countreys. And by this meanes are the customes redoubled, aswel by such thynges as are brought thither, as also by suche as are caryed from thence, forasmuche as great customes aryse of thynges of great value. And that by this voyage infinite and pretious merchaundies were brought from the redde Sea and India, and those of dyuers other sortes then are knowen in our tyme, it appeareth by the fourth volume of the ciuile lawe, wherein is described the commission of Themperours Marcus and Commodus, with the rehearsall of all such stuffe and merchandies, wherof custome shoulde be payde in the redde sea, by suche as

---

[1] The Troglodytes were so called from their practice of dwelling in caves; the name being derived from τρωγλη, a cavern, and δυνω, to enter. They were located in various parts of the east; but their most considerable settlement, called Trogloditica, was on the western shores of the Red Sea, about the region of modern Abyssinia: ancient authors, however, differ as to the extent of their territory.

had the same in fee farme, as were payde the customes of all other prouinces partayning to the Romane Empyre; and they are these folowyng:—

Cinamome.	Xilocassia.
Long pepper.	Myr.
Whyte pepper.	Amome.
Cloues.	Ginger.
Costus.	Malabatrum.
Cancomo.	Ammoniac.
Spikenarde.	Galbane.
Cassia.	Lasser.
Sweete perfumes.	Agarike.
Gumme of Arabie.	Berille.
Cardamome.	Cilindro.
Xilocinamome.	Slaues.
Carpesio.	Cloth of Sarmatia.
Sylkes of diuers sortes.	The sylke called Metaxa.
Lynnen cloth.	Vestures of sylke.
Skynnes and Furres of Parthia and Babylon.	Died cloth, and sylke. Carbasei.
Iuorie.	Sylke threede.
Wood of Heven.	Gelded men.
Pretious stones.	Popingayes.
Pearles.	Lions of India.
Jewelles of Sardonica.	Leopardes.
Ceraunia.	Panthers.
Calamus Aromaticus.	Purple.

Also that iuyce or lyquour whiche is geathered of wooll, and of the heare of the Indians.

By these woordes it doth appeare, that in olde tyme the said nauigation by the way of the red sea was wel knowen, & muche frequented, & perhaps more then it is at this present: Insomuch that the ancient kynges of Egypt, consyderyng the great profite of the customes they had by the viages of the red sea, and wylling to make the same more easie & commodious, attempted to make a fosse or chanel, which should begin in the last part of the said sea, where was a citie named Arsinoe (which perhappes is that that is nowe called Sues), and should have reached to a branch of the riuer of Nilus, named Pelusio, whiche emptieth it selfe in

The great riches the kings of Egypt had by customes.

The noble enterpryses of the kings of Egypt.

Arsinoe.

Pelusio.

Damiata.	our sea toward the East, about the citie of Damiata. They determined also to make three causeys or hygh wayes by land, which shoulde passe from the sayd branch to the citie of Arsinoe: but they founde this too difficult to bryng to passe. In fine, king Ptolomeus, surnamed Philadelphus,
Nilus.	ordeyned another way, as to sayle vppon Nilus, agaynst the
Copto.	course of the riuer, vnto the citie of Copto, and from thence to passe by a desart countrey, vntyl they come aboue the red
Berenice.	sea, to a citie named Berenice, or Miosormo, where they imbarked al their merchandise and wares for India, Ethiope, and Arabie, as appeareth by the wrytyng first of Strabo (who wryteth that he was in Egypt) and then by Plinie, who was in the tyme of Domitian. Strabo also, speaking of the saide
A nauigable trenche made from Egypt to the red sea.	fosse or trenche whiche was made towarde the redde sea, wryteth thus: There is a trenche that goeth towarde the red Sea, & the gulfe of Arabie, and to the citie of Arsinoe, whiche some call Cleopatrida, and passeth by the lakes named
Lacus amari.	Amari (that is) bytter, because in deede they were fyrste bytter: but after that this trenche was made, and the ryuer entred in, they became sweete, and are at this present ful of foules of the water, by reason of their pleasantnesse. This
King Sesostre.	trenche was fyrste begunne by king Sesostre, before the battaile of Troy. Some say that it was begunne by king
King Psammiticus.	Psammiticus, while he was a childe, and that by reason of his death it was left imperfect; also, that afterwarde, King Darius succeeded in the same enterprise, who woulde haue finished it, but yet brought it not to the ende, because he was enfourmed that the redde sea was higher then Egypt, and that if this lande (diuiding both the seas) were opened,
King Ptolomeus.	all Egypt shoulde be drowned thereby. King Ptolomeus woulde indeede haue finished it, but yet left it shut at the head, that he myght, when he woulde, sayle to the other sea, and returne without peryll. Here is the citie of Arsinoe,
The citie Heroum.	and neare vnto that, the citie called Heroum, in the vttermost parte of the gulfe of Arabie, towarde Egypt, with many

portes and habitations. Plinie likewise, speaking of this trenche, sayth: In the furthest parte of the gulfe of Arabie, is a porte called Danco, from whence they determined to bringe a nauigable trenche vnto the riuer of Nilus, whereas is the first Delta. Betweene the saide sea and Nilus, there is a streict of land of the length of .lxii. miles. The firste that attempted this thing, was Sesostre king of Egypt, & after him Darius king of the Persians, whom Ptolomeus folowed, who made a trenche a hundred foote large, and thirtie foote deepe, being .ccc. miles in length, vnto the lakes named Amari, and durst proceede no further for feare of inundation, having knowledge that the red sea was higher by three cubites then all the countrey of Egypt. Other say that this was not the cause: but, that he doubted yf he shoulde haue let the sea come any further, all the water of Nilus shoulde have been thereby corrupted, whiche onely ministreth drynke to all Egypt. *What Plinie wryteth of the nauigable trenche. The largenesse and length of the trenche.*

But notwithstanding all these thinges aforesayde, all this viage is frequented by lande from Egypt to the redde sea, in whiche passage are three Causeyes or hygh wayes. The fyrst begynneth at the mouth of Nilus, named Pelutio: All whiche way is by the sandes, insomuche that if there were not certayne hygh Reedes fixt in the earth, to shew the ryght way, the Causey could not be found, by reason the wynde euer couereth it with sand. The seconde Causey is two myles from the mountayne Cassius: And this also, in the ende of threescore myles, commeth vpon the way or Causey of Pelusius, inhabited with certayne Arabians, called Antei. The thyrde begynneth at Gerro, named Adipson: and passeth by the same Arabians, for the space of threescore myles, somewhat shorter, but full of rough mountaynes, and great scarcenesse of water. Al these Causeyes leade the way to the citie of Arsinoe, builded by Ptolomeus Philadelphus, in the gulfe Carandra, by the redde sea. This Ptolomeus was the fyrst that searched all that part of the red sea, whiche is called *The viage by land from Egypt to the red sea. What king Ptolomeus discouered.*

Trogloditica. Of this trench, described of Strabo and Plinie, there are seene certayne tokens remaynyng at this present, as they do affyrme whiche haue been at Sues beyonde the citie of Alcayr, otherwise called Babylon in Egypt. But the merchauntes that of later dayes trauayle this viage by lande, ryde through the drye and barren desartes, on Camels, both by day and by nyght, directyng theyr waye by the starres and compasse, as do mariners on the sea, and carrying with them water sufficient for many dayes iorneys.

Alcayre.

The places of Arabie, and India, named of Strabo and Plinie, are the selfe same where the Portugales practyse theyr trade at this day, as the maners and customes of the Indians doo yet declare; for euen at this present their women vse to burne themselues alyue with the dead bodyes of their husbandes. Whiche thynge (as wryteth Strabo in his xv book) they dyd in olde time by a lawe, for this consyderation, that sometyme being in loue with other, they forsooke or poysoned their husbandes. And for as muche as accordyng to this custome, the olde Poet Propertius (who lyued about an hundred yeeres before the incarnation of Christ) hath in his booke made mention of the contention that was among the Indian women, which of them shoulde be burned aliue with their husbandes, I haue thought good to subscribe his verses, which are these.

The viage to East India frequented in olde tyme.
The customes and maners of the Indians.

> "Fœlix Eois lex funeris vna maritis,
> Quos aurora suis rubra colorat equis,
> Namque vbi mortifero iacta est fax vltima lecto,
> Vxorum fusis stat pia turba comis,
> Et certamen habent lethi, quæ viua sequatur
> Coniugium, pudor est non licuisse mori.
> Ardent victrices, et flammæ pectora præbent,
> Imponuntque suis ora perusta viris."

As touchyng these viages, both by sea and by lande, to East India and Cathay, many thinges are wrytten very largly by diuers autours, which I omit because they parteyne not

The voyage to Cathay.

so much vnto vs as doth the viage attempted to Cathay by the north seas, and the coastes of Moscouia, discouered in our tyme by the viage of that excellent young man Rychard Chaunceller, no lesse learned in al mathematicall sciences, then an expert pilotte, in the yeere of our Lorde 1554. As concernyng this viage, I have thought good to declare ye communication which was betweene the sayd learned man Galeatius Butrigarius,[1] and that great philosopher and noble gentleman of Italie named Hieronimus Fracastor, as I fynd written in the Italian histories of nauigations. As they were therefore conferryng in matters of learnyng and reasoning of the science of cosmographie, the saide learned man, hauyng in his hand an instrument of Astronomie, declared with a large oration howe much the worlde was bound to the kinges of Portugale, rehearsing the noble factes done by them in India, and what landes and Ilandes they had discouered, and howe by theyr nauigations they made the whole worlde to hang in the ayre. He further declared of what partes of the ball, the earth remayned yet vndiscouered; and sayde, that

Rycharde Chaunceler.

A learned descourse of dyuers voyages.

The voyages of the Portugales.

The worlde hangyng in the ayre.

---

[1] It was upon a conjecture, and that an erroneous one, that Eden connected Galeazzo Botrigari with this conversation in the house of the poet Fracastoro. Ramusio, who was Fracastoro's friend, and present at this conversation, describes the occurrence in the following words:—
"Mi par convenevole di non lassare per modo alcuno che io non racconti un grande ed ammirabile ragionamento che io udi questi mesi passati insieme coll' eccell. architetto M. Michele da San Michele nell' ameno et dilettovo luogo dell' excellente Messer Hieronimo Fracastoro, detto Caphi. In questo luogo essendo andati a visitar detto eccellente Messer Hieronimo, lo trovammo accompagnato con un gentil' huomo, grandissimo philosopho et mathematico, che allhora gli mostrava uno instrumento fatto sopra un moto de cieli trovato di nuovo, il nome del quale per suoi rispetti non si dice." That this "gentil' huomo" could not have been Galeazzo Botrigari, who was Bishop of Gaeta, and is elsewhere referred to by Eden himself, as the pope's legate to the court of Spain (see *Dec.* 2, cap. 1), is shown by the fact, that the latter died in 1518 (see Ughelli, *Italia Sacra*); whereas the conversation occurred some years after the embassy of Paulo Centurione from Pope Leo X. to the court of Russia, which was in 1520.—See *post*, fo. 188.

<small>What is knowen of the lower hemispherie.</small> of the landes of the inferiour hemispherie, or halfe compase of the ball towarde the pole Antartike, there was nothyng
<small>The lande of Brasile.</small> knowen but that litle of the coaste of Brasilia vnto the streyght
<small>Peru.</small> of Magellanus; also a part of Peru; also a litle aboue Affrike towarde the cape of Bona Speranza. Also that he marueyled without measure, that this thyng was no better consydered of
<small>The charg and dutie of Christian princes.</small> Christian Princes, to whom God hath deputed this charge, hauyng euer on theyr counsail men of great learning, which may infourme them of this thing, being so marueylous and noble, wherby they may obtayne glory and fame by vertue, and be imputed among men as gods, by better demerites then
<small>Hercules and Alexander.</small> euer were Hercules & Great Alexander, who traueyled onely into India; and that by makyng the men of this our Hemispherie knowen to them of the other halfe compasse of the ball beneathe vs, they myght by the tytle of this enterpryse, without comparison, farre excell all the noble factes that euer were doone by Julius Cæsar, or any other of the Romane Emperours. Whiche thyng they myght easily bryng to passe, by assigning colonies to inhabite diuers places of
<small>The colonies of the Romans in regions subdued.</small> that Hemispherie, in lyke maner as dyd the Romanes in prouinces newly subdued; whereby they myght not onely atteyne great riches, but also enlarge the Christian fayth and Empire, to the glory of God and confusion of infidels.
<small>The great Ilande of Saynct Laurence or Madagascar.</small> After this, he spake of the Ilande of Saint Laurence, called in olde tyme Madagascar, whiche is greater then the realme of Castile and Portugale, and reacheth from the xii degree towarde the Pole Antartike, unto the xxvi degree and a halfe; lying Northeast from the cape of Bona Speranza, and partly vnder the lyne of Tropicus Capricorni, beyng wel inhabited, and of temperate ayre, with abundance of all thynges necessary for the lyfe of man, and one of the moste excellent Ilandes that is founde this day in the worlde: And that, neuerthelesse there is nothing knowen therof, except onely a fewe
<small>The Ilandes of Taprobana or Giava.</small> small Hauens by the sea syde, as the lyke ignoraunce remayneth of the greatest part of the Ilandes of Taprobana

[Ceylon], Giava, the more and the lesse, and infinite other. Then begynnyng to speake of the partes of our Pole, he caused the bookes of Plinie to be brought hym, where diligently ponderyng the lxvii Chapter of the seconde booke, he founde where he rehearseth the historie of Cornelius Nepos, by these woordes: That in his tyme one Eudorus, escapyng the handes of king Lathyro, departed from the gulfe of Arabie, and came by sea to the Ilande of Calese: Declarying further, that whereas this narration was many yeeres reputed for a fable, was nowe in our tyme, by the vertue of the Portugales, knowen to be true: And that, lykewyse the same Cornelius Nepos reciteth, that at the tyme when Quintus Metellus Celer was Proconsul or Lieuetenant for the Romanes in Fraunce, the kyng of Sueuia gaue hym certayne Indians, whiche saylyng out of India for merchandise, were by tempest dryuen to the coastes of Germanie.

Plinie.

The historie of Cornelius Nepos.

Shypps of India driuen into the sea of Germanie.

When he had redde these woordes, he proceeded, saying that the same thyng myght be verified nowe in our tyme, if the princes which confine vppon that sea woulde endeuoure theyr industry and diligence to bryng it to passe; and that there coulde not any nauigation be imagined so commodious and profitable to all Christendom as this way might be, if by this voiage should be found open to India, to come to the rych countrey of Cathay, whiche was discouered nowe two hundred yeeres since by Marcus Paulus. Then takyng the globe in his hande, he made demonstration that this voyage shoulde bee very shorte, in respect of that which the Portugales nowe followe, and also of that which the Spanyardes may attempt, to the Ilandes of Molucca. He declared furthermore, that the citie of Lubyke, beyng ryche and of great power, and situate vppon the sea of Germanie, and also accustomed with continuall nauigations to trauayle the sea of Norway and Gothlande, and lykewyse the ryght noble kyng of Polonie, whose dominions, with his realme of Lituania, extende to the saide sea, shoulde be apte to discouer this

An enterprise whereby princes may obtayne true fame and glory.

Cathay discouered by Marcus Paulus.

The citie of Lubyke.

The kyng of Polonie.

VOL. II. B B

The Duke of Moscouia. secrete: But that aboue al other, the Duke of Moscouia should perfourme the same, with greater commoditie, & more facilitie then any other Prince.

And here staying awhile, he began to speake againe, and said:—Nowe, forasmuch as we are come to the passe, me thinke it should seeme a great discurtesie if I should not shew you al that I knowe as touching this viage, whereof I greatly mused with my selfe many yeeres by occasion of the woordes of Plinie. Wheras therfore, beyng a young man, I was in Germanie in the citie of Augusta, it so chaunced An ambassadour from the Duke of Moscouia. that in those dayes there came thither an ambassadour of the Duke of Moscouia, a man singulerly learned both in the Greek tongue & the Latine, and of good experience in worldely thynges, hauing been sent to dyuers places by the sayde Prince, and one of his counsayle. Of whose learnyng beyng aduertised, I sought his acquayntaunce, and talkyng with hym one daye of these Indians, dryuen by fortune to the coastes of Germanie, and of the viage that myght be discouered by the North sea to the Ilandes of spices, I perceyued that at the fyrst he marueyeled exceedyngly, as at a thyng that he coulde neuer haue imagined. But restyng a whyle in maner astonyshed in his secrete phantasie, hee The woordes of the ambassadour of Moscouia. tooke great pleasure therein, and sayde: forasmuch as the Portugales haue now compassed about all the South partes, supposed in old tyme to bee inaccessable by reason of great heate, why should we not certaynely thynke that the lyke may bee done about this parte of the North, without feare of colde, especially to men borne and brought up in that clime: Yet proceedyng further, he sayde, that if his Prince and maister had men that would animate him to discouer this vyage, there was no Prince in Christendome that myght doe The way from Moscouia to the North Ocean and Cathay. it with more facilitie. Then calling for a Mappe, in which was the discription of Moscouia, and the prouinces subiect to the same, hee declared that from the citie of Moscouia or Mosca, goyng towarde the North-east for the space of lx

myles, they come to the ryuer of Volochda, and afterwarde   Volochda.
by that, and folowyng the course thereof, to the citie of
Vstiug, so called bycause the ryuer of Iug falleth into the Vstiug. Jug.
ryuer of Succana, where they lose theyr owne names, and Succana.
make the great ryuer Duina, and by that, leauyng on the Duina.
ryght hande the citie of Colmogor, they sayle vnto the Colmogor.
North Ocean. The which way, although it bee a long The North Ocean.
tracte, as more then 800 myles, neuerthelesse he sayd that
in sommer it myght commodiously be sayled. And that
whereas it falleth into the sea, there are infinite woods of Great woods.
goodly trees, apte to make shyppes, and the place so conuenient for this purpose that shypwryghtes and other skylfull
woorkemen for all thinges heerevnto apperteynyng, may easily
come out of Germanie: also, that the men which are vsed to
traueyle the sea of Germanie about the coastes of Gothlande, Gothlande.
should bee best and most apte to attempt this enterpryse,
bycause they are indurate to abyde colde, hunger, and labour. He sayde furthermore, that in the court of his Prince,
they haue much knowledge of the great Cam of Cathay, by The Moscouites haue knowledge
reason of the continuall warres they haue with the Tartars, of of the great Cam of Cathay.
whom the greatest parte gyue obedience to the sayd great
Cam, as to theyr chiefe Emperour.

He made also demonstration in the sayde carde by the
North-east, that being past the prouince of Permia, and the Permia.
ryuer Pescora (which falleth into the North sea), & certeine Pescora.
mountaines named Catena Mundi, there is thentraunce into Catena mundi.
the prouince of Obdora, whereas is Vecchiadoro, and the Obdora. Vecchiadoro
ryuer Obo, whiche also falleth into the sayd sea, and it is the Obo.
furthest border of Thempyre of the Prince of Moscouia. The
sayde ryuer hath his originall in a great lake called Chethai, The lake Chethay.
which is the fyrst habitation of the Tartars, that pay tribute The Tartars.
to the great Cane. And from this lake, for the space of two
moneths vyage (as they were credybly informed by certayne
Tartares taken in the warres) is the most noble citie of Cam- The citie of Cambalu.
balu, beyng one of the chiefest in the dominion of the great

Cane, whom some call the great Cham. He also affyrmed, that if shyppes should be made on the coastes of the sayde sea, and sayle on the backe halfe of the coast thereof (which he knew by many relations made to his Prince, to reach infinitely towarde the North-east), they should doubtlesse in folowyng the same, easily discouer the countrey. Unto these woordes he added, that although there were great difficultie in Moscouia, by reason that the way to the sayde sea is full of thicke woods and waters, whiche in the sommer make great maryshes, and impossible to be traueyled, as well for lacke of victuals, whiche cannot there be founde, not for certayne dayes, but for the space of certeyne monethes, the place beyng desolate without inhabitauntes: neuerthelesse he sayde, that if there were with his Prince, onely two Spanyardes or Portugales, to whom the charge of this viage should be committed, he no wayes doubted but that they would folowe it, and fynde it; forasmuch as with great ingeniousnesse and inestimable patience, these nations haue ouercome much greater difficulties then are these, whiche are but litle in comparison to those that they haue ouerpassed, and doe ouerpasse in all their viages to India. He proceeded, declaryng that not many yeeres since, there came to the courte of his Prince, an Ambassadour from pope Leo, named maister Paulo Centurione, a Genuese, vnder dyuers pretenses. But the princypall occasion of his commyng, was, bycause hee had conceyued great indignation and hatred agaynst the Portugales: And therfore intended to proue if he could open any vyage by land, wherby spyces myght be brought from India by the lande of Tartaria, or by the sea Caspium (otherwyse called Hircanum) to Moscouia, and from thence to be brought in shyppes by the ryuer Riga, which runnyng by the countrey of Liuonia, falleth into the sea of Germanie: and that his Prince gaue eare vnto him, and caused the sayde vyage to be attempted by certaine noble men of Lordo, of the Tartars confinyng next vnto him. But the warres which were then betweene them, and the great desartes which they should *Desartes.* of necessitie ouerpasse, made them leaue of theyr enterpryse: whiche if it had ben purposed by the coastes of this our North sea, it might haue been easily fynyshed. The sayde *The vyage by the North sea.* Ambassadour continued his narration, saying that no man ought to doubt of that sea, but that it may be sayled sixe monethes in the yeere, forasmuche as the dayes are then very long in that clime, and hot, by reason of continuall reuerberation of the beames of the Sunne, and shorte nyghtes: And *The woorthinesse of this vyage.* that this thing were as well woorthie to bee prooued, as anye other nauigation, whereby many partes of the worlde, heeretofore vnknowen, haue been discouered and brought to ciuilitie.

And heere makyng an ende of this talke, he sayde: Let vs now omyt this parte of Moscouia with his colde, and speake somewhat of that parte of the newe worlde, in whiche is the lande of Brytons, called Terra Britonum, and Baccaleos, or Terra Baccalearum, where in the yeere 1534, and *The vyages of the Frenchmen to the lande of Baccalaos.* 1535, Jaques Cartiar, in two vyages made with three great French Gallies, founde the great and large countreys named Canada, Ochelaga, and Sanguenai: which reach from the xlv to the 51 degree, beyng well inhabited, and pleasaunt *Pleasaunt countreys.* countreys, and named by him Noua Francia. And here stay- *New France.* ing a while, and lyftyng vp his handes, he sayde: Oh what doe the Christian princes meane, that in suche landes dis- *Apostrophe to the Christian princes.* couered, they doe not assigne certayne colonies to inhabite the same, to bryng those people (whom God hath so blessed with naturall giftes) to better ciuilitie, and to embrace our religion, then the whiche nothing can bee more acceptable to God. The sayd regions also, beyng so fayre and fruitful, with plentie of all sortes of corne, hearbes, fruites, wood, fyshes, beastes, metals, and ryuers of suche greatnesse that *Great ryuers.* shyppes may sayle more then 180 myles vpon one of them, beyng on both sydes infinitely inhabited: And to cause the *A thyng woorthy to be searched.* gouernours of the sayde colonies to searche whether that lande towarde the North, named Terra de Laborador, doe ioyne as one firme lande with Norway: Or whether there bee any streight or open place of sea, as is most lyke there should be, forasmuch as it is to bee thought that the sayde Indians, dryuen by fortune about the coastes of Norway, came by that streight or sea, to the coastes of Germanie, and by the sayde streight to sayle north-west, to discouer the landes and countreys of Cathay, and from thence to sayle to the Ilandes of Molucca, and these surely should bee enterpryses able to make men immortall. The which thing, that ryght woorthie gentleman maister Antony di Mendoza consyderyng, by the singular vertue and magnanimitie that is in him, attempted to put this thyng in practyse. For being viceroy of the countrey of Mexico (so named of the great citie Mexico, otherwyse called Temistitan, now called new Spayne, beyng in the xx degree aboue the Equinoctiall, and parte of the sayde firme lande) he sent certayne of his Captaines by lande, and also a nauie of shyppes by sea, to search this secrete.

And I remember that when I was in Flaunders, in Themperours court, I saw his letter wrytten in the yeere 1541, and dated from Mexico: wherein was declared howe towarde the Northwest he had founde the kyngdome of Sette Citta (that is) seuen Cities, wheras is that, called Civola, by the reuerende father Marco da Niza: and howe beyonde the sayde kyngdome yet further towarde the Northwest, Captayne Francesco Vasques of Coronado, hauing ouerpassed great desartes, came to the sea syde, where he founde certayne shyppes which sayled by that sea with merchandies, and had in theyr banner vpon the prooes of theyr shyppes, certayne foules made of golde and siluer, which they of Mexico call Alcatrazzi, and that theyr mariners shewed by signes that they were .xxx. dayes sayling, in commyng to that hauen: whereby he vnderstoode that these shyppes could be of none other countrey then of Cathay, forasmuch as it is situate on the contrary parte of the sayde lande discouered. The sayd maister Antonie wrote furthermore, that by the opinion of men well practised, there was discouered so great a space of that countrey vnto the sayd sea, that it passed 950 leagues, which make 2850 myles. And doubtless if the Frenche men, in this theyr newe Fraunce, would have passed by lande towarde the sayd Northwest and by North, they should also haue founde the sea whereby they myght haue sayled to Cathay. But aboue all thynges, this seemed vnto me most woorthie of commendation, that the sayde maister Antonie wrote in his letter, that he had made a booke of all the naturall and marueylous thinges whiche they founde in searchyng those countreys, with also the measures of landes, and altytudes of degrees: A worke doubtlesse which sheweth a princely and magnificall mynd, wherby we may conceiue that if God had giuen him the charge of the other hemispherie, he would or now haue made it better knowen to vs. The which thing I suppose no man doth greatly esteeme at this tyme: beyng neuerthelesse the greatest and most glorious enterpryse that may be imagined. *The sea from newe Fraunce or Terra Britonum to Cathay.* *A great and glorious enterprise.*

And heere makyng a certayne pause, and turnyng himselfe towarde vs, hee sayde: Doe you not vnderstande to this purpose, howe to passe to India towarde the Northwest wynde, as dyd of late a citizen of Venece, so valiant a man, and so well practised in all thinges perteynyng to nauigations, and the science of Cosmographie, that at this present hee hath not his lyke in Spayne, insomuche that for his vertues hee is preferred aboue all other pylottes that sayle to the West Indies, who may not passe thyther without his lycence, and is therefore called Piloto Maggiore (that is), the graunde pylote.[1] And when we sayde that wee knewe him not, hee proceeded, saying, that beyng certayne yeeres in the citie of *Sebastian Cabote, the grand pylot of the West Indies.*

---

[1] For much curious matter connected with this incidental, but extremely interesting, reference to Cabot, see *Memoir of Sebastian Cabot*, by Biddle. London, 1831; 8vo.

Siuile, and desirous to haue some knowledge of the nauigations of the Spanyardes, it was tolde him that there was in the citie a valiant man, a Venecian borne, named Sebastian Cabote, who had the charge of those thinges, beyng an expert man in that science, and one that could make cardes for the sea with his owne hande: and that by this reporte, seekyng his acquayntaunce, hee founde him a very gentle person, who enterteyned him friendly, and shewed him many thinges, and among other a large Mappe of the worlde, with certayne perticular nauigations, as well of the Portugales as of the Spanyardes: and that hee spake further vnto him, in this effecte.

Commendation of Sebastian Cabote.

Sebastian Cabote tolde me that he was borne in Brystow, and that at iiii yeeres olde he was carryed with his father to Venice, and so returned agayne into England with his father after certayne yeeres: whereby he was thought to haue ben borne in Venice.

When my father departed from Venece, many yeeres since, to dwell in Englande, to folowe the trade of merchandyes, hee tooke me with him to the citie of London, whyle I was very young, yet hauing neuerthelesse some knowledge of letters of humanitie, and of the sphere. And when my father dyed, in that tyme when newes were brought that Don Christopher Colonus Genuese had discouered the coastes of India, wherof was great talke in all the court of Kyng Henry the Seuenth, who then reigned: insomuche that all men with great admiration affirmed it to be a thing more diuine then humane, to sayle by the West into the East, where spyces growe, by a way that was neuer knowen before. By which fame and report, there increased in my harte a great flame of desyre to attempt some notable thyng. And vnderstandyng by reason of the sphere, that if I should sayle by the way of the Northwest wynde, I should by a shorter tracte come to India, I therevppon caused the kyng to bee aduertised of my diuise: who immediately commaunded two carauels to be furnyshed with all thynges apperteynyng to the vyage, which was, as farre as I remember, in the yeere 1496, in the begynnyng of sommer. Beginning, therefore, to sayle toward northwest, not thinking to fynde any other lande then that of Cathay, and from thence to turne toward India.

The fyrst vyage of Sebastian Cabote.

But after certayne dayes, I founde that the lande ranne towarde the north, which was to me a great displeasure. Neuerthelesse, saylyng along by the coast, to see if I could fynde any gulfe that turned, I founde the lande styll continent to the fifty-sixth degree vnder our pole. And seeing that there the coast turned toward the east, dispayring to fynde the passage, I turned backe agayne, and sayled downe by the coast of that lande towarde the equinoctiall (euer with intent to fynde the sayde passage to India), and came to that parte of this firme lande whiche is nowe called Florida. *The lande of Florida.* Where, my victualles faylyng, I departed from thence, and returned into Englande, where I founde great tumultes among the people, and preparance for warres in Scotlande, by reason whereof there was no more consideration had to this vyage. Wherevppon I went into Spayne, to the Catholyke king, and queene Elizabeth: who, beyng aduertised what I had done, enterteyned mee, and at theyr charges furnyshed certayne shyppes wherewith they caused me to sayle to discouer the coastes of Brasile, where I founde an exceedyng great and large ryuer, named at this present, Rio della Plata (that is), the ryuer of siluer, into the whiche I sayled, and folowed it into the firme lande more then six hundred leagues, fyndyng it euery where very fayre and inhabited with infinite people, whiche with admiration came runnyng dayly to our shyppes. Into this ryuer, runne so many other ryuers, that it is in maner incredible. After this, I made many other vyages, whiche I now permyt [pretermit]. And wexing olde, I gyue my selfe to rest from suche traueyles, bycause there are nowe many young and lusty Pylotes and mariners of good experience, by whose forwardnesse I doe reioyce in the fruites of my labours, and rest with the charge of this office as you see. And this is as muche as I haue vnderstoode of maister Sebastian Cabote, as I haue geathered out of dyuers nauigations written in the Italian tongue.

The seconde vyage of Cabote to the land of Brasile and Rio della Plata.

Cabote tolde me that in a region within this ryuer he sowed 50 graynes of wheate in September, and geathered therof 50 thousande in December, as wryteth Francisco Lopes.

And whereas I haue before made mention howe Moscouia *The viage to Moscouia.*

was in our tyme discouered by Richarde Chanceler in his
vyage towarde Cathay, by the direction and information of
the sayd maister Sebastian, who long before had this secrete
in his mynd, I shall not neede heere to describe that viage,
forasmuche as the same is largely and faythfully written in
the Latine tongue by that learned young man Clement
Adams, schoolmaister to the Queenes Henshemen, as he receyued it at the mouth of the sayd Richard Chanceler.[1] Neuerthelesse, I haue thought good heere to speake somewhat
of Moscouia, as I haue redde in the booke of John Faber,[2]
written in the Latine tongue, to the ryght noble Prince Ferdinando, Archeduke of Austria, and Infant of Spaine, of the
maners and religion of the Moscouites, as he was partly
instructed by the Ambassadours of the Duke of Moscouia,
sent into Spayne to Themperours maiestie, in the yeere 1525.
He wryteth therefore as foloweth:

I thynke it fyrst conuenient to speake somewhat of the
name of this region whereby it is called at this day, and
howe it was called in olde tyme. Conferryng, therefore, the
moste aunciente of the Greeke and Latine monumentes with
the historyes of later tyme, I perceyue it to bee a thyng
whiche requireth no small iudgement of wytte and learnyng.
For we see in howe shorte tyme the names of thinges are
chaunged, as are also the maners of men. I fynde, therefore,
that those people whom at this day wee commonly call Moscouites, were in tyme past (as wytnesseth Plinie) called

The hystory of Moscouia.

The dyuers names of Moscouia.

[1] This Latin account of Chancelor's voyage, by Clement Adams, was
written in 1554, and published by Hakluyt, together with a translation
into English, in the first edition of his *Principall Navigations*, 1589.
Hence the editors of the *Rerum Moscoviticarum Auctores Varii* were at
fault when they asserted in their dedication to Marquardus Freherus of
the first edition in 1600, " Anglorum Navigationem ad Moscovitas *nunc
primum* damus ex Bibliothecâ tuâ."

[2] See page cxx of Introduction. Fabri's work appeared under
the title, *Joh. Fabri Lencurchensis, Episcopi Viennensis, Epistola de
Moscovitarum juxta mare glaciale religione seu de dogmatibus Moscorum.*
Tubingæ, 1525, 4to.; Spiræ, 1582. Also in *Rerum Moscoviticarum Auctores Varii.* Francofurti, 1600, fo. 130, *et seq.*

Roxolani, whom neuerthelesse by chaungyng one letter, Roxolani.
Ptolome in his eyght table of Europe, calleth Rosolanos, as Rosolani.
doth also Strabo. They were also many yeeres called Ru- Rutheni.
theni, and are that people whyche sometyme fought manfully
agaynst the Captaynes of Mithridates, as Strabo wryteth.
They were called Moscouites, of the chiefe citie of all the
prouince, named Moscouia or Mosca: or (as Volaterane[1]
sayeth) of the ryuer Mosco. They were sometyme gouerned The ryuer Mosco.
by Duke John, whose wife was Helena, of the lynage of
Themperours of Constantinople, of the noble famelie of the
Paleologi. Beyonde these Roxolanos, Strabo sayeth there is
no lande inhabited. These Ruthenians, therfore, or Moscouites, are people of the Northeast parte of the worlde from
vs, and are determined with the limittes of the great ryver The ryuer Boristhenes.
Boristhenes of Scithia: on the one syde with the Lituanians
and Polonians, and on the other syde with the Tartars, who
cease not to vexe them with continuall warres and incur-
sions: Especially the great Emperour Cham of Cathay, the Themperour of Cathay.
chiefe Prince of the Tartars, resydent by the sea syde in
Taurico Chersoneso, molesteth them with sore warres. They
are towarde the North syde inclosed with the frosen sea, the The frosen sea.
lande of whose coastes beyng very large, perteyneth in maner
all to the dominion of the Duke of Moscouie. The sea is it
whiche the olde wryters call Lacus Cronicus, so named of Lacus Cronicus.
the Greeke woorde Cronos, which the Latines call Saturnus, Saturnus.
whom they fayne to be an olde man, of complexion colde and
slowe, and thereby name all suche thinges as are colde and
slowe, Cronica, as by lyke reason they dyd this North sea,
which beyng in maner euer frosen, is slow and cold, and in
maner immoueable. And for lyke consideration (as sayeth
Plinie) Heathens nameth it in the Scithian tongue, Amal- Amaltheum.
theum, which woorde signifieth as much as congealed or
frosen. But that I wander not farre from my purpose: The dominion of the Duke of Moscouia.
Thempyre and dominion of the Duke of Moscouie, reacheth

---

[1] Raffaello Maffei, surnamed Volaterranus. His work is entitled *Commentarii Rerum Urbanarum*, published in Paris, 1515, fo.

so farre, that it comprehendeth certayne partes of Asia, and also of Europe.

The citie of Moscouia. The citie of Moscouia, or Mosco, is counted twyse as byg as Colonia Agrippina [Cologne], as they faythfully reporte which know both. Vnto this they haue also an other, not *The chief cities of Moscouia.* vnequall in bygnesse, called Fladimer. Also Blescouia, Nouogradia, Smolne [Smolensko], and Otifer [Tver], all which, theyr Ambassadours affyrme to be of princely and magnificall buyldynges, and strongly defended with walles both of bricke and square stone. Of these, Blescouia is strongest, and enuironed with three walles. Other whiche they haue innumer-*The Duke of Moscouia & Emperour of Russia.* able, are not so famous as are these wherof this Duke of Moscuvie and Emperoure of Russia taketh thinscription of his title. For euen at this present, when so euer, eyther by his ambassadours or his letters, he doth signifie hym selfe to *The duke of Moscouia his tytle.* be Emperour of Muscouie, he is accustomed to vse this title, Basilius, by the grace of God Emperour of al Russia, and great Duke of Fladamer, Moscouie, Nouigrade, Blascouia, Smolne, and Otifer, etc. And this is the tytle whereby the sayde ambassadours saluted your maiestie in the name of great Basilius when they began theyr oration.

Duke Basilius. This prince of Moscouia, hath vnder hym prynces of many prouinces, and those of great power: Of the whiche, that olde whyte bearded man, whom this Emperour of the Ruthians sent for his ambassadoure to Themperours maiestie into Spaine, is not one of the least. For euen he, when necessitie *Theyr power.* of warre requireth, is accustomed to make for his Emperour *Theyr obedience to theyr prynce.* a bande of .xxx. thousand horsemen. But this is to their singular commendation, that they are so obedient to theyr prince in all thynges, that beyng sommoned by hym by neuer so meane an heralde, they obey incontinent, as if it were to *Theyr warres & conquestes.* God, thynkyng nothing more glorious then to die in ye quarel of theyr prince. By reason of which obedience, they are able, in short tyme, to assemble an army of two or three hundred thousand men against theyr enimies, eyther the Tartars, or

the great Cham: And haue hereby obtayned great victories
and triumphes, aswell agaynst the Turks, as the Tartars, by
the exceeding multitude of theyr horsemen, and continuall
experience in warres. At such time as Themperour Maximilian made a league with them, they kept warre against the
kyng of Polonie. They vse not onely bowes and dartes, after
the maner of the Parthians, but haue also the vse of gunnes *Gunnes.*
as we haue. And to be briefe, only the Moscouites may *Only the Muscouites*
seeme that nation which hath not felte the commodities of *haue not felt the commo-*
peace: Insomuch that if theyr region were not strongly de- *dities of peace.*
fended by the nature of the place, beyng impreignable, it
had or now been oftentymes conquered. Theyr language *Theyr language.*
agreeth much with the tongue of ye Bohemians, Crotians,
and Sclauons, so that the Sclauon doth playnely vnderstande
the Moscouite, although the Moscouian tongue be a more
rude and hard phrase of speech. The historiographers wryte
that the Sclauons tongue tooke the name of the confusion
whiche was in Babell in the tyme of that stoute hunter Nem-
roth, of whom mention is made in the Genesis. But I can not
enough marueyle at this thyng, that whereas betweene Dal- *Dalmatia.*
matia (now called Sclauonia) and Moscouia, both the Panno- *Pannonia.*
nies are situate, yet this notwithstandyng, the Hungarians *Hungarie.*
tongue nothyng agreeth with the Moscouites. Whereby we
may coniecture that these nations were sometymes diuided
by legions, and that they came out of Dalmatia thyther:
whiche thyng also Volateranus affirmeth, saying that the language of the Ruthenians (which are the Moscouites) is Semi-
dalmatic (that is, halfe Sclauone); howe so euer it be, this is *The Scla-*
certaine, that the Bohemians, Crotians, Sclauons, and Mos- *uion tongue reacheth farre.*
couites, agree in language, as we perceiued by thinterpre-
tours whiche your maiestie had then in your courte. For
whereas the sayd interpretours were borne among the Croa-
tians and Sclauons, and none of them had euer been in Moscouia, or before that tyme had any conversation with them,
yet dyd they well vnderstande the ambassadours woordes.

There are in Moscouia, wooddes of exceedyng byggenesse, in the whiche blacke woolues and whyte beares are hunted. The cause whereof may bee thextreme colde of the North, whiche doth greatly alter the complextions of beastes, and is the mother of whitenesse, as the Philosophers affirme. They haue also great plentie of Bees, wherby they haue such abundaunce of hony and waxe, that it is with them of smale price. When the commoditie of theyr countrey is neglected by reason of long warres, their chiefe aduantage wherby they haue all thynges necessarie towarde theyr lyuynge, is the gaynes whiche they haue by theyr ryche furres, as Sables, Marternes, Luzernes,[1] most whyte Armins, and such other, whiche they sell to merchauntes of dyvers countreys. They bye and sell with the simple fayth of woordes, exchaungyng ware for ware, without any curious bondes or cautels. And albeit they haue the vse of both golde and siluer mynes, yet do they for the moste parte exchaunge theyr furres for fruites, and other things necessarie to mainteine their life. There are also some people under the dominion of this Emperour, which haue neither wyne nor wheate, but lyue only by fleshe and mylke, as do the wylde Tartars theyr borderers, which dwell in wods by the coastes of the frosen sea. These people are bruitishe and lyve in maner lyke wylde beastes. But they of the citie of Mosca and Nouigrade, and other cities, are ciuile people, and agree with vs in eatyng of fyshe and fleshe, although theyr maner of coquerye is in many thynges differyng from ours. Volaterane wryteth that the Ruthenians vse money vncoyned.

And enquiryng further, I was infourmed that the money of Hungary is much current with them. But this is cheeflye to be considered, that they embrace the Christian fayth, whiche they affirme to haue been preached to them fyrst by Sainct Andrewe the Apostle, and brother to Simon Peter. Suche doctrine also as vnder Constantine the great, in the

---

[1] Lupus cervarius, a kind of wolf, called the stag-wolf.

yeere .ccc.xviii., was concluded in the fyrst generall coun- *The counsayle of Nicene.*
sayle holden in the citie of Nicene in Bethynia, and there
determined by ccc.xviii. Byshops, and also suche as hath
been wrytten and taught by the Greeke Doctours Basilius *Basilius Magnus.*
Magnus and Chrisostomus, they beleeue to be so holy, fyrme, *Chrisostomus.*
and syncere, that they thynke it no more lawfull one heare
to transgresse or go backe from the same, then from the Gos-
pell of Christ. For theyr constancie and modestie is suche,
that no man dare call those thynges into question whiche *Their constancie in theyr religion.*
have once been decided by holy fathers in theyr generall
counsailes. They do therfore with a more constant mynde
perseuer in theyr first faith, which they receiued of Sainct
Andrew thapostle, and his successoure and holy fathers, then
do many of vs, beyng diuided into scismes and sectes, which
thing neuer chaunceth among them. But if any difficultie
chaunce to rise as touching the faith or custome of religione,
all is referred to the Archebyshop and other byshops, as to be *The bishops define controuersies in religion.*
defined by theyr spirite: not permyttyng any iudgement to
the inconstant and ignoraunt people. Their Archbishop is re-
sident in the citie of Mosca, where also the Emperour keepeth
his court. They haue lykewyse diuers other Byshops: as one *Theyr bishops.*
in Nouigradia, where also Isodorus was Byshop vnder pope
Eugenius. They haue an other in Rosciuia [Rostov], an other
in Sustali, an other in Otiferi, also in Smolne, in Resan, in Col-
mum, and in Volut [Vologda], all whiche haue theyr Dioces.
They acknowledge theyr Archebyshop as the cheefe. Before *The archbishop.*
the Patriarche of Constantinople was oppressed by the tiranny *The patriarke of Constantinople.*
of the Turkes, this Archebyshop recognised hym as his
superiour: Insomuche that this Duke of Moscouia, and
Emperour of Russia, not vnmyndeful hereof, but a diligent
obseruer of his accustomed religion, doth at this daye yeerely
sende a certayne stypend, in maner of almes, to the Patri- *A notable example of a Christian Prince.*
arche of Constantinople, that he may with more quiet mynde
looke for the ende of this his Egyptian seruitude, vntil it
shall please almightie God to restore hym to his former

churche and aucthoritie. For he iudgeth it muche impietie,
if he shoulde nowe forsake hym whose predicessours haue
ruled and gouerned so many churches, and of whom the
fayth and religion of so many regions and prouinces haue
depended.

Theyr religion.

But to speake briefly of theyr religion, they agree in manye
thynges with vs, and in some thynges folowe the Greekes.
They haue Munkes and religious men. Not farre from the
citie of Mosca, they haue a great Monasterie, in the whiche

A monasterie of ccc. Munkes.

are three hundred Munkes, lyuyng vnder the rule of Basilius
Magnus, in the whiche is also the sepulchre of S. Sergius
the Abbot. They obserue theyr vowe of chastitie, whiche
none may breake that haue once professed. Yet such as haue
maried Virgins of good fame, may be admitted to thorder of

Priestes.

priesthood, but may neuer be a Munke. The priestes and
Byshops whiche are admitted to orders vnmaried, may neuer
after be maried: nor yet such as haue wiues marry agayne
when they are dead, but liue in perpetual chastitie. Such
as commit adulterie or fornication, are greuously punissed by
the Byshops, and depriued of the benefices. They celebrate

Masse.

masse after the maner of the Greekes, whiche differeth from
ours in dyuers thynges, as in fermented bread, after the maner of the Greekes. They put in the Chalice as muche water
as red wine, which water they vse to heate, because (not with-

A misterie.

out a great mysterie) there ishued foorth of the syde of our
Lord, both blood and water, which we ought by good reason
to thynke was not without heat: for els should it scarcely
haue been iudged for a miracle. In fine, they affirme that
al theyr customes and rites are according to the institutions

The primitiue churche.
A strange custome.

of the primitive church, and the doctrine of Basilius Magnus,
and Chrisostomus. In this thyng they differ greatly from
vs, that they minister the communion to young chyldren of
three yeeres of age, which they do with fermented bread dypt
in a sponefull of wine, and geue it to them for the bodye and
blood of Christ.

A Briefe Description of Moscouia, after the Later
WRITERS, AS SEBASTIAN MUNSTER,[1] AND JACOBUS GASTALDUS.[2]

The prouince of Moscouia, is so named of the ryver Mosca, whiche passeth by the metropolitane citie of Moscouia, called Mosca by the name of the ryuer Mosco. This prouince was called of the olde writers, Sarmatia Asiatica. The borderers or confines to the Moscouians on the one syde towarde the East, are the Tartars, called Nogai, and the Scianbanians, with the Zagatians. Towarde the West, the prouinces of Liuonia and Lituania. Towarde the South the ryver of Tanais, and the people confining with the ryver of Volga, called of the olde wryters Rha. And towarde the North, the Ocean sea, called the Scythian sea, and the region of Lapponia. Moscouia is in maner all playne, and full of Maryshes, wooddes, and many very great ryvers, whereof the ryver of Volga is the principall. Some call this Ledib, as the olde authours named it Rha. It begynneth at the great lake called Lacus Albus (that is) the white lake, and runneth into the sea of Bachau, named of the auncient wryters, the sea of Caspian or Hircanum. Under the dominion of Moscouia, are certayne regions and Dukedomes: as Alba Russia (that is whyte Russia). Also Colmogora, Plescouia, Basrida, Nouogradia, with also manie places of the Tartars, whiche are subiecte to the Duke of Moscouia. The chiefe cities of Moscouia, are Mosca, Plescouia, Nouogradia, Colmogora, Oto-

Sarmatia Asiatica.
The Scythian Ocean.
The ryuer Volga.
Lacus albus.
The Caspian Sea.
Theyr chiefe cities.

---

[1] Sebastian Munster, a learned Hebraist, born at Ingelheim in 1489, whose *Cosmographei*, published at Basle, 1550, fol., is well known. For his notice of Russia, see Introduction, under article Nicolaus Cusanus.

[2] Jacobus Gastaldus, a native of Villafranca, in Piedmont. His geographical observations are inserted in the first Italian translation of Ptolemy, published by Pier Andrea Mattioli, Venice, 1548, 8vo.

geria, Viatra, Smolenser, Percastauia, Cologna, Volodemaria, Rostania, and Cassam. The people of Moscouia are Christians and haue great abundaunce of honey and waxe: also rych furres, as Sables, Marternes, Foynes,[1] and dyuers other. All the Tartars whiche inhabite towarde the east beyonde the ryuer of Volga, haue no dwellyng places, nor yet cities or Castles, but cary about with them certayne cartes or wagens couered with beastes hydes, vnder whiche they reste, as we do in our houses. They remoue togeather in great companyes, whiche they call Hordas. They are warlyke people, and good horsemen, and are all Macometistes [Mahometans].

<small>The wylde Tartars.</small>

<small>Hordas.</small>

Sebastian Munster, in his booke of "Uniuersall Cosmographie", wryteth, that the citie of Mosca or Moscouia conteyneth in circuite xiiii. myles, and that it is twise as bygge as the citie of Praga in Bohemie. Of the countrey of Moscouia, besyde other prouinces subiecte to the same, he wryteth thus: It extendeth in largenesse foure hundreth myles, and is rych in syluer. It is lawful for no man to go out of the realme, or come in, without the Dukes letters. It is playne, without mountaynes, and full of woodds and marishes. The beastes there, by reason of the colde, are lesse then in other countreys more southwarde. In the middest of the citie of Mosca, beyng situate in a playne, there is a Castell with .xvii. toweres, and three bulwarkes, so strong & fayre, that the lyke are scarcely seene in any other place. There are also in the Castell .xvi churches, and three very large courtes, in the whiche the noble men of the courte haue theyr lodgynges. The Dukes pallaice is buylded after the maner of the Italian buyldyng, and very fayre, but not great. Theyr drynke is mede and beere, as is the maner of the most part of the people that inhabite the North partes of the woorlde. They are exceedyngly geuen to droonkennesse. Yet (as some saye) the princes of the lande are prohibite on payne of death to absteine from such strong drinkes as are of force to ine-

<small>The bygnes of the citie of Moscouia.</small>

<small>Syluer.</small>
<small>The region of Moscouia.</small>
<small>Beastes.</small>

<small>A fayre and stronge castel in the citie of Mosca.</small>

<small>The Dukes pallaice.</small>

<small>Theyr drynke.</small>

<small>They are geuen to drunkennesse.</small>

---

[1] A species of weasel (*mustela foina?*).

briate, excepte at certayne times when licence is graunted them, as twise or thrise in the yeere. They plowe the ground with horses, and plowes of wood. Theyr corne and other grayne, by reason of long colde, do seldome waxe rype on the ground, by reason wherof they are sometimes inforced to rype and drye them in their stooves and hot houses, and then grynd them. They lacke wyne and oyle. Moscouia is extended vnto Iurham and Corelia, which are in Scithia. The famous ryuer of Tanais, the Moscouites call Don, hauyng his sprynges and originall in Moscouia, in the Dukedome of Rezense. It ryseth out of a ground that is playne, baren, muddy, full of maryshes and wooddes. And where it proceedeth toward the East to the mountaynes of Scythia and Tartarie, it bendeth to the South: and commyng to the maryshes of Meotis, it falleth into them. The ryuer of Volga (sometyme called Rha, and now called of the Tartars Edell) runneth towards the North certaine myles, to whom is ioyned the ryuer Occa or Ocha, flowing out of Moscouia, and then bendyng into the South, and encreased with many other ryuers, falleth into the sea Euxinum, which diuideth Europe and Asia.

The wood or forest called Hircania silua, occupieth a small portion of Moscouia: Yet is it somewhere inhabited, and by the long labour of men, made thynner and barer of trees. In that part that lieth toward Prusia, is a kinde of great & fierce Bulles, called Vri or Brisonts, as writeth Paulus Jouius. There are also Alces, much lyke vnto Hartes, with long snowtes of flesh, and long legges, without any bowyng of theyr houx or pasternes. These beastes the Moscouites cal Lozzi, and the Almaines, Helenes.[1] The iorney that is betweene Vlna of Lituania by Smolence to Mosca, is trauayled in winter on Sledes, by the snow congeled by long frost, and made very slypperie and compact lyke Ise, by reason of much wearyng and tredyng, by meanes wherof this viage is per-

---

[1] Elan, or Allam, a name given in Buffon.

fourmed with incredible celeritie. But in the Sommer, the playne countreyes can not be ouercome without difficult labour :—For when the snow beginneth to be dissolued by contynuall heate, it causes maryshes and quagmyres, inextricable and dangerous both for horse and man, were it not for certaine Causeis made of timber with in maner infinite labour. The region of Moscouia (as I haue said) beareth neither Wines nor Oliue trees, nor yet any other trees that beare any apples or fruites of very pleasant and sweete sauour or taste, except Cherry trees, forasmuch as al tender fruites and trees, are burnt of the cold blasts of the North wynde. Yet do the fieldes beare al kyndes of corne, as wheate, and the grayne called Siligo,[1] wherof the fynest kynde of breade is made : Also Mylle, and Panycke, whiche the Italians call Melica : Lykewyse al kyndes of pulse, as Beanes, Peason, Tares, and such other. But theyr cheefe haruest consisteth of Honye and Waxe, forasmuch as the whole region is replenished with fruitefull Bees, which make most sweete Hony, not in the husband mens hyues, but euen in hollow trees. And hereby commeth it to passe, that both in the wooddes and shadowed launes, are seene many swarmes of Bees hangyng on the bowes of trees, so that it shall not be necessarie to call them togeather, or charme them with the sound of Basens. There are often tymes founde great masses of Hony combes, conserued in trees, of the olde Hony, forsaken of bees, forasmuche as the husbandmen can not seeke euery tree in so great and large woods : Insomuch that in the stockes or bodies of exceedyng great and hollow trees, are sometymes founde great pooles or lakes of Hony. Demetrius, thambassadour of the Duke of Moscouia, whom he sent to the Bishop of Rome not many yeeres since, made relation that a husbandman of the countrey, not farre from the place where he remayned, seekyng in the woods for Hony, descended into a great hollowe tree full of Honye, into the

[1] *Query*, Siliqua, whence *seigle*, barley.

which he slypt vp to the breast, and lyued there only with Hony for the space of two dayes, calling in vaine for helpe in that desart of woodds: and that in fine dispayryng of helpe, he escaped by a marueylous chaunce, beyng drawen out by a great Beare that descended into the tree, with her loynes downewarde after the maner of men. For when the man (as present necessitie and opertunitie serued) perceyued the Beare to be within his reache, he sodenly clasped her about the loynes with his armes, and with a terrible crye prouoked the beast to enforce her strength to leape out of the tree, and therewith to drawe hym out, as it chaunced in deede. *A marueylous chaunce.*

These regions abounde with Beares, whiche euery where seeke both Honye and Bees, not only herewith to fyll theyr bellyes, but also to helpe theyr syght: For theyr eyes are oftentymes dulled, and theyr mouthes wounded of the Bees: both which greefes are eased by eatyng of Honye. They haue weakest heades, as Lions haue strongest: Insomuche that when (beyng thereto enforced) they cast them selues downe headlong from any rockes, they couer theyr heades with theyr feete, and lye for a tyme astonished, and halfe deade with knockes. They walke sometymes on two feete, and spoyle trees, backewarde. Sometyme also they inuade Bulles, and so hang on them with all theyr feete, and they weerye them with weight. The Beare (as sayeth Plinie) bringeth foorth her byrth the thirtie day, and often tymes two. Theyr birth is a certaine white mass of flesh without fourme, and litle bigger then a mouse, without eyes, and without heare, with only the nayles or clawes commyng foorth: but the damme with continuall lyckyng, by litle and litle figureth the informe byrth. When she entreth into the denne which shee hath chosen, shee creepeth thyther with her belly vpwarde, least the place should be founde by the steppes of her feete. And beyng there deliuered of her byrth, remaineth in the same place for the space of .xiiii. *Beares feede of hony and bees. Beares inuade Bulles. The Beares byrth. The Beares denne.*

dayes immoueable, as wryteth Aristotle. They lyue without meat .xl. dayes, and for that tyme susteyne them selues only by lyckyng and suckyng theyr ryght foote. At the length chaunsing to finde meate, they fyll them selues so full, that they remedy that surfeyte by vomyte, which they prouoke by eating of Antes. Theyr byrth is oppressed with so heauy a sleepe for the space of .xiiii. dayes, that it cannot be raysed eyther with prickyng or woundes, and in the meane tyme growe exceedyng fatte. After fourtiene dayes they wake from sleepe, and begyn to lycke and sucke the soles of theyr fore feete, and lyue thereby for a space: Nor yet is it apparent that they lyue by any other meate, vntyll the spring tyme of the yeere. At whiche tyme begynnyng to runne abrode, they feede of the tender buddes and young sprygges or braunches of trees, and other hearbes correspondent to theyr lyppes.

<small>Beares lyue without meate xl. dayes.</small>

<small>The sleape of Beares.</small>

Before fiue hundred yeeres, the Moscouites honoured the Goddes of the Gentyles: And they fyrst receyued the Christian fayth when the Byshoppes of Grecia began to discent from the church of the Latines: and therefore receyued the rites of the Greekes. They minister the sacrament with fermented breade vnder both kyndes: And thynke that the soules of dead men are not helped with the suffragies of priestes, nor yet by the deuotion of theyr friendes or kynsfolke: Also that the place of Purgatorie is a fable. In the tymes of diuine seruice, the hystorie of the myracles of Christ, and the Epistles of sainct Paule are rehearsed out of the Pulpitte. Beyond Moscouia, are many people which they call Scythians, and are partely subiecte to the Prince of Moscouia. These are they which Duke Juan subdued, as are the people of Perm, Baskird, Cezriremissa, Jubra, Corela, and Permska. These people were Idolatours before the Duke compelled them to baptisme, & appointed a byshop ouer them named Steuen, whom the Barbarians, after the departure of the Duke, flayed alyue, and slue. But the

<small>The religion of the Moscouites.</small>

<small>The Scythians subiect to the Duke of Moscouia.</small>

Duke returnyng shortly after, afflicted them sore, and assigned them a newe byshop.

It is here also to be noted, that the olde Cosmographers fayned, that in these regions towarde the North pole, there should be certayne great mountaynes, which they called Ripheos and Hyperboreos, which neuerthelesse are not founde in nature. It is also a fable, that the ryuers of Tanais & Volham doe spring out of hygh mountaynes, whereas it is apparent that both these ryuers, and many other, haue theyr originall in the playnes. <small>It was then an opinion that all ryuers sprong out of mountaynes.</small>

Next to Moscouia, is the fruitful region of Colmogora, through the whiche runneth the ryuer of Diuidna, beyng the greatest that is knowen in the North partes of the worlde. This ryuer increaseth at certayne tymes of the yeere, as the ryuer of Nilus in Egypt ouerfloweth the fieldes rounde about, and with abundaunce of fatte moysture resisteth the coldnesse of the ayre. Wheate sowen in the grounde, groweth abundauntly without ploughyng: and fearyng the newe iniurie of the proude ryuer, springeth, groweth, and rypeth, with wonderfull celeritie of hastyng nature. <small>The fruitful region of Colmogora. The great ryuer Diuidna. Wheate without plowing.</small>

Into the ryuer of Diuidna runneth the ryuer of Juga: And in the very angle or corner where they meete, is a famous marte towne named Vstiuga, beyng a hundred and fyftie myles distant from the chiefe citie of Mosca. To this marte towne, from the higher countreis, are sent the precious furres of Marternes, Sables, Woolues, & such other, which are exchaunged for dyuers other kyndes of wares & merchandies. Hytherto Munsterus. <small>The ryuer of Juga. Vstiuga. Furres.</small>

And forasmuche as many doe marueyle that such plentie of hony should bee in so coole a countrey, I haue thought good to declare the reason and naturall cause hereof. It is therefore to be considered, that lyke as spices, gums, and odoriferous fruites are engendred in hotte regions, by continuall heate duryng all the whole yeere, without impression of the mortifying qualitie of colde, whereby all thynges are <small>The naturall cause of much hony in colde regions. Gummes and spyces in hotte countreys.</small>

constrayned as they are dilated by heate, euen so in colde and moyst regions (whose moysture is thynner and more wateryshe then in hot regions) are flowers engendred more abundauntly, as caused by impression of lesse and faynter heate, workyng in thynne matter of wateryshe moysture, lesse concocte then the matter of gummes and spyces, and other vnctuous fruites and trees growyng in hot regions. For although (as Munster sayeth here before) the region of Moscouia beareth neyther vines or oliues, or any other fruites of sweet sauour, by reason of the coldnesse thereof, neuerthelesse, forasmuch as floures (wherof hony is chiefly geathered) may in sommer season growe abundauntly in the playnes, maryshes, & woods, not onely on the ground, but also on trees in colde regions, it is agreeable to good reason, that great plentie of hony should be in suche regions as abounde with floures, which are brought foorth with the fyrst degree of heate, and fyrst approche of the sunne, as appeareth in the spryng tyme, not only by the spryngyng of floures in fieldes and gardeynes, but also of blossomes of trees spryngyng before the leaues or fruite, as the lyghter and thynner matter fyrst drawne out with the lowest and least degree of heate: as the lyke is seene in the arte of styllyng, whereby all thynne and lyght moystures are lyfted vp by the fyrst degree of the fyre: and the heauyest and thyckest moystures are drawne out with more vehement fyre. As we may therefore in this case compare the generation of floures to the heate of May, the generation of gummes to the heat of June, and spyces to the heate of July: Even so, in suche colde regions whose summer agreeth rather with the temperate heate & moysture of May, then with thextreme heate of the other monethes, that heate is more apte to bring foorth aboundance of floures, as thinges caused by moderate heate, as playnly appeareth by their tast and sauour, in which is no sharpe qualitie of heate, eyther byting the tongue, or offendyng the head, as is in spices, gums, and fruites of hotte regions. And as in colde and playne regions, moderate heate, with aboundance of moisture, are causes of the generation of floures (as I haue sayde) so lykewyse the length of the dayes and shortnesse and warmenesse of the nyghtes in sommer season, in such colde regions, is a greate helpe herevnto. Cardanus writeth in his booke " De Plantis", that bramble & fearne growe not but in colde regions, as doeth wheate in temperate regions : and that spices and hot seedes, can not growe in colde regions; forasmuch as beyng of thynne substance, they should soone bee mortified & extinct by excessiue colde. For (as he sayeth) nothing can concocte, rype, and attenuate the substance of fruites without the helpe of ayre, agreeable to the natures of such thinges as are brought foorth in the same, although it may doe this in rootes. But in maner all floures are of sweete sauoure, forasmuch as the moysture that is in them, being thynne and but litle, is by meane heate soone and easily concocte or made rype. Suche also as are soon rype, are soone rotten, accordyng to the prouerbe. Plinie, although in the .xi booke of his " Naturall Hystorye", cap. viii. he wrytheth that hony is geathered of the floures of all trees and settes or plantes, except sorell and the hearbe called Chenopode (which some call Goose foote) yet he affirmith that it descendeth from the ayre : for in the .xii Chapter of the same booke, he wryteth thus :

This cometh from the ayre at the rysyng of certayne starres, and especially at the rysyng of Sirius, and not before the rysyng of Vergilis (which are the seuen starres called Pleiades) in the spryng of the day. For then at the mornyng spryng, the leaues of trees are founde moist with a fatte dewe. Insomuche that suche as haue been abrode vnder the firmament at that tyme, haue theyr apparell annoynted with lyquor, and the heare of theyr head clammy. And whether this bee the swette of heauen, or as it were a certayne spettyl of the starres, eyther the iuise of the ayre purgyng

Long dayes and shorte nyghtes.

Bramble and fearne.
Spyces.

The sauour of floures.

What Plinie wrytheth of hony.

Sirius is otherwyse called Canicula, that is, the Dogge, of whom the canicular dayes haue theyr name.

What is hony?

it selfe, I would it were pure, liquide, & simple of his owne nature, as it first falleth from aboue. But now descendyng so farre, and infected, not only with suche vncleane vapours and exhalations as it meeteth by the way, but afterwarde also corrupted by the leaues of trees, hearbes, and floures of sundry tastes and qualities, and lykewyse as well in stomackes of the bees (for they vomite it at their mouthes) as also by long reseruyng the same in Hives; it neuerthelesse reteyneth a great parte of the heauenly nature, etc. Agayne in the .xiiii. Chapter of the same booke he wryteth, that in certayn regions towarde the North, as in some places of Germanie, hony is founde in such quantitie, that there haue been seene hony coombes eyght foote long, and blacke in the holow parte. By the which woordes of Plinie, and by the principles of naturall philosophie, it doeth appeare that aboundaunce of honey should chiefly be engendred in suche regions, where the heate of sommer is temperate and continuall, as well by nyght as by day, as it is not in hot regions, where the nyghtes be long and colde, as is declared in the Decades. For like as such thinges as are fyned by continuall heate, mouyng, and circulation, are hyndered by refrigeration or colde (as appeareth in the arte of styllyng and hatchyng of egges) euen so by the action of temperate and continuall heate, without interposition of contrarie and mortifying qualitie, crude thinges are in shorte tyme made rype, sower made sweete, thicke made thinne, heauie made lyght, grosse made subtyle, harde made softe, dead made lyuyng, and in fine, bodyes made spirites, as manifestly appeareth in the marueylous woorke of dygestion of lyuyng beastes, whereby the finest parte of theyr nouryshment is turned into blood, and the finest of that blood conuerted into spirites, as the lyke is also seene in the nouryshment of trees, plants, and hearbes, and all other thinges that growe on the grounde, all which are moued, digested, subtiliate, attenuate, ryped, and made sweete by the action of this continuall heate whereof

I haue spoken. To conclude therefore, if hony be eyther the swette of the starres, or the iuise of the ayre purgyng it selfe (as Plinie wryteth) or otherwyse engendred of subtyle and fine vapours rysing from the earth, and concocte or digested in the ayre by the sayde continuall and moderate heate, it may seeme by good reason that the same should be engendred in sommer season more aboundantly in colde regions then in hot, for the causes aforesayde. And that it may by aucthoritie and reason more manifestly appeare, both that the heate of sommer in colde regions is continuall (as I haue sayde) and also that the colde in wynter is not there so intollerable to thinhabitauntes of those regions as other doe thynke, I haue thought good for the better declaration hereof, to adde herevnto what I haue geathered out of the booke of Ziglerus, wrytten of the North regions.

Subtyle vapours digested by heate.

Colde regions.

Ziglerus.

Of the North Regions, and of the Moderate and
CONTINUAL HEATE IN COLDE REGIONS, ASWELL IN THE NYGHT AS IN THE DAY IN SOMMER SEASON: ALSO HOWE THOSE REGIONS ARE HABITABLE TO THINHABITAUNTES OF THE SAME, CONTRARY TO THE OPINION OF THE OLDE WRYTERS.

Of this matter, Ziglerus[1] in his booke of the North regions in the description of Scondia, wryteth as foloweth.

Ziglerus.

We will intreate of this matter, not as putting the same in question as did the olde writers, nor geathering iudgement deducted of reasons in way of argument, forasmuche as we are already more certayne by hystorie that these colde regions are inhabited. We will first therfore shew by natu-

---

[1] Jacob Ziegler, a celebrated theologian and mathematician, born at Landau in Bavaria. His *Schondia* occurs in a collective geographical work published at Strasburg, 1582, fol.

rall reason, and by consideration of the sphere, declare howe by the helpe of man and arte, colde regions are inhabited without domage or destruction of lyuyng beastes: And will first speake of the qualitie of sommer, declaryng howe it is there augmented. Yet intend I not to comprehende all that may be sayde in this matter, but only rehearse suche reasons and similitudes as are most apparent and easie to be vnderstoode.

<small>The qualitie of sommer in colde regions.</small>

In such regions therefore, as are extended from the burnt lyne or Equinoctiall towarde the North, as much as the sunne ryseth higher ouer them, so much are they the more burnt with heat, as Affrica, bycause it ryseth highest ouer them, as they are nearest to the Equinoctiall: & taryng with them so much the shorter tyme, causeth shorter dayes, with longer and colder nyghtes, to restore the domage of the day past, by reason of the moisture consumed by vapour. But in such regions ouer the which the sun ryseth lower (as in Sarmatia) it remayneth there the longer in the day, and causeth so much the shorter and warmer nyghtes, as reteynyng warme vapours of the day past, which vapours helpe the woorke of the day. I speake as I haue founde by experience, sayth Vpsaliensis:[1] For I haue felte the sommer nyghtes scarsely tollerable for heate in Gothlande, whereas I felte them colde in Rome. This benefit of the increase of the day doeth augment so much the more in colde regions, as they are nearer the poles: and ceaseth not vntyll it come directly ouer the center or poynte of the axes or axceltree of the worlde, where the sunne beyng at the hyest in sommer, is eleuate about .xxiiii. degrees: In which regions, one continuall day consisteth of .vi. monethes from the spryng tyme,

<small>The course of the Sunne.</small>

<small>Vapours.</small>

<small>Short and warme nyghtes.</small>

<small>Gothlande.</small>

<small>One day of vi. monethes.</small>

---

[1] Joannes Magnus, named Stor in Swedish, was archbishop of Upsala. Ziegler, in the preface to his *Schondia*, speaks of him as a private friend from whom he derived information. His work, entitled *Historia de omnibus Gothorum Suenonumque regibus*, was subsequently published by his brother Olaus Magnus. Rome, 1554, fol.

by the standyng of the sunne (called Solstitium) in the signe of Cancer, to Autumne. The Sunne therfore, without any offence of the nyght, gyueth his influence vpon those landes with heate that neuer ceaseth duryng that tyme, which maketh to the great increase of sommer, by reason of continuaunce. Wee haue now therefore thought good to geather, by a certayne coniecture, howe greatly we thynke the sommer to be increased heereby. *Howe the sommer is increased in colde regions.*

We haue before declared howe hygh the sunne is eleuate ouer the regions that are vnder the poles at the staye of the sunne. And so many partes is it eleuate in Rome at the staye of the sunne in wynter (that is) at the shortest day in the yeere. But here, in the myd wynter, the sunne at noonetyde is beneficiall, and bryngeth foorth floures, Roses, and Ielefloures. I haue gathered some in winter in the moneth of December, not procured at home by humane arte, but growyng in open Gardens in maner in euery bed vnder the bare heauen, brought foorth only by the sunne. But this benignitie of the sunne, continueth not past fyue houres in the naturall day, forasmuch as the operation thereof is extinct by the coldenesse of the nyght folowyng. But if this benefite myght be receyued without hinderaunce of the nyght, as it is vnder the poles, and so continue many monethes in hot regions vnto wynter, it should surely bring foorth many wonderfull thinges, if moysture fayled not. And by this condition thus propounded, we may well conceyue that the Romayne wynter, although it be not hotte, yet to be equall in heate to the full spryng tyme in the same citie, duryng the tyme of the sayd fyue houres. And thus by a similitude of the height of the sunne vnder both places, and of the knowen qualitie of the Romane heauen, and by the accesse of the sunne to such places where the longest day continueth certayne monethes, we may geather that sommer, in places vnder the pole, is lyke vnto and equall with the full Romane spryng. *Rome.* *Colde nyghtes in hot regions.* *The Romane wynter.*

One night of vi monethes.

Obiections.

But the more difficult question, is of the tyme of the .vi. monthes in the whiche the Sunne leaueth those regions, and goeth by the contrary or ouerthwarte circle towarde the south in wynter. For they say that at that tyme, those regions are deformed with horrible darknesse, and nyghtes not increased, whiche may be the cause that beastes can not seeke theyr foode : And that also the colde should then bee intollerable. By which double euyls all thynges constrayned should dye, so that no beast were able to abyde the iniuryes of wynter and famyne insuyng thereof: but that all beastes should peryshe before the sommer folowyng, when they should bryng foorth theyr broode or succession : and that for these causes, the sayde colde clyme should be perpetually desolate and vnhabitable. To all which obiections we answere in this maner.

The twylightes.

As touchyng the nyghtes not increased, I say, that it was not conuenient to assume that for any reason. For not as the Sunne falleth, so sodeynly commeth the darke nyght : but that the euenyng doeth substitute and prolong the day long after, as also the day spryng or dawnyng of the day, gyueth a certayne lyght before the rysyng of the Sunne : After the which, the residue of the nyght that receyueth no lyght by the sayde euenyng and mornyng twilightes, is ac-

The lyght of the Moone.

complyshed by the lyght of the Moone, so that the nyghtes are sildome vnaugmented. Let this bee an example proued by our temperate regions, whereby we may vnderstande the

The nyght vnder the pole.

condition of the nyght vnder the pole : Therefore euen there also the twilightes helpe the nyght a long tyme, as we will more presently demonstrate. It is approoued by the Astronomers, that the Sunne descendyng from the highest halfe sphere by eightiene paralels of the vnder horizon, maketh

A demonstration.

an ende of the twilight, so that at the length the darke nyght succeedeth : And that the Sunne approchyng, and rysyng aboue the hyghest halfe sphere by as many paralels, doeth dyminyshe the nyght and increase the twylight. Agayne, by the position or placyng of the sphere vnder the pole, the same is the horizontall that is the Equinoctiall. Those paralelles therefore that are paralelles to the horizontall lyne, are also paralelles to the Equinoctiall. So that the Sunne descendyng there vnder the horizon, doeth not bryng darke nyghtes to those regions, vntyll it come to the paralels distant xviii. partes from the Equinoctiall.

Duryng the tyme of the sayde syxe monethes of darkenesse vnder the pole, the nyght is destitute of the benefite of the Sunne and the sayde twylyghtes, onely for the space of three monethes, in the whiche the Sunne goeth and returneth by the portion of the ouerthwarte circle. But yet neyther this tyme of three monethes is without remedy from heauen. For the Moone with her full globe increased in lyght, hath access at that tyme, and illuminateth the monethes lackyng lyght, euery one by them selues, halfe the course of the moneth: by whose benefite it commeth to passe that the nyght, named as vnaugmented, possesseth those regions no longer then one moneth and a halfe, neyther that continually or all at one tyme: but this also diuided into three sortes of shorter nyghtes, of the whiche euery one endureth for the space of two weekes, and are illuminate of the Moone accordyngly. And this is the reason conceyued of the power of the sphere, whereby we testifie that the sommers and nyghtes vnder the pole are tollerable to lyuyng beastes. But we wyll nowe declare by other remedies of nature and arte, that this colde so greatly feared, is more remisse and tollerable then our opinion: so that, compared to the nature of suche beastes as lyue there, it may be abydden. And there is no doubte but there are autours of more antiquitie then that age in the whiche any thyng was exactly knowen or discouered of the North regions. The olde wryters therefore persuaded onely by naked coniecture, dyd geather what they myght determyne of those places: Or rather, by the estimation of heauen, the whiche, because they felte it to be

<small>The Moone.</small>

<small>Remedies of nature and art.</small>

<small>The olde wryters persuaded by coniecture.</small>

hardely tollerable to them selues, and lesse to men borne in the clyme of Egypt and Grecia, tooke thereby an argument of the whole habitable earth. The hystorie of Strabo is knowen, that a potte of brasse, whiche was broken in sunder with frozen water, was brought from Pontus, and shewed in Delphis in token of a greuous wynter. Here therefore, they that so greatly feared the wynter (suche as chaunceth to the earth vnder the .xlviii. paralele) and therefore consecrated that broken potte to the temple of Apollo: what could suche men truely define vpon regions so farre without that paralele, whether they were inhabited or not: But suche as folowed these, beyng contented with thinuentions of the olde autours, and borne in maner vnder the same qualitie of heauen, persysted wyllyngly in the same opinion, with more confidence then consideration of the thynges whereof we nowe intreate: so lyghtly was that opinion receyued as touchyng the vnhabitable clime vnder the poles. But we with better confidence and faith (forasmuche as we are not instructed with coniectures) intende to stande against the sentence of the olde autours, affyrmyng the North regions within the colde clime to be inhabited with herrynges, coddes, haddockes, and brettes,[1] tunnyes, and other great fyshes, with thinfinite number whereof tables are furnyshed through a great parte of Europe: All whiche are taken in the North sea extended beyonde our knoweledge. This sea at certayne tymes of the yeere poureth foorth his plentifulnes, or rather driueth foorth his increase to seeke newe mansions, and are here taken in theyr passage. Furthermore also, euen the mouthes of the riuer of Tiber receiued a fyshe as a newe gest sent from the North sea: this swamme twise through Fraunce, and twise through Spayne, ouerpassed the Ligurion and Tuscan sea, to communicate her selfe to the citie of Rome. The lakes also and ryuers of those regions are replenyshed with fyshe: insomuch that no power of

---

[1] A local name for a flat-fish of the turbot and flounder kind.

colde is able to extinguyshe thincrease of the yeere folowing, and the succession reparable so many hundred yeeres. And I plainely thinke, that if it should of necessitie folowe, that one of these two elementes, the earth and the water, <small>The qualitie of water.</small> should be destructive to lyuyng creatures, the water should chiefely haue wrought this effecte. But this is founde so tractable, that in the depe wynter, both that increase is brought foorth, and fyshyng is also exercised. The lande is lyke- <small>The land.</small> wyse inhabited with like plentifulnesse. But that we wander not to farre, let the fayth hereof rest in therposition folowyng, wherein we intend to declare howe by the power of nature and industry of man, this commoditie may come to passe.

Therefore as touchyng nature, we suppose that the diuine <small>The diuine prouidence in moderatyng the elementes.</small> prouidence hath made nothyng vncommunicable, but to haue geuen suche order to all thynges, whereby euery thyng may be tollerable to the next. The extremities of the elementes consent with theyr next. The ayre is grosse about the earth and water: but thynne and hot about the fyre. By this pro- <small>The nature of the sea.</small> uidence of nature, the vttermost sea is very salt. And salt <small>Salt.</small> (as witnesseth Plinie) yeldeth the fattnesse of Oyle. But Oyle, by a certayne natyue heate, is of propertie agreeable to fyre. The sea then, beyng al of such qualitie, powreth foorth it selfe farre vpon thextreeme landes, whereby by reason of the saltnesse thereof, it moueth and stirreth vp generatiue heate, as by fatnesse it norisheth the fecunditie <small>Generatyue heate.</small> of thynges generate. It geueth fruitefulnesse to the earth at certayne floods, although the earth also it selfe haue in his inner bowels the lyuely and norishing heate, wherby not <small>Outward cold is cause of inwarde heate.</small> only the Dennes, Caues, and hollow places, but also sprynges of water are made warme: & this so much the more, in howe muche the wynter is more vehement. This thyng doth more appeare by this example, that the mountaines of Norway and Swethlande are fruitfull of metales, in the which, siluer <small>Metals.</small> and copper are concocte and molten into veines, which can scarcely be done in fornaces. By this reason also, the vapoures and hot exhalations pearsyng the earth and the waters, and through both those natures breathyng foorth into the ayre, tempcrateth the qualitie of heauen, & maketh it tollerable to beastes, as witnesseth the huge bygnesse of the Whales in those seas, with the strength of body, and long lyfe of such beastes as lyue on the lande : which thyng coulde not be, except all thynges were there commodiously norished by the benefite of the heauen and the ayre. For nothyng that in the tyme of encrease is hyndred by any iniurie, or that is euyl fedde al the tyme it lyueth, can prosper wel. Neyther are such thynges as liue there, offended with theyr natural wynter, as though an Egyptian or an Ethiopian were sodenly conueighed into those cold regions. For they were in long tyme, by litle and litle, brought fyrst acquaynted with the nature of that heauen, as may be prooued both by the lyfe of man, and by the hystorie of holy scripture. They that were led from Mesopotamia, and that famous Tower of Babilon towards the North partes of the worlde, in the fyrst dispertion of nations, did not immediately passe to the extreme boundes, but planted theyr habitations first vnder a myddle heauen, between both, as in Thracia, and Pontus, where there posteritie was accustomed better to susteyne the rigour of Scythia and Tanais, as he that commeth from winter to sommer, may the better after abyde yse and snow, beyng fyrst hardened thereto by the frostes of Autumne. In lyke maner mortal men, accustomed to beare the hardnesse of places next vnto them, were thereby at the length more confirmed to sustayne the extremities. And here also, if any sharpnesse remaine that may seeme intollerable, nature hath so prouided for the same, with other remedies. For the land and sea hath geuen vnto beastes deepe and large caues, dennes, and other hollowe places, and secreete corners in mountaynes and rockes, both on the land and by sea banckes, in the which are euer conteyned warme vapoures, so muche the more intent and

vehement, in how much they are the more constrayned by
extreme cold. Nature hath also geuen valleyes diuerted *Valleis.*
and defended from the North windes.

She hath lykewyse couered beastes with heare, so muche
the thycker, in how much the vehemencie of cold is greater:
by reason wherof the best and richest furres are brought *The best furres.*
from those regions, as Sables, whose pryce is growne to great *Sables.*
excesse, next vnto gold and precious stones, and are esteemed
princely ornamentes. The beastes that beare these furres
are hunted cheefelye in winter (whiche thyng is more
strange), because their heare is then thicker, and cleaveth
faster to the skin. How greeuous then shal we thinke the
wynter to be there, where this litle beast liueth so wel, and *Beastes that lye hyd in wynter.*
where the hunters may search the dennes and hauntes of
such beastes through the woods and snow: But such beastes,
the condition of whose bodies is so tender that they are not
able to abide thiniurie of the cold, either lye hyd in wynter,
or change their habitation, as do certaine beasts also in our
clime. Nature hath furthermore geuen remedie to man,
both by arte and industry, to defende him selfe both abrode
and at home. Abrode with a thicke vesture, and the same
well dowbeled. At home, with large fyres on Harthes,
Chymneyes, and in Stooues for the daye, with close Chaum-
bers, and Couches, soft and warme Beddes for the nyght:
by whiche remedies they mittigate the wynters, which seeme
rigorous to straungers, although they are to thinhabitantes *All beustes haue the*
more tollerable then our opinion, as in deede by the fyrst *nature of the place where*
naturall mixture or composition of theyr bodies such thynges *they are engendred.*
are agreeable to them as seeme very hard to other. The
lion in Affrik, and the beare in Sarmatia, are fierce, as in
theyr present strength and vigoure: but translated into a
contrary heauen, are of lesse strength and courage. The
foule called Ciconia (which some thinke to be the Storke)
doth not tary the wynter: yet do the Cranes come at that
tyme.

The Scythian wyll accuse the Romane heauen as inducyng feuers, whereas neuerthelesse there is none more holsome. Such as haue been tenderly brought vp, if they come suddeynely into the campe, can not away with hunger, watchyng, heate, passages through ryuers, battayles, sieges, and assaultes: But the olde souldier, exercised in the warres, vseth these as meditations of the fielde, as hardened therto by long experience. He that hath been accustomed to the shadowe of the citie, and wyll attempte the saying of the poet Virgil, *Nudus ara, sero nudus*, (that is), naked and bare, without house and home, shal to his peryl make an end of the verse, *Habebis frigora februm*, (that is), he shal haue the cold ague. Suche thynges therfore as seeme hard vnto us, beyng accustomed by litle and litle, become more tollerable: Insomuch that this exercise of sufferaunce by such degrees doth oftentimes growe to prodigious effectes, farre beyonde our expectation. And thus we seeme to haue made sufficient demonstration, by heauen, nature, and art, wherby it may appeare that no parte of the land or sea is denied to liuing creatures. The reader may also perceiue howe large matter of reasons and examples may be opened for the declaryng of our opinion, wherin we rest. Let therfore thauctoritie of the auntient auctours geue place, and the consent of the newe writers agree to this history, not as nowe at the length comprehended (wheras before many hundred yeeres Germanie and Scondia had entercourse of merchandies not seuered by the large gulfe of Gothia), but as nowe by our commentaries brought to lyght: and hauyng sayde thus muche in maner of a preface, we wyll nowe proceede to wryte of the North regions.

Marginalia: What exercise may do. Vse maketh masteries. Scondia.

Laponia.

The region of Laponia was so named of the people that inhabite it. For the Germanes call all suche Lapones as are simple or vnapte to thinges. This people is of small stature, and of suche agilitie of bodie, that hauyng theyr quyuers of arrowes gerte to them, and theyr bowes in theyr handes, they can with a leape cast themselues through a circle or hope of the diameter of a cubite. They fight on foote, armed with bowes and arrowes, after the maner of the Tartars. They are exercised in hurlyng the darte, and shootyng, from theyr youth: insomuche that they gyue theyr chyldren no meate vntyll they hyt the marke they shoote at, as dyd in old tyme thynhabitauntes of the Ilandes called Baleares. They vse to make theyr apparell streight and close to theyr bodyes, that it hynder not theyr woorke. Theyr wynter vestures are made of the whole skynnes of Seales or Beares, artificially wrought, and made supple. These they tye with a knotte aboue theyr heads, leauyng onely two holes open to looke through, and haue all the residue of theyr bodyes couered, as though they were sowed in sackes, but that this beyng adopted to all partes of theyr bodyes, is so made for commoditie, and not for a punyshment, as the Romanes were accustomed to sow paricides in sackes of leather, with a Cocke, an Ape, and a Serpent, and so to hurle them alyue altogeather into the ryuer of Tiber. And heereby I thynke it came to passe, that in olde tyme it was rashly beleeued, that in these regions there were men with rough & heary bodyes lyke wylde beastes, as parte made relation through ignoraunce, parte also takyng pleasure in rehearsall of suche thinges as are straunge to the hearers. The Lapones defended by this arte and industry, goe abrode and withstand the sharpenesse of wynter and the North wyndes, with all the iniuryes of heauen. They haue no houses, but certayne Tabernacles lyke tentes or hales, wherewith they passe from place to place, and chaunge their mansions. Some of them lyue after the maner of the people of Sarmatia, called in olde tyme Amaxobii, which vsed waynes in the steade of houses. They are much giuen to huntyng, and haue suche plentie of wylde beastes, that they kyll them in maner in euery place. It is not lawful for a woman to goe foorth of the tent at that doore by the which her husbande went out on huntyng the same day, nor yet to touche with her hande any parte of the beast that is taken, vntyll her husbande reache her on the spytte suche a portion of fleshe as he thynketh good. They tyll not the grounde. The region nourysheth no kynde of Serpentes: yet are there great and noysome Gnattes. They take fyshe in great plentie: by the commoditie whereof they lyue after the maner of the Ethiopians, called Ichthiophagi. For as these drye theyr fyshe with feruent heate, so doe they drye them with colde, and grynde or stampe them to pouder as small as meale or floure. They haue suche aboundaunce of these fyshes, that they hourd great plentie thereof in certeyne store houses, to carry them vnto other landes neare about them, as Northbothnia, and Whyte Russia. Theyr shyppes are not made with nayles, but are tyed togeather and made fast with cordes and wythes. With these they sayle by the swyft ryuers betweene the mountaynes of Laponia, beyng naked in sommer that they may the better swymme in the tyme of perill, and geather togeather such wares as are in daunger to be lost by shypwracke. Parte of them exercise handie craftes, as imbroderyng and weauyng of cloth, interlaced with gold and siluer. Suche as haue deuised any necessary Arte, or doe increase and amende the inuentions of other, are openly honoured, and rewarded with a vesture, in the which is imbrodered an argument or token of the thyng they deuised. And this remayneth to the posteritie of theyr famelie, in token of theyr desartes. They frame shyppes, buylde houses, and make dyuers sortes of housholde stuffe artificially, and transporte them to other places neare about. They buye and sell both for exchaunge of wares, and for money. And this only by consent of both parties, without communication: yet not for lacke of wytte, or for rudenesse of maners, but bycause they haue a peculiar language vnknowen to theyr borderers. It is a valiant nation, and lyued long free, and susteyned the warres of Norway and Suetia, vntyll at the length they submitted themselues, and payde ryche furres for theyr tribute. They chose themselues a gouernour, whom they cal a kyng: But the kyng of Suetia gyueth him aucthoritie and administration. Neuerthelesse, the people in theyr suites and doubtful causes resorte to Suetia to haue theyr matters decised. *Bargeynyng without woordes.*

In theyr iourneys, they go not to any Inne, nor yet enter into any house, but lye all nyght vnder the firmament. They haue no horses, but in the steade of them they tame certayne wylde beastes which they call Reen, beyng of the iust bygnesse of a Mule, with rough heare lyke an Asse, clouen feete, and braunched hornes lyke a Harte, but lower and with fewer antlettes. They will not abyde to be rydden. But when theyr peytrels or drawyng-collars are put on them, and they so ioyned to the Chariotte or sleade, they run in the space of .xxiiii. houres, a hundred and fiftie myles, or .xxx. Schœnos, the whiche space they affyrme to chaunge the horizon thryse, that is, thryse to come to the furthest signe or marke that they see a far off. Which, doubtlesse, is a token both of the marueylous swiftnesse & great strength of these beastes, beyng able to continue runnyng for so great a space, in the meane whyle also spendyng some tyme in feedyng. I suppose that this thyng was somewhat knowen to the olde wryters, although receyued in *No horses. A beast of marueylous strength and swiftnesse. What Schœnus is, looke in Gronlonde. The chaunge of the horizon. The olde aucthours called all the north people Scythyans.*

maner by an obscure and doubtful fame: For they also wryte that certayne Scythians doe ryde on Hartes.

They neyther folow the Christian religion, nor yet refuse it, or are offended therewith, as are the Iewes: but doe sometymes receyue it fauourably, to gratifie the princes to whom they obey. And that no more of them imbrase the Christian fayth, the faulte is somewhat to be imputed to the Bysshoppes and Prelates that haue eyther reiected this cure & charge of instructyng the nation, or suffered the fayth of Christ to be suffocate euen in the fyrst spryng. For vnder the pretence of religion, they would haue aduaunced theyr owne reuenues, and ouerburdened the people by an intollerable example, none otherwyse here then in all Christendome, which thyng is doubtlesse the cause of most greeuous defections. I heard John, a byshop of Gothlande, say thus: We that gouerne the churche of Vpsalia, and haue vnder our diocesse a great parte of that nation, lyke as it is not conuenient to declare many thinges of our vigilance and attendaunce ouer the flocke committed to our charge, euen so absteynyng from mischeeuous couetousnesse, whereby religion is abused for luker, we doe in all places our diligent endeuour, that wee minister none occasion, whereby this nation, as offended by our sinnes, may be the lesse wyllyng to embrase the Chrystian fayth. This is the state of the religion among the Lapones: although of theyr owne institution and custome receyued of theyr predicessours, they are Idolatours, honouryng that lyuyng thyng that they meete fyrst in the mornyng, for the God of that day, and diuinyng thereby theyr good luck or euyll. They also erecte Images of stone vpon the mountaynes, whiche they esteeme as Goddes, attributyng to them diuine honour. They solemne mariages, and begyn the same with fyre and flynt, as with a mysterie so aptely applyed to the Image of stone, as if it had been receyued from the myddest of Grecia. For in that they adhibite a mysterie to fyre, as they doe not this alone (forasmuch as the Romanes obserued the same custome), euen so are they herein partly to be commended, in that they vse the ceremonies of so noble a people. The mysterie of the flinte is no lesse to be praysed, both forasmuch as this is domesticall philosophie, and hath also a neare affinite and signification to these solemnities. For as the flynt hath in it fyre lying hyd, whiche appeareth not but by mouyng & force: so is there a secrete lyfe in both kynds of man and woman, which by mutuall coniunction commeth foorth to a lyuyng byrth.

They are furthermore experte inchaunters. They tye three knottes on a stryng hangyng as a whyp. When they lose one of these, they rayse tollerable wynds. When they lose an other, the wynde is more vehement: but by losyng the thyrd, they rayse playne tempestes, as in olde tyme they were accustomed to rayse thunder and lyghtnyng. This arte doe they vse agaynst such as sayle by theyr coastes; and staye or moue the ryuers and seas more or lesse, as they lyst to shew fauour or displeasure. They make also of leade certayne shorte magicall dartes of the quantitie and length of a fynger. These they throwe agaynst such, of whom they desyre to be reuenged, to places neuer so farre distant. *Experte inchaunters.* *Magicall dartes.*

They are sometymes so vexed with the canker on theyr armes or legges, that in the space of three dayes they dye through the vehemencie of the payne. *The canker.*

The Sunne falleth very lowe in these regions: and prolongeth one continuall nyght for the space of three monethes in wynter, durynge whiche tyme they haue none other lyght but lyke vnto the twilight of eueninges & mornynges. This is very cleare, but continueth but fewe houres, and is lyke the bryght shynyng of the Moone. Therefore, that day that the Sunne returneth to the hemispherie, they keep holy day and make great myrth with solemne festiuitie. *One nyght of three moneths.*

And these are the maners of this nation, not so brutyshe or

saluage, as woorthy therefore to be called Lapones for theyr vnaptenesse or simplicite, as when they lyued vnder theyr owne Empyre, and vsed no familiaritie or entercourse with other nations, & knew not the commoditie of their owne thinges, neyther the pryce and estimation of theyr furres in our regions, by reason whereof they solde great plentie of them for some of our wares of small value.

<small>Riche furres.</small>

The boundes or limittes of Laponia (beyng the extreeme land of Scondia knowen towarde the North pole) are extended towarde this parte of the North, to the world yet vnknowen to vs : And furthermore towarde the same parte of the vttermost sea, accordyng to this description.

The fyrst coast	70	72.
The coast folowyng	80	7.
That that yet foloweth . .	90	70.

<small>Plentie of sea fyshe.</small>

From the fyshyng places and store houses of this sea, they carry foorth to Nordbothnia and whyte Russia, landes confinyng to them, great plentie of fyshe. Whereby we may coniecture that this sea is extended on euery syde towarde the North. Towarde the West, it is limitted with the most inwarde gulfe at the Castle of Wardhus, at the degree . . . . . . 54 70 30.

<small>Wardhus.</small>

Towarde the South, it is limitted by a lyne drawen from thence vnto the degree . . . 90 69.

Finland, and Eningia.

Finlandia is as much to saye as a fayre land, or fyne lande, so named for the fertilitie of the ground. Plinie seemeth to call it Finnonia: for he saieth that, about the coastes of Finland are many Ilands without names, of the which there lyeth one before Scithia called Pannonia. The gulfe called Sinus Finnonicus, is so named at this day of the land of Finnonia. Finnonia confineth with Scithia, and runneth without all Tanais, (that is to say) without the lymittes of Europe to the confines of Asia. But that the name of Finlande seemeth not to agree hereunto, the cause is, that this place of Plinie is corrupted, as are many other in this aucthour. So that from the name of Finnonia, or Phinnonia, it was a lykely errour to call it Pannonia, forasmuche as these wordes doo not greatly differ in wrytyng and sounde: so that the counterfect name was soone put in the place of the true name, by hym that knew Pannonia, and read that name before, beyng also ignorant of Phinnonia. *Pannonia falsly taken for Finnonia.*

Eningia had in the olde tyme the tytle of a kyngdome; it is of such largenesse, but hath now only the title of an inferiour gouernor, beyng vnder the dominion of the Slauons, and vsyng the same tongue. In religion, it obserued the rytes of the Greekes of late yeeres, when it was vnder the gouernance of the Moscouites. But it is at this present vnder the kyng of Suecia, & obserueth thinstitutions of the Occidentall churche. *Eningia.*

Spanyshe wynes are brought thither in great plentie, which the people vse meryly and cheerefully. It is termined on the North side by the South lyne of Ostrobothnia, and is extended by the mountaynes. Toward the West, it is termined with the sea of Finnonia, accordyng to this description, and hath degrees 71. 66. &c. *Spanishe wines.*

The History, written in the Latin Tongue by Paulus

JOUIUS, BYSHOP OF NUCERIA IN ITALIE, OF THE LEGATION OR AMBAS-
SADE OF GREAT BASILIUS PRINCE OF MOSCOUIA, TO POPE CLEMENT
THE VII. OF THAT NAME : IN WHICH IS CONTEYNED THE DESCRIPTION
OF MOSCOUIA WITH THE REGIONS CONFINYNG ABOUT THE SAME, EUEN
VNTO THE GREAT AND RYCH EMPIRE OF CATHAY.

I intend first briefly to describe the situation of the region which we plainely see to have ben litle knowen to Strabo and Ptoleme, and then to proceede in rehearsing the maners, customes and religion of the people. And this in maner in the like simple stile and phrase of speach as the same was declared unto us by Demetrius the Ambassadour, a man not ignorant in the Latin tongue, as from his youth brought up in Liuonia, where he learned the first rudiments of letters, and being growne to mans age, executed thoffice of an Ambassadour into dyuers Christian prouinces. For whereas by reason of his approued faithfulnesse & industrie, he had before ben sent as Oratour to the kynges of Suecia and Denmarke, & the great maister of Prussia, hee was at the last sente to Themperour Maximilian, in whose courte (beinge replenyshed with all sortes of men) while he was conuersant, if any thyng of barbarous maners yet remayned in so docible & quiet a nature, the same was put away by framyng hym selfe to better ciuilitie. The cause of his legacie or ambassade, was given by Paulus Centurio a Genuese, who when he had receiued letters commendatory of pope Leo the tenth, & came to Moscouia for the trade of marchaundies, of his owne mynde

[margin: Demetrius the ambassadour of Moscouia.]

[margin: Paulus Centurio.]

conferred with the familiars of Duke Basilius as touching the conformation of the rites of both churches.

He furthermore of great magnanimitie, and in maner outragious desire, sought how by a new and incredible viage, spices myght be browght from India. For whyle before hee had exercised the trade of marchandies in Syria, Egypte, & Pontus, he knewe by fame that spices myght be conueighed from the further India up the riuer Indus against the course of the same, and from thence by a small vyage by land passing ouer the mountaines of Paropanisus, to be caried to the riuer Oxus in Bactria, which hauing his originall almost from the same mountaynes from whence Indus doeth spryng, and violently carying with it many other ryuers, falleth into the sea Hircanum or Caspium, at the porte cauled Straua. And he earnestly affirmed that from Straua, in an easy and safe nauigation unto the marte-towne of Citrachan or Astrachan and the mouth of the ryuer Volga, and from thence ouer against the course of the ryuers, as Volga, Occha and Moscho, unto the citie Moscha, and from thence by lande to Riga, and into the sea of Sarmatia and all the West regions. For he was vehemently and more then of equitie, accensed and prouoked by the iniuries of the Portugales, who hauyng by force of armes subdued a great parte of India, and possessed all the marte-townes, takyng holy into theyr handes all the trade of spyces to bryng the same into Spayne, and neuerthelesse to sell them at a more greeuous aud intollerable price to the people of Europe then euer was hard of before: And furthermore kepte the coastes of the Indian sea so straightly with continuall nauies, that those trades are thereby left of, which were before exercised by the gulfe of Persia, and towarde the ryuer of Euphrates, and also by the streightes of the sea of Arabia, and the ryuer of Nilus, and in fine by our sea: by which trade all Asia and Europe was aboundantly satisfied and better cheape than hathe been since the Portugales

Spices brought from India to Moscouia.

The ryuer Indus.

Oxus or Hoxina, a ryuer of Asia, runneth through the desartes of Sythia.

The sea Hircanum is now called Mare Abacuk, or Mare de Sala.

Citrachan, or Astracan.

Sarmatia is that great countrey wherein is conteyned Russia, Livonia, and Tartaria, and the North and East part of Polonia.

Agaynst the Portugales.

The trade of spices in owld tyme.

had the trade in theyr handes with so many incommodities of such long viages, whereby the spyces are so corrupted by thinfection of the pompe and other filthnesse of the shippes, that theyr naturall sauour, taste, and qualitie, as well hereby as by theyr long reseruyng in the shoppes, sellers, and warehouses in Lusheburne, vanysheth and resolueth, so that reseruynge euer the freshest and newest, they sell only the woorst and most corrupted. But Paulus, although in all places he earnestly and vehemently argued of these thinges, and styrred great malice and hatred agaynst the Portugales, affyrmyng that not only thereby the customes and reuenues of princes should be much greater, if that vyage might be discouered, but also that spyces myght bee better cheape bought at the handes of the Moscouites, yet could he nothyng auayle in this suite, forasmuche as Duke Basilius thought it not good to make open or disclose vnto a straunger and vnknownen man, those regions which gyue enterance to the sea Caspium and the kyngdomes of Persia. Paulus therefore excludyng all hope of further traueyle, and become nowe of a marchaunte an Ambassadour, brought Basilius letters (Pope Leo beyng now departed) to Adrian his successour, in the which he declared with honourable and reuerende woordes, his good will and fauorable mynde towarde the Bysshopp of Rome. For a fewe yeeres before, Basilius (then keepyng warres agaynst the Polones, at suche tyme as the generall counsayle was celebrate at Laterane) requyred by John, Kynge of Denmarke (the father of Christierne who was of late expulsed from his kyngdome) that safe passage myght be graunted to the Ambassadours of Moscouia to goe to Rome. But wheras it so chaunced, that kynge John and pope Julius dyed both in one day, whereby he lacked a conuenient sequester or solicitour, he omitted his consultation as touchyng that legacie. After this, the warre waxed hot betweene him and Sigismunde the kyng of Polonie: who obteynyng the victorie agaynst the Moscouites at Boristhene, supplications were decreed in Rome for the ouerthrowe and vanysshyng the enemyes of the Christian fayth, whiche thing greatly alienated both kyng Basilius him selfe, and all that nation from the Bysshoppe of Rome.

But when Adriane the VI departed from this lyfe, and lefte Paulus now readie to his seconde vyage, his successour, Clement VII, perceyung that Paulus styll furiously re- uolued and tossed in his unquyet mynde that vyage towarde the Easte, sente hym agayne with letters to Moscouia, by the whiche with propense and friendly persuations, hee exhorted Basilius to acknowledge the maiestie of the Romane churche, and to make a perpetuall league and agreement in matters of religion, which thyng should bee not only for the health of his soule, but also greatly to the increase of his honour: And further promysed, that by the holy aucthoritie of his office he would make him a kyng, and gyue him kyngly ornamentes, if reiectyng the doctrine of the Greekes, hee would confourme him selfe to the aucthoritie of the Romane churche. For Basilius desyred the name and tytle of a kynge by thassignation of the bysshoppe of Rome, forasmuch as he judged that to apperteyne to the catholyke right and the bysshoppes maiestie, of whome (as he knewe ryght well) euen Themperours them selues by an aunciente custome haue receaued there insignes of honoure with the diademe and scepter of the Romane Empire: althowghe it is sayde that he required the same of Themperour Maximiliane by many ambassades. But Paulus, who with more prosperous iourneyes then great vauntage, had from his youth traueyled a great parte of the worlde, although hee were nowe aged and sore vexed with the strangurie, came with a prosperous and speedy iourney to Moscouia, where he was gentelly receyued of Basilius, and remayned in his Courte for the space of twoo monethes. But in fine, mystrustyng his owne strength, and deterred by the difficultie of so greate a iourney, when he had utterly put away all his imaginations and hope of this

The seconde viage of Paulus to Moscouia.

The Pope persuadeth Basilius to acknowledge the Romane churche.

The Emperoures receaue there diademe of the bysshoppes of Rome.

trade to India, returned to Rome with Demetrius the Ambassadour of Basilius, before we yet thought that he had been in Moscouia. The Byshoppe commaunded that Demetrius should bee lodged in the most magnificent and princely parte of the houses of Vaticane, the rooffes of whose edifies are gylted and embowed, and the chambers rychly furnysshed with sylken beddes and cloth of Arresse.

Demetrius intertaynement at Rome.

Wyllynge furthermore that he should be honorably receyued and vestured with silke, he also assigned Franciscus Cheregatus the Byshoppe of Aprutium (a man that had often tymes been Ambassadour to diueres regions), to accompany him and shew him the order and rytes of our religion, with the monumentes and maners of the citie. Furthermore, when Demetrius had certayne dayes rested and recreated him selfe, washing away the fylth he had gathered by reason of the long vyage, then apparelled with a fayre vesture after the maner of his countrey, he was brought to the byshops presence, whom he honoured kneelyng with greate humilitie and reuerence (as is the maner), and therwith presented unto his holinesse certeyne furres of Sables in his owne name, and in the name of his prince, and also delyuered the letters of Basilius, which they before, and then the Illyrian or Slauon interpretour Nicolaus Siccensis translated into the Latine tongue in this effecte as foloweth.

Demetrius is brought to the Popes presence.

To Pope Clemente, shepard and teacher of the Romane churche, great Basilius, by the grace of God, lord, Emperour, and dominatour of all Russia, and great Duke of Volodemaria, Moscouia, Nouogrodia, Plescouia, Smolenta, Ifferia, Iugoria, Periunia, Vetcha, Bolgaria, etc., Dominator & great prince of Nouogrodia in the lower countrey : Also of Ceruigouia, Razania, Volotchia, Rezeuia, Belchia, Rostouia, Iaroslauia, Belozeria, Vdooria, Obdoria, & Condiuia, etc. You sent vnto vs Paulus Centurio, a citizen of Genua, with letters, whereby you doe exhort vs to ioyne in power and counsayle with you and other Princes of Christendome against the enemies

Basilius letters to Pope Clement.

of the christian fayth : & that a free passage & redy way may bee opened for both your Ambassadours & ours to come & go to & fro, whereby by mutual dutie and indeuour on both parties, we may haue knowledge of the state of thinges perteynyng to the wealth of vs both. We certes, as we haue hitherto happely by the ayde and helpe of almightie God constantly and earnestly resisted the cruell & wicked enemies of the Christian faith, so are we determined to doe hereafter : and are likewise redy to consent with other christian princes, & to graunt free passage into our dominions. In consideration wherof, we haue sent vnto you our faithful seruant Demetrius Erasmus with these our letters : & with him haue remitted Paulus Centurio : desiring you also shortly to dismisse Demetrius, with safegard and indemnitie vnto the borders of our dominions. And we wil likewise do the same if you send your Ambassadour with Demetrius, whereby both by communication and letters, we may bee better certified of thorder and administration of such thinges as you require : so that being aduertised of the mindes and intent of all other christian princes, we may also consult what is best to be done herein.

Thus fare ye wel. Giuen in our dominiō in our citie of Moscouia, in the yeere from the creation of the world, vii thousande and 300, the third day of Aprill.

But Demetrius, as he is experte in diuine and humane thinges, and especially of holy scripture, seemed to haue secrete commaundement of greater matters, whiche we thinke he will shortly declare to the senate in priuate consultations. For he is now deliuered of the feuer, into the which he fell by change of ayre, and hath so recouered his strength & natiue colour, that being a man of .lx. yeeres of age, he was not only present at the Popes masse, celebrated with great solemnitie in the honour of S. Cosmus & Damian, but came also into the Senate, at such tyme as Cardinal Campegius, commyng fyrst from the legacie of Pannonia,

Cardinall Campegius.

was receiued of the pope & all the nobilitie of the court: And furthermore also viewed the Temples of the holye citie with the ruines of the Romane magnificence, and with woondring eyes beheld the lamentable decay of the auncient buildinges. So that we thinke that shortly after he hath declared his message, he shal return to Moscouia with the byshop of Scarense the Popes legate, not vnrecompensed with iust rewardes at the handes of his holinesse.

The ruynes of Rome.

The name of Moscouites is nowe newe, although the Poete Lucane maketh mention of the Moschos confynyng with the Sarmatians : and Plinie also placeth the Moschos at the sprynges of the great ryuer of Phasis, in the region of Colchos, aboue the sea Euxinus towarde the East. Theyr region hath very large boundes, and is extended from the Aultars of great Alexander about the sprynges of Tanais, to the extreme landes and North Ocean in maner vnder the North starres, called charles wayne, or the great Beare, beyng for the most parte playne, & of fruitfull pasture, but in sommer in many places full of marishes. For whereas all that lande is replenyshed with many and great ryuers, which are greatly increased by the wynter, snowe, and Ise, resolued by the heate of the sunne, the playnes and fieldes are thereby ouerflowen with marishes, and all iourneyes incombred with continuall waters and myrie slabbynesse, vntyll by the benefite of the newe wynter the riuers and marishes be frosen agayne, and giue safe passage to the sleades that are accustomed to iourney by the same.

The description of Moscouia.

The altares of great Alexander.

Marisshes in sommer.

The wood or forest of Hercynia (and not Hyrcania as is red in some false copies) occupyeth a great parte of Moscouia, and is heere and there inhabited, with houses builded therein and so made thinner by the long labour of men that it doeth not now shewe that horrour of thicke & impenetrable woods and landes as many thinke it to haue. But beyng replenished with many wylde beastes, is so farre extended through Moscouia, with a continuall tract be-

The forest of Hercynia.

Wylde beastes.

tweene the East and the North towarde the Scythian Ocean, that by the infinite greatnesse therof, it hath deluded the hope of suche as haue curiously searched the ende of the same. *The Scythian Ocean.*

In that parte that reacheth towarde Prussia, are founde the greate and fierce beastes cauled Vri, or Bisontes, of the kynde of Bulles: Also, Alces lyke vnto Hartes, which the Moscouites call Lozzi, and are called of the Germaynes Helenes. *The beastes cauled Uri or Bisontes. Helenes.*

On the East syde of Moscouia are the Scythians, which are at this day called Tartars, a wandryng nation, and at all ages famous in warres. In the stead of houses they vse wagons, coured with beastes hydes, whereby they were in oulde tyme called Amaxouii. For cities and townes, they vse great tentes and pauilions, not defended with trenches or walles of tymber or stone, but inclosed with an innumerable multitude of archers on horsbacke. The Tartars are diuided by companyes which they call Hordas, which worde in theyr tongue signifieth a consentyng company of people, geathered together in forme of a citie. Euery Horda is gouerned by an Emperour, whom eyther his parentage or warlyke prowes hath promoted to that dignitie. For they oftentimes keepe warre with theyr borderers, and contende ambiciously and fiercely for dominion. It doeth hereby appeare, that they consist of innumerable Hordas, in that the Tartars possesse the most large desartes, euen vnto the famous city of Cathay, in the furdest Ocean of the East. *Of the Scythyans and Tartars. Amaroüi. Horda. The large dominion of the Tartars. Cathay.*

They also that are nearest to the Moscouites, are knowen by theyr trade of marchaundies, and often incursions. In Europe, neare vnto the place called Dromon Achillis,[1] in Taurica

---

[1] Supposed to be the Island of Tendra, at the mouth of the Dnieper. Cellarius speaks of the Dromos Achilleos as follows (lib. ii, cap. VI, 14):—"Post Achillis insulam est peninsula, Dromos Achilleos nominata, Græce, Δρομος Αχιλλειος. ** Plinius dicto loco: *Ab ea* [*insula*] *cxxv millibus passuum peninsula, ad formam gladii in transuersum porrecta,*

The Tartars of Europe. Chersoneso, are the Tartars called Precopites, the doughter of whose prince, Selymus the Emperour of the Turkes tooke to wyfe. These are most infest to the Polones, and waste the regions on euery syde, betweene the riuers of Boristhenes and Tanais. They that in the same Taurica possesse Caffam, a colonie of the Ligurians (called in olde tyme Theodosia), doe both in religion and all other thinges agree with the Turkes. But the Tartars that inhabite the regions of Asia betweene Tanais and Volga, are subiect to Basilius the kyng of the Moscouites, and choose them a gouernour at his assignement. Amonge these, the Cremii afflicted with ciuile seditions, where as heeretofore they were ryche and of great power, haue of late yeeres lost theyr dominion and dignitie. The Tartars that are beyonde the riuer of Volga, do religiously obserue the frendship of the Moscouites, and professe them selues to be their subiectes. Beyond the Cassanites towarde the North, are the Sciambani, rych in heardes of cattaylle, and consistyng of a great multitude of men. After

The Tartars of Asia are subiecte to the Duke of Moscouia.

The Tartars beyonde the riuer of Volga.

exercitatione ejusdem [Achillis] *cognominata Dromos Achilleos, cujus longitudinem octoginta millium passuum tradit Agrippa.* Et Pomponius Mela (lib. ii, cap. 1), *Achilles infesta classe mare Ponticum ingressus, ibi ludicro certamine celebrasse victoriam, et quum ab armis quies erat, se ac suos cursu exercitavisse memoratur. Ideo dicta est,* Δρομος Αχιλλειος. *De figura gladii idem. Terra tum longe distenta excedens, tenui radice litori adnectitur. Post spatiosa modice paullatim se ipsa fastigat, et quasi in mucronem longa colligens latera, facie positi ensis adlecta est.*

" Quam ergo Melam peninsulam, et ex illo Plinius, comparaverunt formæ gladii jacentis. Strabo (pag. 213) cum ταινια fascia conferendam duxit : et similitudinis rationem dat, quia longitudo sit circiter cιɔ stadiorum ; latitudo maxima, duorum stadiorum ; minima τεσσαρα πλεθρων, quatuor jugerum. Ptolemæus (lib. iii, cap. v) peninsulæ hujus in transuersum oblongæ singulatim ισθμον, *isthmum;* et promontoria laterum sive extremitatum enarrat, occidentale, ιερον ἄκρον, *sacrum promontorium;* et orientale μυσαριν ἄκραν *Mysarin promontorium.* Arrianus insulam Achillis Leucam cum hoc Dromo sive Cursu ejusdem confundit, quasi eadem fuerit insula et Dromos : quæ vero ab aliis diligenter, ut insula et peninsula, distinguuntur.

these, are Nogai, whiche obteyne at this daye the chiefe fame of ryches and warly affayres. Theyr Horda, although it be most ample, yet hath it no Emperour, but is gouerned by the wysedome and vertue of the most aunciént & valiant men, after the maner of the common wealth of Venese. Beyonde the Nogais, somewhat towarde the South & the Caspian sea, the noblest nation of the Tartars, cauled Zagathai, inhabite townes buylded of stone, and haue an exceedyng great and fayre citie, called Samarcanda, which Iaxartes the great ryuer of Sogdiana runneth through, and passyng from thence about a hundred myles, falleth into the Caspian sea. With these people in our dayes, Ismael the Sophi and kyng of Persia hath often tymes kepte war with doubtfull successe. Insomuche that fearyng the greatnesse of theyr power, whiche he resysted with all that he myght, he lefte Armenia and Taurisium the chiefe citie of the kyngdome, for a praye to Selimus the victourer of one wyng of the battayle. From the citie of Samarcanda, descended Tamburlanes the myghty Emperour of the Tartars, whom some call Tanberlanis: But Demetrius sayth that he shoulde be called Themircuthlu. This is he that about the yeere of Christ .m.ccc.xcviii, subdued almost all the Easte partes of the worlde: And lastly with an innumerable multitude of men inuaded the Turkes dominions, with whom Baiasetes Ottomanus theyr kyng (and father to the great grandfather of this Solyman that nowe lyueth), meeting at Ancira in the confines or marches of Galatia and Bythinia, gaue hym a sore battayle, in the which felle on the Turkes parte .20000. men, and Baiasetes hym selfe was taken prisoner, whom Tamburlanes caused to be locked in an Iron cage, and so caryed hym about with hym through all Asia, which he also conquered with a terryble army. He conquered all the landes betwene Tanais and Nilus, and in fine vanquished in battayle the great Soltane of Egypte, whom he chased beyonde Nilus, and tooke also the citie of Da-

margin notes: Nogai. Sigismundus cauleth them Nogaysri. The noblest nation of the Tartars. The ryuer Jaxartes. Ismael the Sophi kyng of Persia. The citie of Samarcanda the myghtie Emperour of the Tartars. The conquestes of Taburlanes. Baiasetes.

mascus. From the region of these Tartars, called Zagathei, is brought great plentie of sylken apparell to the Moscouites. But the Tartares that inhabite the mydlande or inner regions, bryng none other wares then trucks or droues of swift runnyng horses, and clokes made of whyte feltes: also hales or tentes, to withstande the iniuries of colde and rayne. These they make very artificially & apte for the purpose. Thei receiue againe of the Moscouites, coates of cloth, and Syluer monie, conteynynge all other bodyly ornaments, and the furnyture of superfluous housholde stuffe. For beyng defended agaynst the violence of wether and tempestes onely with such apparel and couerture wherof we haue spoken, they trust onely to theyr arrowes, which they shoote aswell backwarde flying as when they assayle theyr enemies face to face: Albeit, when they determined to inuade Europe, theyr princes and captaynes had helmets, coates of fense, and hooked swoordes, whiche they bought of the Persians.

This apparell they haue of the Persians.

The Tartars trafficke with the Moscouites.

Towarde the Southe, the boundes of Moscouia are termined by the same Tartars whiche possesse the playn regions neere vnto the Caspian sea, aboue the maryshes of Meotis in Asia, and about the ryuers of Borysthenes and Tanais, in part of Europe.

The Tartars of the South syde of Moscouia.

The people called Roxolani, Gete, and Bastarne, inhabited these regions in oulde tyme, of whom I thynke the name of Russia tooke originall. For they call part of Lituania, Russia the lower, wheras Moscouia it selfe is called whyte Russia. Lituania therefore, lyeth on the Northwest syde of Moscouia. But toward the full West, the mayne landes of Prussia and Liuonia are ioyned to the confines or marches of Moscouia, wher the Sarmatian sea, breakyng foorth of the streightes of Cimbrica Chersonesus (nowe called Denmarke), is bended with a crooked gulfe towarde the North. But in the furthest bankes of that Ocean, where the large kyngdomes of Norway and Suecia are ioyned to the continent, and almost enuironed with the sea, are the people

Gete and Roxolani.
Russia.
Moscouia called Whyte Russia. Lituania.
Prussia. Liuonia.
Denmarke.
Norwaye. Suecia.
The people of Laponia.

called Lapones: a nation exceedyng rude, suspitious, and fearefull, flying and astonyshed at the syght of al straungers and shyppes. They knowe neyther fruites nor apples, nor yet any benignitie eyther of heauen or earth. They prouide them meate onely with shootyng, and are appareled with the skynnes of wylde beastes. They dwell in caues fylled with drye leaues, and in holowe trees, consumed within eyther by fyre, or rotten for age. Such as dwell neare the sea syde, fyshe more luckelye then cunnyngly, and in the stead of fruites, reserue in store fyshes dryed with smoke. They are of small stature of bodie, with flat visagies, pale and wannie coloure, and very swyft of foote. Theyr wyttes or dispositions, are not knowen to the Moscouites theyr borderers, who thynke it therfore a madnesse to assayle them with a smal power, and iudge it neyther profitable nor glorious with great armies to inuade a poore & beggerly nation.

They exchange the most white furres, which we cal Armelines, for other wares of dyuers sortes: Yet so, that they flye the syght and coompanie of all merchantes. For comparyng and laying theyr wares togeather, and leauyng theyr furres in a mydde place, they bargayne with simple fayth, with absent and vnknowen men. Armeline furres. Barganyng without wordes.

Some men of great credite and aucthoritie, do testifie that in a region beyond the Lapones, betwene the West and the North, oppressed with perpetuall darknesse, is the nation of the people called Pigmei, who being growen to theyr ful grought, do scarcely excede the stature of our chyldren of ten yeeres of age. It is a fearefull kynde of men, and expresse theyr wordes in suche chatteryng sort, that they seeme to be so muche the more lyke vnto Apes, in howe muche they dyffer in sence and stature from men of iust heyght. The dark region: by this dark region and Pigmei is the way to Chathay by the North sea.

Towarde the North, innumerable people are subiect to the Empire of the Moscouites. Theyr regions extend to the Scythian Ocean for the space of almost three moonethes iorney. The Scythian Ocean.

Nere vnto Moscouia, is the region of Colmogora, abound- The region of Colmogora.

yng with fruites. Through this runneth the ryuer of Diuidna, being one of the greatest that is knowen in the North partes, and gaue the name to an other lesse ryuer which breaketh foorth into the sea Baltheum. This increasyng at certayne tymes of the yeere, as dooth the ryuer Nilus, ouerfloweth the feeldes and playnes, and with his fatte and nourishyng moysture, doth maruelously resist the iniuries of heauen and the sharp blastes of the North wynde. When it riseth by reason of molten snow, and great showres of rayne, it falleth into the Ocean by vnknowen nations, and with so large a trenche, lyke vnto a great sea, that it can not be sayled ouer in one day with a prosperous wynde. But when the waters are fallen, they leaue here and there large and fruitfull Ilandes: For corne there cast on the grounde, groweth without anye helpe of the Plowe, and with meruaylous celeritie of hasteng nature, fearyng the newe iniurie of the proude ryuer, doth both spryng and rype in short space. Into the ryuer Diuidna, runneth the ryer Iuga: And in the corner where they ioyne togeather, is the famous Marte towne called Vstiuga, distant from the cheefe citie Mosca .vi. hundre myles.

"Note[1] that whereas Paulus Iouius wryteth here that the ryuer of Diuidna, otherwyse called Dwina, runneth through the region of Colmogora: it is to bee understood that there are two ryuers of that name, the one on the Northeast side of Moscouia, toward the frosen sea, & the other on the Southwest syde fallyng into the sea Baltheum, or the gulfe of Finnonia, by the citie of Riga in Liuonia. And forasmuche as the true knowledge of these and certayne other is very necessarie for all such as shal trade into Moscouia, or other regions in those coastes by the North sea, I haue thought good to make further declaration hereof as I haue founde in the hystorie of Moscouia, most faythfully and largly wrytten by Sigismundus Liberus, who was twyse sent Embassa-

[1] This note which is here marked by inverted commas is by Eden.

dour in Moscouia, as fyrst by Maximilian the Emperour, and then agayne by Ferdinando kyng of Hungarie and Boheme. This haue I done the rather, for in al the mappes that I haue seene of Moscouia, there is no mention made of the ryuer of Duina, that runneth through the region of Colmogor, and by the citie of the same name, although the prouince of Duina be in all cardes placed Northwarde frome the ryuer of Vstiug or Succana, which is the same Duina wherof we now speake, and whereof Paulus Iouius wryteth, although it be not so named but from the angle or corner, where ioynyng with the ryuer of Iug and Succana, *The ryuer Suchana.* it runneth Northwarde towards the citie of Colmogor, and from thence falleth into the North or frozen sea, as shall *The frosen sea.* hereafter more playnely appeare by the wordes of Sigismundus, that the one of these be not taken for the other, beyng so farre distant, that great errour myght ensue by mistaking the same, especially because this whereof Paulus Iouius writeth, is not by name expressed in the cardes, but only in the other, wherby the errour myght be the greater. Of that therfore that runneth by the confines of Liuonia, and the citie of Riga, Sigismundus writeth in this maner."

" The lake of Duina is distant from the sprynges of Borysthenes, almost ten myles, and as many from the marishe of Fronovvo. From it a ryuer of the same name towarde the West, distant from Vuilna twentie myles, runneth from thence towarde the North, where by Riga, the cheefe citie of Liuonia, it falleth into the Germane sea, whiche the Moscouites caule Vuareczkoie morie. It runneth by Vuitepsko, Polotzo, and Dunenburg, and not by Plescouia as one hath wrytten. This ryuer, beyng for the most part nauigable, the Liuons calle Duna. Of the other Duina whereof Paulus Iouius speaketh, he wrytteth as foloweth."

" The prouince of Duina, and the ryuer of the same name, *Dwina and Suchana.* is so named from the place where the ryuers of Suchana and Iug, meetyng togeather, make one ryuer so called. For

Duina in the Moscouites tongue, signifieth two. This ryuer, by the space of two hundred myles, entreth into the North Ocean, on that part where the sayde sea runneth by the coastes of Suecia and Norway, and diuideth Engreonland from the vnknowen lande. This prouince situate in the full North, perteyned in tyme past to the segniorie of Nouogorode. From Moscouia to the mouthes of Duina, are numbered ccc. myles: Albeit as I haue sayde, in regions that are beyond Volga, the accompt of the iourney can not be wel obserued, by reason of many maryshes, ryuers, and very great wooddes that lye in the way. Yet are we led by coniecture to thinke it to be scarsely two hundred myles: forasmuch as from Moscouia to Vuolochda, from Vuolochda to Vstiug, somewhat into the East; and laste of al from Vstiug by the ryuer Duina, is the ryght passage to the Northe sea. This region, besyde the Castel of Colmogor and the citie of Duina, situate almost in the mydde way betwene the sprynges and mouthes of the ryuer, and the Castell of Pienega, standyng in the very mouthes of Duina, is vtterly without townes and Castels: Yet hath it many vyllages, which are farre in sunder, by reason of the barennesse of the soyle, etc."

Grenland or Engronland.

Understand myles of Germany, that is, leagues.

" In an other place he wryteth, that Suchana and Iug, after they are ioyned togeather in one, loose theyr fyrst names and make the ryuer Duina, etc. But let vs nowe returne to the hystorie of Paulus Iouius."

Unto Vstiuga, from the Permians, Pecerrians, Inugrians, Vgolicans, and Pinnegians, people inhabytyng the North and Northest prouinces, are brought the precious furres of Marterns and Sables, also the cases of Woolfes and Foxes both whyte and black: And lykewyse the skynnes of the beastes called Ceruarii Lupi (that is), harte Woolfes, beyng engendered eyther of a Woolfe and a Hynde, or a Harte and a bytch Woolfe. These furres and skynnes they exchaunge for dyuers other wares. The best kynde of Sables and of the finest

Rych furres.

Lupi Ceruarii.

Sables.

heare wherewith nowe the vestures of princes are lyned, and
the tender neckes of delicate dames are couered, with the
expresse similitude of the lyuynge beast, are brought by the
Permians and Pecerrians, whiche they themselues also receyue at the handes of other that inhabite the regions neyre
vnto the North Ocean. The Permians and Pecerrians, a
litle before our tyme, dyd sacrifice to Idols after the maner of the Gentyles: but do nowe acknoweledge Christe
theyr God. The passage to the Inugrians and Vgolicans,
is by certayne rough mountaynes, which perhappes are they *The mountains cauled Hyperborei.*
that in olde tyme were cauled Hyperborei. In the toppes
of these, are founde the best kyndes of Falcons: whereof *Haukes of diuers kyndes.*
one kynde (cauled Herodium) is white, with spotted fethers.
There are also Jerfalcons, Sakers, and Peregrines, whiche
were vnknowen to the ancient princes in theyr excessiue and
nise pleasures.

Beyonde those people whom I last named (beyng all try-
butaries to the kynges of Moscouia) are other nations, the
last of men, not knowen by any voyages of the Moscouites, *The passage from Moscouia to Cathay.*
forasmuche as none of them haue passed to the Ocean, and
are therefore knowen onely by the fabulous narrations of
merchauntes. Yet is it apparante that the ryuer of Diuidna
or Dwina, draweyng with it innumerable other ryuers, runneth with a vehement course towarde the North: and that
the sea is there exceedyng large: so that saylyng by the
coast of the ryght hande, shyppes may haue passage from
thense to Cathay, as is thought by most lykely coniecture, *Cathay.*
except there lye some lande in the way. For the region of
Cathay perteyneth to thextreme and furthest partes of the
Easte, situate almost in the paralel of Thracia, and knowen
to the Portugales in India when they sayled neere there-
unto by the regions of Sinara and Malacha to Aurea Cher- *Master Eliot calleth Cathay the regions of Sinarum.*
sonesus, and brought from thense certayne vestures made of
Sables skynnes, by whiche onely argument it is apparente that
the citie of Cathay is not farre from the coastes of Scithia.

But when Demetrius was demaunded whether eyther by
the monumentes of letters or by fame lefte theym of theyr
predicessours, they had any knowledge of the Gothes, who
nowe more then a thousande yeeres since, subuerted Thempire
of the Romane Emperours, and defaced the citie of
Rome : He answered, that both the nation of the Gothes
and the name of kyng Totilas theyr chiefe captayne, was of
famous memorie amonge them : And that dyuers nations of
the North regions conspired to that expedition, and especially
the Moscouites ; Also that that armie increased of the
confluence of the Barbarous Liuons and wanderyng Tartars:
But that they were all called Gothes, forasmuche as the
Gothes that inhabited Scondania and Iselande, were the
auctours of that inuasion.

And with these boundes are the Moscouites inclosed on
euery syde, whom we thinke to be those people that Ptolome
called Modocas : but haue doubtlesse at this day theyr
name of the ryuer Mosco, which runneth through the cheefe
citie Mosca, named also after the same. This is the most
famous citie in Moscouia, as well for the situation thereof
beyng in maner in the myddest of the region, as also for the
commodious oportunitie of ryuers, multitude of houses, and
stronge fence of so fayre and goodly a Castell. For the citie
is extended with a long tract of buildynges by the bankes
of the ryuer for the space of fyue myles. The houses are
made all of tymber, and are diuided into Parlours, Chambers,
and Kychyns, of large roomes : yet neyther of vnseemely
heyght or to lowe, but of decent measure and proportion.
For they haue great trees, apte for the purpose, brought
from the forest of Hercinia : Of the which, made perfectly
round like ye mastes of shyps, and so layd one vppon an other,
that they ioyne at the endes in ryght angles, where beyng
made very fast and sure, they frame theyr houses therof, of
meruaylous strength with smal charges, and in verye short
tyme. In maner all the houses haue priuate gardens, aswell

for pleasure as commoditie of hearbes, wherby the circuite of the dispersed citie appeareth very great. All the wardes or quarters of the citie haue theire peculiar Chappels.

But in the cheefest and highest place therof, is the Church of our Lady, of ample and goodly workemanshyppe, whiche Aristoteles of Bononie, a man of singular knowledge and experience in Architecture, builded more then threescore yeres since. At the very head of the citie, a little ryuer, called Neglina, which driueth many corne mylles, entereth into the ryuer Moscus, and maketh almost an Ilande, in whose end is the Castel, with many strong towers and bulwarkes, builded very fayre by the diuise of Italian Architecturs that are the maisters of the kynges woorkes. In the fieldes about the citie, is an incredible multitude of Hares, and Roe Buckes, the which, it is lawful for no man to chase or pursue with dogges or nettes, except only certayne of the kynges familiars and straunge Ambassadours, to whom he geueth licence by speciall commaundement. Almost three partes of the citie is inuironed with two ryuers, and the residue with a large Mote that receiueth plentie of water from the sayde ryuers. The citie is also defended on the other syde with an other ryuer named Jausa, whiche falleth also into Moscus, a litle beneath the citie. Furthermore, Moscus runnyng towards the South, falleth into the ryuer Ocha or Occa, muche greater then it selfe at the towne Columna: and not very farre from thence Ocha it selfe increased with other ryuers, vnladeth his streames in the famous ryuer Volga, where at the place where they ioyne, is situate the citie of Nouogradia the lesse, so named in respect of the greater citie of that name, from whence was brought the fyrst colonie of the less citie. *The ryuer Ocha. Wolga. Nouogrodia.*

Volga, called in olde tyme Rha, hath his originall of the greate marishes, named the whyte Lakes. These are aboue Moscouia, betweene the North and the West, and send foorth from them almost all the ryuers that are dis- *Rha. The whyte lakes.*

persed into dyuers regions on euery syde, as we see of the Alpes, from whose toppes and sprynges descend the waters, of whose concourse the ryuers of Rhene, Po, and Rodanum, haue theyr increase. For these maryshes in the steade of mountaines full of sprynges, minister abundant moysture, forasmuche as no mountaynes are yet founde in that region by the long trauayles of men, insomuche that many that haue been studious of the old Cosmographie, suppose the Ryphean and Hyperborean, mountaines, so often mentioned of the auncient writers, to be fabulous. From these maryshes therfore, the ryuers of Duina, Ocha, Moschus, Volga, Tanais, and Boristhenes, haue theyr originall. The Tartares call Volga Edel: Tanais they call Don: And Boristhenes is at this time called Neper.

The Ryphean and Hyperborean mountaynes.

Tanais and Borysthenes

This, a litle beneath Taurica, runneth into the sea Eurinus. Tanais is receyued of the maryshes of Meotis, at the noble Marte Towne Azoum. But Volga, leauyng the citie of Mosca towardes the South, and runnyng with a large circuite, and great Wyndynges, and Creekes first towardes the East, then to the West, and lastly to the South, falleth with a full streame into the Caspian or Hircan sea. Aboue the mouth of this, is a citie of the Tartars called Cytrachan, which some call Astrachan, where Martes are kept by the Merchauntes of Media, Armenia, and Persia. On the further bancke of Volga, there is a towne of the Tartars called Casan, of the whiche the Horda of the Casanite Tartars tooke theyr name. It is distant from the mouth of Volga and the Caspian sea 500 myles. Aboue Casan 150 myles, at the entraunce of the ryuer Sura, Basilius that now reigneth, buylded a towne called Surcium, to thintent that in those desartes, the marchantes and traueylers which certifie the gouernours of the marches of the doinges of the Tartars, and the maners of that vnquiet nation, may haue a safe mansion among theyr customers.

The sea Eurinus.

Sura. Surcium.

The Emperours of Moscouia at dyuers tymes, eyther moued

thereto by occasion of thinges present, or for the desyre they had to nobilitate newe and obscure places, haue kepte the seate of theyr courte and Empyre in dyuers cities. For Nouogrodia, which lyeth toward the West, and the Lyuon sea, not many yeeres past, was the head citie of Moscouia, and obteyned euer the chiefe dignitie, by reason of the incredible number of houses and edifies, with the oportunitie of the large lake replenyshed with fyshe, and also for the fame of the most aunciente & venerable Temple, which more then foure hundred yeeres since was dedicated to Sancta Sophia, Christ, the sonne of God, accordyng to the custome of the Emperours of Byzantium, now called Constantinople. Nouogrodia is oppressed in maner with continuall wynter and darkenesse of long nyghtes. For it hath the pole Artike eleuate aboue the Horizon threescore and foure degrees: and is further from the Equinoctiall then Moscouia by almost six degrees. By which dyfference of heauen, it is sayde, that at the sommer steye of the sunne, it is burnt with continuall heate, by reason of the shorte nyghtes. *The Temple of Sancta Sophia.* *The eleuation of the pole at Nouogrodia & Moscouia.* *Heate by reason of short nyghtes.*

The citie also of Volodemaria, beyng more then twoo hundred myles distant from Mosca towarde the Easte, had the name of the chiefe citie and kynges towne, whyther the seate of the Empire was translated by the valiaunt Emperours for necessarie considerations, that such ayde, furniture, and requisites, as appertayne to the warres, myght be neare at hande, at suche tyme as they kepe continuall warre agaynst the Tartars theyr borderers. For it is situate without Volga, on the bankes of the ryuer Clesma, whiche falleth into Volga. *The citie of Volodemaria.*

But Moscha, as well for those gyftes and commodities whereof we haue spoken, as also that it is situate in the myddest of the most frequented place of all the region and Empyre, and defended with the ryuer and Castell, hath in comparyson to other cities been thought most woorthie to *The citie of Moscha.*

be esteemed for the chiefe. Moscha is distant from Nouogrodia fiue hundred myles; and almost in the myd way is the citie of Ottoferia (otherwyse called Otwer, or Tuwer), vppon the ryuer of Volga. This ryuer, neare vnto the fountaynes and sprynges of the same, not yet increased by receyuyng so many other ryuers, runneth but slowlye and gentelly, and passeth from thence to Nouogrodia, through many woods and desolate playnes. Furthermore from Nouogrodia to Riga, the nexte porte of the Sarmatian sea, is the iorney of a thousande myles, litle more or lesse. This tract is thought to be more commodious then the other, bycause it hath many townes, and the citie of Plescouia in the way, beyng imbrased with two ryuers. From Riga (perteynyng to the dominion of the great master of the warres of the Liuons) to the citie of Lubecke, a porte of Germanie, in the gulfe of Cymbrica Chersonesus (now called Denmarke), are numbered about a thousande myles of daungerous saylyng.

From Rome to the citie of Moscha, the distance is knowen to be two thousande and sixe hundred myles, by the nearest way, passyng by Rauenna, Taruisium, the Alpes of Carnica: also, Villacum, Noricum, and Vienna of Pannonie: and from thence (passyng ouer the ryuer of Danubius) to Olmutium of the Marouians, and to Cracouia, the chiefe citie of Polonie, are compted .xi. hundred myles. From Cracouia to Vilna, the head citie of Lithuania, are compted fiue hundred myles: and as many from that citie to Smolenzko, situate beyonde Boristhenes, from whence to Moscha are compted sixe hundred myles. The iourney from Vilna by Smolenzko to Moscha, is traueyled in wynter with expedite sleades, and incredible celeritie vppon the snowes, hardened with long frost and compacte lyke Ise, by reason of muche wearyng. But in sommer, the playnes can not bee ouerpassed but by difficulte and laborious trauayle. For when the snowes by the continuall heate of the Sunne begyn to melte and dissolue, they cause great maryshes and quamyres, able to intangle both horse and man, were it not that wayes are made through the same with brydges and causes of wood, and almost infinite labour. *Maryshes in sommer. Other writers deny this.*

In all the region of Moscouia, there is no vayne or mine of golde or syluer, or any other common metall, except Iron; neyther yet is there any token of precious stones: and therefore they buye all those thinges of straungers. Neuerthelesse, this iniurie of nature is recompensed with abuundance of rich furres, whose price, by the wanton nysenesse of men is growen to suche excesse, that the furres parteynyng to one sorte of apparell, are now solde for a thousande crownes. But the tyme hath been that these haue been bought better cheape, when the furthest nations of the North, being ignorant of our nyse finenesse and breathyng desyre towarde effeminate and superfluous pleasures, exchaunged the same with muche simplicitie, often tymes for tryfles and thinges of small value. Insomuche, that commonly the Permians and Pecerrians, were accustomed to giue so many skinnes of Sables for an Iron Axe or Hatchet, as being tyed harde togeather, the marchantes of Moscouia could drawe through the hole where the hafte or handle entereth into the same. But the Moscouites sende into all partes of Europe the best kynde of flaxe to make lynnen cloth, and hempe for ropes. Also many Oxe hydes, and exceedyng great masses of waxe. *Rych furres. The price of furres. How many Sable skynnes for an Axe. Flaxe. Oxe hydes. Waxe.*

They proudely deny that the Romane churche obteyneth the principate and preeminent aucthoritie of all other.

They so abhorre the nation of the Jewes, that they detest the memorie of them, and will in no condition admyt them to dwell within theyr dominions: esteemyng them as wycked and mischieuous people, that haue of late taught the Turkes to make gunnes. Beside the bookes that they haue of the ancient Greeke doctours, they haue also the commentaries and homelies of saynte Ambrose, Augustine, Jerome, & Gregorie, translated into the Illirian or Slauon tongue, *They abhorre the Jewes. Their bookes and religion.*

which agreeth with theyrs: For they vse both the Slauon tongue and letters, as doe also the Sclauons, Dalmates, Bohemes, Pollones, and Lithuanes. This tongue is spredde further then any other at this day: For it is familiar at Constantinople, in the court of the Emperours of the Turks: and was of late hearde in Egypt, among the Mamalukes, in the court of the Soltane of Alcayre, otherwyse cauled Memphis, or Babilon in Egypte. A great number of bookes of holy scripture are translated into this tongue by the industrie of Saynte Jerome and Cyrillus. Furthermore, besyde the hystories of theyr owne countreys, they haue also bookes, conteyning the facts of great Alexander, and the Romane Emperours, and lykewyse of Marcus Antonius, & Cleopatra. They haue no maner of knowledge of philosophie, Astronomie, or speculatiue phisicke, with other liberal sciences. But such are taken for phisitians as professe that they haue oftentimes obserued the vertue and qualitie of some vnknowen hearbe.

The Slauon tongue spred further then any other.

Sainct Jerome was borne in Dalmatia, now called Sclauonia.

They number the yeeres, not from the byrth of Christ, but from the begynnyng of the world. And this they begin to accompt, not from the moneth of January, but from September.

Howe they number the yeeres.

They haue fewe and simple lawes throughout all the kyngdome, made by the equitie and conscience of theyr prynces, and approued by the consent of wyse and good men; and are therfore greatly for the wealth and quyetnesse of the people, forasmuche as it is not lawfull to peruerte them with any interpretations or cauillations of lawyers or atturneys. They punysh theeues, rouers, priuie pyckers, and murtherers. When they examyne malefactours, they poure a great quantitie of could water vppon such as they suspecte, whiche they say to bee an intollerable kynde of torment. But somteymes they manacle suche as are stubborne, and will not confesse apparent crymes.

Fewe and simple lawes.

Theyr youth is exercised in dyuers kyndes of games and

The exercise of youth.

plays, resemblyng the warres, whereby they both practise policie and increase theyr strength. They vse runnyng, both on horsebacke and afoote. Also runnyng at the tylt, wrestlyng, and especially shootyng. For they gyue rewardes to such as excell therein. <small>Shootyng.</small>

The Moscouites are vniuersally of meane stature, yet very square set, and myghtyly brawned. They haue all grey eyes, long beardes, shorte legges, and bygge bellyes. <small>The corporature of the Moscouites.</small>

They ryde very shorte, and shoote backewarde very cunnyngly, euen as they flye. At home in theyr houses, theyr fare is rather plentifull then deyntie. For theyr tables are furnyshed for a small pryce with all suche kyndes of meates as may bee desyred of suche as are gyuen to most excessiue gluttony. <small>Theyr fare.</small>

Hennes and Duckes are bought for litle syluer pence the peece. There is incredible plentie of beastes and cattayle, both great and small. The fleshe of beefe that is kylled in the myddest of wynter, is so coniealed and frosen, that it putrifieth not for the space of two monethes. Theyr best and most delicate dyshes are gotten by huntyng and haukyng, as with vs: For they take all sortes of wylde beastes with Houndes, and dyuers kyndes of nettes. And with Faulcons and Erens, or Eagles of a marueylous kynde, which the region of Pecerra bryngeth foorth vnto them, they take not onely Fesantes and wylde Duckes, but also Eranes and wylde Swannes. <small>Flesshe preserued longe by reason of coulde. Haukynge and huntynge.</small>

They take also a foule of darke colour, about the bygnesse of a Goose, with redde ouerbrowes, whose fleshe in taste passeth the pleasauntnesse of Phesauntes. These in the Moscouites tongue are called Tetrao, whiche I suppose to be the same that Plinie calleth Erythratao, knowen to the people of the Alpes, and especially to the Rhetians which inhabite the landes about the sprynges of the ryuer Abdua. The ryuer of Volga ministreth vnto them great fyshes, and of pleasaunt taste: especially sturgions, or rather <small>Plentie of fyshe.</small>

a kynde of fyshe lyke vnto Sturgions : which in the wynter season, beyng inclosed in Ise, are long reserued freshe and vncorrupte.

<small>Fyshe long reserued in Ise.</small>

Of other knydes of fyshes, they take in maner an incredible multitude in the whyte lakes whereof we haue spoken before. And whereas they vtterly lacke natyue wynes, they vse such as are brought from other places. And this only in certeyne feastes and holy mysteries, especially the pleasaunt Maluasies of the Ilande of Creta, now called Candy, are had in most honour : and vsed eyther as medicines, or for a shewe of excessiue aboundaunce, forasmuch as it is in maner a miracle that wines brought from Candy by the streightes of Hercules pyllers and the Ilandes of Gades, & tossed with such fluddes of the inclosed Ocean, should be droonke among the Scythian snowes in theyr natiue puritie and pleasauntnesse.

<small>Wyne.</small>

<small>Maluasie.</small>

<small>All the North parte of the fyrme lande was called Scythia, and the people Scythians.</small>

The common people drinke meade, made of hony & hoppes sodden togeather, whiche they keepe long in pitched barrelles, where the goodnesse increaseth with age. They vse also beere and ale, as doe the Germanes and Polones. They are accustomed, for delicatenesse in sommer, to coole theyr beere and meade with putting Ise therein, which the noble men reserue in theyr sellars in great quantitie for the same purpose. Some there are that delight greatly in the iuise that is pressed out of Cherries before they be full rype, which they affyrme to haue the colour of cleare and ruddy wyne, with a very pleasaunt taste.

<small>Drinke cooled with Ise.</small>

<small>Wyne of cherryes.</small>

Theyr wyues & women, are not with them in such honour as they are in other nations : for they vse them in maner in the place of seruantes. The noblewomen & gentlewomen do diligently obserue their walkes, and haue an eye to theyr chastitie. They are sildom bydden foorth to any feastes : neither are permitted to resorte to churches farre of, or to walke abrode without some great consideration. But the common sorte of women, are easily and for a

<small>Their women.</small>

small price allured to lechery, euen of straungers: by reason wherof, the Gentlemen doe litle or nothyng esteeme them.

John the father of king Basilius, dyed more then .xx. yeeres since. He maryed Sophia, the daughter of Thomas Paleologus, who reigned far in Peloponnesus (now called Morea), & was brother to Themperour of Constantinople: She was then at Rome when Thomas her father was dryuen out of Grecia by the Turks. Of her were fiue children borne, as Basilius hymselfe, George, Demetrius, Symeon, and Andreas. Basilius tooke to wife Salomonia, the daughter of George Soboronius, a man of singuler fidelitie & wysedome, and one of his counsayle: the excellent vertues of whiche woman, only barennesse obscured.

_{Thomas Paleologus.}

_{The conquest of the Turkes in Grecia.}

When the Princes of Moscouia deliberate to marry, their custome is to haue choyse of all the vyrgynes in the realme, and to cause suche as are of most fayre and beutifull vysage and personage, with maners and vertues accordyng, to bee brought before them: Whiche afterwarde they commyt to certayne faythful men, and graue matrones to be further viewed, insomuche that they leaue no parte of them vnsearched. Of these, shee whom the Prince most lyketh, is pronounced woorthie to bee his wyfe, not without great and carefull expectation of theyr parentes, lyuyng for that tyme betweene hope and feare. The other virgins also whiche stoode in election, and contended in beautie and integritie of maners, are oftentymes the same day, to gratifie the Prince, marryed to his noble men, Gentlemen, and Capytaynes: wherby it sometymes commeth to passe, that whyle the Princes contemne the lynage of royall descent, suche as are borne of humble parentage are exalted to the degree of princely estate, in lyke maner as the Emperours of the Turkes were accustomed to be chosen, by comelynesse of personage, and warly prowesse.

_{Howe the princes choose theyr wyues.}

Basilius was under thage of fourtie and seuen yeeres, of

_{Duke Basilius.}

comly personage, singular vertue, & princely qualities, by all meanes studious for the prosperitie & commodities of his subiectes : furthermore, in benevolence, liberalitie, and good successe in his doinges, to be preferred before his progenitours. For when he had .vi. yeeres kepte warre with the Lyuons that moued .lxxii. confetherate cities to the cause of that warre, he obteyned the victorie, & departed w^t few conditions of peace, rather giuen then accepted. Also at the beginning of his reigne, he put the Polones to flight, and tooke prisoner Constantine, the Capitayne of the Ruthens, whom he brought to Moscouia tyed in chaynes : But shortly after, at the ryuer Boristhenes, aboue the citie of Orsa, he him selfe was ouercome in a great battayle, by the same Constantine, whom he had dismissed : Yet so, that the towne of Smolenzko, which the Moscouites possessed before, and was nowe woon by the Polones, should styll parteyne to the dominions of Basilius. But agaynst the Tartars, and especially the Tartars of Europe, called the Precopites, the Moscouites haue oftentymes kepte warre with good successe, in reuenge of the iniuries done to them by theyr incursions.

Basilius is accustomed to bryng to the fielde more then a hundred and fiftie thousande horsemen, diuided into three bandes, and folowyng the banners or ensignes of theyr Captaynes in order of battayle.

On the banner of the kynges wyng, is figured the Image of Josue, the Captayne of the Hebreues, at whose prayer the Sonne prolonged the day and stayed his course, as witnesse the hystories of holy scripture. Armies of footemen are in maner to no vse in those great wyldernesses, as well for theyr apparel being loose and long, as also for the custome of theyr enemies, who in theyr warres trust rather to the swyftnesse of their light horses, then to trye the matter in a pyght fielde.

Theyr horses are of lesse then meane stature ; but very

War betweene the Polones and Moschouites.

War betweene the Moschouites and Tartars.

The Moscouites army.
Their banner.

strong and swyfte. Theyr horsemen are armed with pykes, Ryuettes, Mases of yron, and arrowes. Fewe haue hooked swoordes. Theyr bodyes are defended with rounde Targets, after the maner of the Turkes of Asia: or with bendyng and cornarde Targettes after the maner of the Greekes: also with coates of mayle, Brygantines, and sharpe Helmettes. Basilius dyd furthermore instytute a bande of hargabusiers on horsebacke: and caused many great brasen peeces to be made by the workemanshyp of certaine Italyans: and the same with theyr stockes and wheeles to be placed in the Castle of Mosca. *Theirhorses and horsemen. Theire armure. Hargabusiers. Gonnes.*

The kynge him selfe, with princely magnificence and singular familiaritie (wherwith neuerthelesse no parte of the maiestie of a kyng is violate) is accustomed to dyne openly with his noble men, & strange Ambassadours, in his owne chamber of presence, where is seene a marueylous quantitye of syluer & gylt plate, standyng vppon two great and high cubbardes in the same chamber. He hath not about him any other garde for the custody of his person, sauing only his accustomed familie. For watch and warde is deligently kept of the faithful multitude of the citizens. Insomuch, that euery warde or quarter of the citie is inclosed with gates, rayles, and barres: neyther is it lawfull for any man rashely to walke in the citie in the nyght, or withowt lyght. All the courte consisteth of noble men, Gentelmen, and choyse souldyers, which are called out of euery region by theyr townes and vyllages, and commaunded to wayte course by course at certayne monethes appoynted. Furthermore when warre is proclaymed, all the armie is collected, both of the oulde souldyers and by musteryng of newe in all prouinces. For the Lieuetenantes and Capytaynes of the army are accustomed in al cities to muster the youth, & to admyt to the order of souldyers such as they thynke able to serue the turne. *The prince dyneth openly. Sigismundus sayth that much of this is golde. The custodie of the citie. The dukes courte.*

Theyr wages is payde them of the common treasury

euery prouince which is geathered, and partely payde also in the tyme of peace, although it be but litle. But such as are assigned to the warres, are free from all tributes, and inioye certayne other priuilegies, wherby they maye the more gladly and cheerfully serue theyr kyng, and defende theyr contrey. For in the tyme of warre, occason is mynistred to shewe true vertue and manhood, where in so great and necessarie an institution, euery man accordyng to his approued actiuitie and ingenious forwardenesse, may obtayne the fortune eyther of perpetuall honour, or ignominie.

Souldyers wages of the common treasury.

> Vix olim vlla fides referentibus horrida regna
>   Moschorum, et Ponti, res glacialis erat.
> Nunc Iouio autore, illa oculis lustramus, et vrbes,
>   Et nemora, et montes cernimus et fluuios.
> Moschouiam, monumenta Ioui, tua culta reuoluens,
>   Cœpi alios mundos credere Democriti.

THE END.

INDEX.

A.

Abrahemin, king of Kazan, ii, 58
Achus, Town of, ii, 12
Aculpa, king of the Tartars, ii, 51
Adultery unpunished, i, 93
All Saints' Day, celebration of, i, 82
Altar, one in each temple, i, 57
Altar of Alexander, ii, 12
Ambassadors, manner of receiving and treating in Russia, ii, 112
Andrew, St., the Apostle of the Russians, i, 53
Animals of Russia, ii, 3
Anointing and confirmation, ceremonies of, i, 63
Aphgasi, the people, ii, 77
Archbishops, authority of amongst the Russians, i, 53
———— election of, i, 54
———— privileges of, i, 58
Archimandrites, i, 58
Arigo, Luchino, lviii
Artillery, use of, unknown to the Russians, i, 98
Ascelin, xxiii
Astrachan, the city, ii, 76
Azov, the city, ii, 76

B.

Baptism, ceremony of, i, 73-66
Barbara, wife of Sigismund king of Poland, i, 47
Barbaro, Josafa, lxvi
Barmai, i, 44
Barni, ii, 82
Bartholomew, metropolitan of Russia, i, 54
Bassalich, i, 96
Bati, king of the Tartars, i, 17
Bears, i, 205
Bears, white, abundance of, ii, 37, 39
Bears, kept for exhibition in games, ii, 137
Beaver skins, i, 115
Beluga, a large fish, i, 39; ii, 13

Berdebeck, king of the Tartars, ii, 51
Beresina, the river, i, 27; ii, 85, 153
Bibliography of the "Rerum Moscoviticarum Commentarii", cxxxvii
Biela, the fortress of, i, 23
———— the principality of, ii, 20
Bieloiesero, city of, ii, 31
Bielski, Dimitry, leader of the Russians against the Tartars, ii, 14, 66
Bishops, their functions, i, 58; mitres of various kinds, i, 58; their privileges, i, 58; their vestments, croziers, i, 58
Bison, the, ii, 95
Blud, the councillor and betrayer of Yaropolk, i, 14
Bona, wife of Sigismund king of Poland, i, 47
Boranets, ii, 74
Boris, Grand Duke, ii, 23
Borisov, the town, i, 27
Borysthenes, the river, ii, 21
Botrigari, Galeazzo, i, 183
Boyars, i, 36
Brandy drunk before dinner, ii, 128
Breslaw, the town, ii, 147
Bread, a token of favour among the Russians, ii, 128
———— of the Blessed Virgin, ii, 137
Brensko, the city, i, 23
Buda, ii, 47
Buffaloes, ii, 96
Bulgaria, i, 6; taken possession of by Vasiley, i, 19; by the Tartars, ii, 50
Bulgarians conquered by Svatislaus, i, 12
Bull of Alexander VI respecting the baptism of the Russians, i, 74

C.

Cabot, Sabastian, i, 191; first voyage, 192; second voyage, 193, 223
Cæsar's altar, ii, 12
Calmucks, ii, 76
Calor, or the Heat, a common disease in Russia, ii, 6
Cameniporas Mountain, ii, 39

Capha, a Genevese, the Barma taken from him, i, 44
Casimir, Duke of Lithuania, i, 46; canonized, 46
Cassimovgorod, town of, ii, 9
Castroma, city, ii, 33
Castromovgorod, city, ii, 44
Catalan, Jourdain, lii
Catching a Tartar, i, 81
Catskins, i, 116
Cauldron, miracle of the wild asses, ii, 97
Cazan, its kings, i, 24; its territory, ii, 8
—— the kingdom of attacked by the Russians, i, 30
Chancelor, Richard, his voyage to Muscovy, i, 183-194
Chelealeck, king of Cazan, ii, 58
Chidir, king of the Tartars, ii, 51
Chloppigrod, ii, 27, 32
Chrysostom Slatousta, i, 83
Circas, the town, i, 5; ii, 82
Circassians, ii, 83
Cirpach, the town, ii, 13, 14
Codaiclu, a Tartar, is baptized, ii, 59
Colchis, ii, 77
Colmogor, ii, 36, 37
Communion, ceremonies of, i, 78
Confession, i, 77
Constantinople besieged by Oleg, i, 9; delivered from the Turkish siege, ii, 53
Contarini, Ambrogio, lxxiv
Cor, Jean de, li
Corela, the river, ii, 30, 104
Corn, wonderful fertility in, ii, 7
Corsa, the idol, ii, 16
Corsira, the town, ii, 14
Corsula, ii, 149
Corsun, a city of Greece, is besieged and taken, ii, 27; is restored to the emperor of Constantinople, i, 17
Cosatzkii, the people, ii, 76
Coseri, the people, exact tribute from the Russians, i, 7
Cosle, the town, ii, 174
Cossin, the fortress, ii, 41
—— the river, ii, 41
Cotelnitz, ii, 45
Cotoroa, the river, ii, 33
Councils or Synods, authority of among the Russians, i, 60
Cracow, praise of, ii, 156
Crepitza, the city, ii, 168
Cronon, the river, ii, 146, 147
—— the town, ii, 86
Cropivna, the river, i, 28
Crubin, Simon, ii, 10
Cumeri, idols, i, 16
Cupa, the river, ii, 77

Cures, Prince of the Pieczenigi, i, 13
Cureti, the people, ii, 100
Cusanus, Nicolaus, lxix
Customs' dues, i, 116
Cyril, questions of, to Bishop Niphon, i, 68
Czar, title of sovereign, i, 33
Czarigrad, name of Constantinople, i, 34
Czeladin, Ivan, i, 27
Czeremissi, the people, ii, 8, 45, 47
—— swift runners and skilful archers, ii, 48, 58
—— they harrass the Russians, ii, 69
Czerna, the river, ii, 155
Czernigov, the town, ii, 14, 18
Czilme, the river, ii, 38
Czimburgis, married to Ernest, Archduke of Austria, i, 47
Czubaschi, skilful archers, ii, 58
Czutzko, the lake, ii, 28

D.

Daniel, Archbishop of Russia, i, 54
Dantiscus, John, ii, 143
Dantzic, the town, ii, 100
Dasva, the idol, i, 16
Deacons, obliged to marry, i, 56
Demetriovich, the town, ii, 19
Deng, the coin, i, 109
Derbt, the town, ii, 101
Desna, the river, ii, 14
Dignity, titles of, among the Tartars, ii, 82
Dimitriov, the fortress, ii, 30
Dimitry Danielovich, ii, 74
Dimitry Michailovich, Duke, i, 18
Dimitry, the Grand Duke, overcomes the king of the Tartars, i, 18; his posterity, ii, 18
Ditciloppi, the country, ii, 107
Disla, the city and lake, ii, 147
Divorce, i, 93
Dnieper, the river, i, 5, ii, 21, 83, 84, 85
Dnyepersko, the village, ii, 21
Dobrina, daughter of Calufcza, i, 12
Dogs used for draught by the Russians, ii, 46
Don, the river, 5; ii, 11-13
—— the lesser river, ii, 13
Donco, the town, ii, 10, 12, 13
Dowry, things given in, i, 92
Dress, mode of, i, 100
Drevlians, the people, i, 7; are conquered by Olga, Empress of the Russians, i, 10
Drogobusch, citadel of, i, 23
Drogobusch, the town, ii, 19
Dront, ii, 107, 108

INDEX. 259

Drunken priests whipped at Moscow, i, 56
Dubna, the river, ii, 30
Dukes of Muscovy, election and inauguration, i, 39
Duna, the river, ii, 22, 145
Dverschak, the town, ii, 151
Dwina, the river, i, 83, 145; ii, 35, 36, 147
—— the province, ii, 35, 36
—— the lake, ii, 22
—— the principality, ii, 25

E.

Emanuel, king of Constantinople, i, 21
Emperor, name of, why given to the Dukes of Russia, i, 33
Englishman, anonymous, xvii
Engroneland, ii, 36, 43, 87
Eraclea, the river, ii, 77
Erlingen, the town, ii, 143
Ermine skins, i, 115
Eucharist, ceremonies with which it is celebrated, i, 78
Eustace Tascovitz, ii, 63, 64, 83

F.

Falcons, abundance of in Muscovy, ii, 135
Fasts, i, 62
Fasts of monks and priests, i, 83
Fasts of the Russians, i, 82
Feast days, i, 79
Feast of unleavened bread, i, 63
Ferdinand, is crowned king of the Bohemians, ii, 174
Finland, i, 6; ii, 100
Finlapeia, people of, ii, 106
Fish of a human shape, ii, 42
Floating bridge, ii, 149
Forehead, custom of striking the, as a salutation, ii, 124
Fox skins, i, 115
Foxes, black and ash-coloured, ii, 35
Frederick of Brandenburgh, the younger, 46
Frederick, the emperor, 47
Frenchmen, voyages of, to the land of Baccalaos, 189
Freystadt, the town, ii, 156
Fronov, the marsh, ii, 21
Frozen Ocean, ii, 105-112
Furs, i, 219

G.

Gabriel, Grand Duke, his exploits, i, 25
Galitz, the principality, ii, 44
Gargni, ii, 82

Gastaldus, Jacobus, i, 201
George Danielovich, Duke, i, 18
George, the Little, i, 50, 84; ii, 46
George, Grand Duke, routed and slain by the Tartars, and death, ii, 50
George Pisbeck, a German knight, ii, 90
Gerodin, the town, ii, 151
Girdle of the world, mountain, ii, 42
Givoites, worshipped reptiles, ii, 99
Golden Old Woman, ii, 41
Gostinovosero, the island of merchants, ii, 68
Gostomissel, Prince of Novogorod, i, 9
Gostomissel, advises the Russians to choose princes and emperors for themselves, i, 9
Gothland, island of, ii, 101
Gothland, i, 212
Grand Dukes, power of over their subjects, i, 30
Greeks, war of, with Svyatoslav', i, 12
Gregory Istoma, ii, 105; account of his itinerary, ii, 105-108
Grinki, the town, ii, 146, 154
Grodno, town of, ii, 86, 154
Grustina, the fortress, ii, 40
Grustintzi, the people,
Gustavus, king of Sweden, ii, 103
Gyr-falcons, ii, 43; abundance of in Muscovy, ii, 135

H.

Hafnia or Copenhagen, metropolis of Denmark, ii, 108
Haitho, xliii
Hamerstete, Lucas, a valiant soldier, ii, 102
Hares of various colours, abundance of, ii, 20
Hedwige, wife of Joachim of Brandenburgh, i, 47; Queen of Poland, 45
Helen, Duchess of Lithuania, i, 22
Helen or Olga, Empress of the Russians, is canonized, i, 12
Herberstein, Sigismund von, his title of "Discoverer of Russia", ii; birth and parentage, lxxxviii; anecdote of his family, lxxxix; hereditary estate, xc; his education, xci; enters the army, xciv; made standard-bearer, xcvii; diplomatic missions to the Archbishop of Salzburg, &c., xcvii; mission to Christian II of Denmark, xcviii; first journey to Russia, cii; arrives at

Moscow, cvi; leaves Moscow after a stay of eight months, cxii; the estates of Styria appoint him their councillor, cxv; ordered to appear at the celebrated diet of Worms, cxvii; his marriage, cxviii; his second journey to Poland and Russia, cxviii; reception at Moscow, cxxiv; retires to his estate to recover his health, and is publicly thanked by Ferdinand, cxxxiii; receives the title of freyherr, or baron, cxxxvi; dies in his eightieth year, cxxxvi
Herberstein, route on his second embassy, ii, 16; journeys into Russia, ii, 143
Holmia, *see* Stockholm
Holy Nose, the headland, ii, 106
Homicide, punishment of, i, 101
Honey, i, 204, 207, 209
Hordes, division of the Tartars into, ii, 53
Horses in Russia, i, 96; their speed, i, 108; care of among the Tartars, ii, 55
Hranitza, the city, ii, 157
Hungary, i, 5; digression on its miserable condition, ii, 159-166
Hunting, as practised by the Russian sovereigns, ii, 133
Hyperborean mountains, ii, 43

I.

Ibn Batuta, li
Ibn-Fodhlan, vii
Igor, Emperor of the Russians, i, 9; his actions, i, 10
Igumens, i, 57
Ihedra, the lake and town, ii, 50
Ikhri, i, 70
Ilmen, the lake, i, 3, 53; ii, 27
Interiano, Giorgio, lxxi
Irtische, the river, ii, 40
Ivan, the Scribe, i, 31
Ivan, great lake of, ii, 11
Ivan Vasilievich, monarch of all Russia, i, 24; occupies the principality of Obskov, ii, 29; his decrees, i, 102; war with Novogorod, ii, 25; life and character, i, 24; death, i, 25; success in war, 24
Ivan, Duke, war with his son-in-law Alexander, i, 22

J.

Jachroma, the river, ii, 30

Jacobites, heresy of, i, 62
Jagellon, king of Poland, exploits, i, 45
Jaick, the river, ii, 47, 73, 74
Jamma, the fortress, ii, 29
Jamschnick, master of posts, i, 108
Januza, the river, ii, 152
Japhet, settles himself near the Danube, i, 6
Jaroslav, the city, ii, 9, 33, 34
Jasonica, the river, ii, 154
Jausa, the river, ii, 5
Jepiphanovlies, the wood, ii, 11
Jerom, the citadel, ii, 40
Jester with brooms, ii, 17
Jews, passover of the, i, 63
John the Baptist, fast of, i, 82
John's (St.) headland, i, 2, 77
John Albert, king of Poland, i, 46
John, metropolitan of Russia, letter to the Roman archbishop, i, 59; canons, i, 66
Jordan, Johann, an artilleryman, a German, in the Russian service, ii, 64, 65
Jug, the river, ii, 37
Jugaria, or Juharia, the province, ii, 46
Juhrici, the people, ii, 45
Jurgenci, the people, ii, 75
Justice, venality of among the Muscovites, i, 105

K.

Kaiemai, the people, ii, 106
Kama, the river, ii, 45
Kantinger, Justus, lxxxiv
Kesleni, i, 96
Kestud, dies in prison, i, 45
Khurland, ii, 100
Kiev, metropolis of Russia, ii, 84
Kitai, the lake, ii, 40
Kitaisko, the lake, ii, 39
Knesi, i, 36, 82
Koninskawoda, the river, i. 72
Koninzki, the river, i, 82
Koroll, i, 33
Kovar, Ivan, ii, 64
Kral, Kyrall, or Koroll, Slavonic name for king, i, 33
Kretzet, the birds, ii, 135
Krim, the city, ii, 77
Ksi, ii, 82
Kulvio, the river and lake, ii, 38
Kuthia, how made, 70; consecration of, i, 70
Kwas, i, 70
Kyrall, i, 33
Kysaleczki, Michael, i, 81

L.

Ladoga, the lake, i, 54, ii, 24, 27
Lamas, the town, ii, 154
Lapland,
Laplanders, ii, 109; manners and customs, ii, 110
Lech, prince of the Poles, i, 3, 6
Lechi, the people, i, 6
Lent among the Russians, i, 82
Lepin, the fortress, ii, 39
Leytha, the river, ii, 159
Limidis, the lake, ii, 27
Linski, Michael, a valiant soldier, ii, 88; his wonderful liberty of speaking, captivity, exploits, and death, ii, 91-93
Linz, the town, ii, 144
Lipnik, the town, ii, 157
Lithuania, i, 6; is laid waste by the Muscovites, i, 29; description of, ii, 82; its produce, ii, 87; bishoprics in, ii, 87, 112; inhabitants of, manners and customs, ii, 94
Lithuanians, war with the Muscovites, i, 22, 29
Livonia, description of, ii, 101
Lopata, Feodor, is taken prisoner and ransomed, ii, 64
Loss, the animal, ii, 97
Lovat, the river, 53, ii, 22, 27
Lublin, the palatinate, ii, 145
Lucomorya, the people of, die every year in the month of November, and rise again in April, ii, 40; description of, ii, 41
Lutinitsch, the lake, ii, 150
Lynxes, skins of, i, 115

M.

Macedonian heresy, i, 66
Machmethemin, king of the Tartars, i, 23
Machmetgerei, king of Taurida, his warlike actions, ii, 61-65; is slain, ii, 81
Macosch, the idol, i, 16; Grand Duke of Muscovy, i, 6
Magnus, Joannes, i, 212
Maldittus, prince of the Drevlians, i, 10
Malpont, the river, ii, 168
Maluscha, daughter of Kalufcza, i, 12
Mamaii, king of the Tartars, i, 18, ii, 80
Mandeville, Sir John, liii
Marco Polo, xxviii
Marriages, i, 91
Mary, the Virgin, fast of, i, 82
Master Merchants, hall of the, ii, 114
Matthæus, cardinal of Saltzburg, ii, 158

Maximilian, the Monk, a religious reformer, i, 83
Meeting, day of, mode of celebrating it among the Russians, ii, 52
Melnik, the town of, ii, 145
Memel, or Mumel, the city, ii, 86, 146
Men of monstrous shape, ii, 42
Mengarlia, ii, 77
Merchants, island of, ii, 73
Merchandize, articles of, and mode of carrying it on, i, 111-116; mutual exchange of, ii, 40
Merula, the river, ii, 77
Meseriz, the town of, ii, 145
Metals of Norway and Sweden, 217
Methodius Patanczki, bishop, ii, 49
Metropolitans of the Russians, whence they derive their authority, i, 53; election of, i, 54
Mezen, the river and village, ii, 38
Michael, emperor of Constantinople, the first who introduced the Slavonic letters into Bulgaria, i, 7
Midwives, i, 73
Miesko, the citadel is occupied, ii, 89
Miracle of the cauldron, i, 8
Misceveck, a marshy place, ii, 13
Moabites, the people, ii, 49
Mohilev, ii, 85
Mologa, the city, ii, 32
Moloscha, the river, ii, 18
Moncastro, i, 5
Money among the Russians, i, 109
Monks, their fastings, i, 83
Monte Corvino, Giovanni di, xliii
Montecroce, Riccoldo da, xlvii
Moon, light of, i, 214
Moravia, ii, 47
Moravians, i, 6
Mordwa, the people, ii, 9, 48; their manners and customs, ii, 9
Morse, the animal, ii, 39, 111; its teeth, i, 112
Mosaisko, a fortified town, ii, 20
Moscow, prince of, why called the White King, i, 34; the city, capital and metropolis of Russia, description of, ii, 1; is occupied by the king of the Tartars, i, 18; is beseiged by Andrew and Dimitry, i, 20; is fortified by Ivan Vasilievich, i, 24; Grand Duchy of, i, 19
Mosier, the city, ii, 95
Mosqwa, the river, ii, 1, 5, 9
Motka, the promontory, ii, 807
Mountains, burning, ii, 111
Msta, the river, ii, 150
Munster, Sebastian, 201
Muscovite hermits, i, 58; money, i, 109

INDEX.

Muscovy, Prince of, the facility of his making Northern discoveries, i, 186; his truce with the King of Poland, ii, 139; war with the Tartars, ii, 59; his robes, ornaments, etc., ii, 133, 137; extent of his territory, ii, 37
Murom, the town, ii, 8
Muromani, principality of the, ii, 8
Mursa, ii, 82
Music, contempt of, i, 58

N.

Nagai Tartars, ii, 73
Nali, the city, ii, 4
Narev, the town and river, ii, 145
Nawer, the lake, ii, 147
Neglima, the river, ii, 5
Nemen, the river, ii, 146
Neva, the lake, ii, 24; the river, ii, 27, 29, 54
Nerel, the river, ii, 33
Nerva, the fortress, ii, 28; the river, ii, 28, 101
Nicholas of Bari, Saint, miracles, i, 81
—— Czaplitz, ii, 157
—— Radovil, palatine of Vilna, ii, 154
—— of Spier, a celebrated bombardier, ii, 62; is held in great estimation by Vasiley, ii, 66
Niklspurg, the fortress, ii, 158
Nischa, the city and lake, ii, 148
Niepretz, the river, ii, 21
Northern Ocean, i, 187 189-195
North Sea, fishes of, i, 216
Nortpoden, ii, 106
Novogorod, city of, description, ii, 8; conquered by Ivan Vasilievich, i, 24; ii, 25; principality and town of, ii, 24; their idolatry, ii, 26; inhabitants of, besiege Corsun, a town in Greece, ii, 27; their wives, during the absence of their husbands, marry their slaves, ii, 27; is laid waste by the king of Kazan, ii, 61; market transferred to, from Kazan, i, 104; money of, i, 109
Novogrodeck, the town, ii, 18
Norway, description of, ii, 104
Noss, a name given to headlands, ii, 42
Nugaroli, Leonard, narrowly escapes drowning, ii, 117
Nuptials, celebration of, ii, 92
Nuremburg, ii, 28

O.

Oath, form of, 80; neglect of, i, 113
Obdora, the province, ii, 41
Oby, the river, ii, 39
Obskov, the principality, ii, 39
Occa, the river, i, 6; ii, 8, 9; its source, ii, 13; the river, island of, ii, 9
Ochakov, the fortress, i, 5
Ocolnick, i, 106
Ohthere, iv
Okonitzkilies, the wood, ii, 11
Olboadula, ii, 82
Olbond, ii, 82
Oleg, a warlike administrator of the kingdom of the Russians, i, 9; king of the Drevlians, is conquered by his brother, i, 14
Olga, empress of the Russians, her warlike actions, i, 10; is baptized, i, 11
Olgird, Grand Duke of Lithuania, i, 45
Opotzka, the town, ii, 28, 149, 152
Opscha, the river, ii, 20
Oreschak, the fortress, ii, 27, 30
Orlov, the town, ii, 45
Orsa, the city, i, 15, 110
Ossoga, the town, ii, 151
Ostra, the town, ii, 144
Ostrava, the town, ii, 157
Ostravitza, the river, ii, 144, 157
Osventzin, the town, ii, 156
Otwer, or Tver, a principality of Russia, ii, 23
Ovka, is married to Voleslaus, Duke of Teschen, i, 47
Ovoyov', the fortress, ii, 11
Ozechi, i, 6

P.

Papin, or Papinovgorod, the city, ii, 43
Parcho, the city, ii, 149
Passover, i, 64
Pegolotti, Francesco Balducci, lvii
Pelas, the river, ii, 28
Pereaslav', the city, ii, 33; the seat of the Russian kings, i, 11; is taken by Svyatoslav', i, 12; is burned, ii, 50; the lake, i, 44
Permia, the province and city, ii, 45
Perun, an idol of the inhabitants of Novogorod, ii, 26
Perunski, the monastery, ii, 26
Pessetz, the animal, i, 116
Petchora, the river, ii, 38, 39, 43
Peter, Saint, the miraculous, i, 39
Peter Tomitzki, bishop of Premisl, ii, 146
Peti, i, 7
Phasis, the river, ii, 77
Piecenigi, the people, ii, 49
Pienega, the fortress, ii, 36; the river, ii, 38
Piescoya, the river, ii, 38

Pieski, the town, ii, 170
Piesza, the river, ii, 33
Pietza, the river, ii, 173
Plague, not prevalent in Russia, ii, 6
Plano Carpini, Joannes de, xviii
Plants, wonderful, ii, 74, 75
Plescovia, the river and city, ii, 28; money of, ii, 109; inhabitants of, their integrity, etc., ii, 29
Plussa, the river, ii, 29
Poland, kings of, their genealogy, i, 45
Poleni, the people, i, 7
Poleutzani, the people, i, 7
Poloniza, the city, ii, 155
Polovitza, the town, ii, 169
Polovtzi, the people, ii, 50
Polta, the river, i, 7
Poltin, the coin, i, 109
Pootzko, the principality, i, 148
Poppel, Niclaus, lxxvi
Pordenone, Oderico di, xlix
Possetzen, Ivan, ii, 34
Possoch, an episcopal staff, i, 59
Post Stations, i, 108
Potivlo, the town, ii, 14, 15, 18
Prague, the city, ii, 174
Prayer, upon inauguration of the Grand Duke, i, 40, 41
Precop, the city, ii, 81, 84; king of, ii, 97
Precopskii, the kings, ii, 77
Prepetz, the river, ii, 85
Prince of Muscovy, called the chamberlain of God, i, 32
Priests, election of, i, 56; marriage of, allowed by the most ancient councils, i, 63; their privileges, i, 56; maintenance, dress, i, 57; drunken, publicly whipped, i, 56; in the Russian Church allowed to have wives, i, 56; honour and dignity of among the Tartars, ii, 68
Princes, their avarice, i, 31; of Muscovy, election and inauguration, i, 30; ceremonies after inauguration, i, 42
Ptzima, the principality, ii, 156
Priors, how chosen, i, 55; their oath, i, 55, 56
Proscura, i, 88
Proscurnicæ, the women, i, 88
Prukh, the town, ii, 158
Pschega, the river, ii, 149
Pskov, the principality, ii, 29
Purgatory, where situated, ii, 111; not an article of belief in the Russian Church, ii, 80
Pustoosero, the town, ii, 38

R.

Raba, the river, ii, 159
Rack, Theodoric, i, 51
Rechenberg, Johann von, a German knight, ii, 90
Reigning, memorable example of the lust of, i, 7
Reindeer, abundance of, ii, 107; their use in Norway, ii, 107
Reptiles worshipped in Samogithia, ii, 99
Revel, the town, ii, 101
Rezan, the town, ii, 13; the principality and province, ii, 10, 11, 44
Rhecitza, the river, ii, 45
Rhiphæan mountains, ii, 43
Riga, metropolis of Livonia, ii, 22, 29, 101
Rochmida, daughter of the Prince of Plescov', i, 14
Rochvolochda, Prince of Plescov', i, 14
Roden, the town, besieged by Vladimir, i, 15
Romish Church, errors, i, 61
Rosseia, i, 3
Rostov, the city, ii, 33, 34; the province, is laid desolate, ii, 50
Roxolania, i, 3
Rsova of Demetrius, the city, ii, 21
Rsova, called the Deserted, the city, ii, 21
Rubicho, the river, ii, 38
Rubo, the river, ii, 101
Rubruquis, xxv
Rurick, Prince of Novogorod, i, 9
Russ, the town, ii, 28
Russia, Princes of, said to be sprung from the Romans, i, 9; Grand Dukes of, their titles, i, 32; their hostility to the Pope, i, 35; Princes of, form of inauguration, i, 30; ancient, ii, 29; is laid waste by the Tartars, i, 18; how long without monarchs, i, 20; origin of name, i, 3; princes of, tributaries of the Tartars, i, 18; its situation and extent, i, 5; is ravaged by the Tartars, ii, 61
Russian abbots, i, 57; prisoners are sold by the Tartars, ii, 65
Russians, prefer slavery to freedom, i, 95; are defeated by the Lithuanians, i, 28; war of the, with the Lithuanians, i, 27; their drunkenness, i, 136; bishops of the, i, 58; abbots of the, i, 57; dress of the, i, 100; their war with the master of Livonia, ii, i, 102; Sabbath, observance of the, i, 61, 83; the people, i, 4; their language, i, 4; their religion, i, 53; how

long ignorant of letters, i, 7; contentions among them for the sovereignty, i, 9; tribute imposed on them by the Corsari, i, 7
Russum, the town, i, 3
Russus, Prince of the Poles, i, 3

S.

Sables, black, ii, 43
Sable skins, i, 114
Saint Quentin, Simon de, xxiv
Saints, worship of, i, 81, 82; images of in private dwellings, i, 107
Salomea, daughter of Ivan Sapur, is forcibly thrust into a convent, i, 50
Salt, a token of affection among the Russians, ii, 128
Samara, the river, ii, 18
Samoged, the people, ii, 39
Samogithia, the province, 6; ii, 97-100; inhabitants of, their manners and customs, ii, 98, 99
Samogithia, reptiles worshipped in, ii, 99
Samstin, the lake, ii, 150
Sandomir, town, ii, 155
Sapgirei, king of Kazan, ii, 61
Satabellum, the island, ii, 77
Savolha, kings of, ii, 74
Savorsinski, Ivan, ii, 88, 89, 146
Scandia, description of, ii, 104
Schapka, a hat so called, i, 44
Scharaitzick, the city, ii, 74
Schamachia, the city and country, ii, 76
Schatibeck, king of Savai, ii, 52
Schat, the river, ii, 11
Scheachmet, king of Savolha, ii, 79, 154
Scheale, king of Kazan, ii, 66
Schibanskii, the people, ii, 76
Schildberger, Johann von, lxiii
Schirni, ii, 82
Schlingva, the river, ii, 151
Scholona, the river, i, 24; ii, 27, 149
Schocksna, the river, ii, 31
Schorna, the city and river, ii, 152
Schosna, the river, ii, 14
Scripture, Holy, the authority of, i, 66
Scythians, subject to the prince of Muscovy, i, 206
Selva, the river, ii, 170
Sem, the river, ii, 14
Semecka, Dimitry, i, 20
Semeczitzi, origin of the name, i, 20
Semeczitz Vasiley, i, 20; ii, 16; his lust of power, ii, 16; is accused to the prince of the crime of rebellion, ii, 17
Semes, the rock, ii, 107
Semla (Chamiska-), the country, ii, 30
Semnor Poyas, the mountains, ii, 42

Semovisten, Duke of Mazovia, i, 47
Serbli, the people, i, 6
Sergius, Saint, grave of, i, 85
Serponiotzi, the people, their manners and customs, ii, 40
Sest, the river, ii, 30
Sewera, the principality, ii, 15; the province, i, 5; princes of, their origin, ii, 18
Seweri, or Sewerski, the people, i, 7
Seyd, chief-priest of the Tartars, ii, 68
Siberia, the province, ii, 47
Sibut, the river, ii, 39
Sigismund, king of Poland, i, 48, 49
Sigismund, duke of Lithuania and king of Poland, i, 26
Sigismund, king of Poland, truce with the prince of the Muscovites, ii, 139-142
Sigismund, king of Poland, his actions, i, 27
Simaergla, the idol, i, 16
Simeon Federovitz, ii, 34, 43
Simeon Ivanovich, duke, i, 18
Sinaus, prince of the Russians, i, 9
Skins, different kinds of, among the Muscovites, i, 114, 115, 116
Slata Baba, the idol, ii, 41
Slavery among the Muscovites, i, 95
Slaves' Fortress, ii, 27
Slavonic language, i, 4
——— race, its antiquity, i, 6
Solovoda, ii, 45
Smolensko, the city, i, 7; ii, 19; is besieged by the Lithuanians, i, 29
Sna, the river, ii, 18, 24
Snups, Michael, lxxxiii
Sola, the river, ii, 145, 150
Salovki, the island, ii, 30
Sonca, i, 46
Sophia, wife of Ivan Vasilievich, i, 21
Sossa, the river, ii, 39, 40
Squirrel skins, i, 115
Staradub, the town, ii, 15, 16
Starosta, ii, 97
Stephen, palatine of Moldavia, i, 24
Stephen, bishop of the Russians, enrolled amongst the number of the gods, ii, 46
Stephen, count of Zips, i, 47
Steschicza, the town, ii, 173
Stockholm, the city, ii, 103
Stolph, the mountain, ii, 43
Stolpniki, hermits, i, 58
Stratagem of the Tartars, ii, 60
Streltze, the town, ii, 37
Stretimue, ii, 52
Striba, the idol, i, 16
Sturb, the island, ii, 19

INDEX. 265

Strupili, the fortress, ii, 39
Strupin, the river, ii, 149
Sturgeon, three kinds of, ii, 14
Stzuchogora, the river, ii, 39
Suchana, the river, ii, 35, 36
Suchenwirt, Peter, lix
Sula, the river, i, 7
Sultan, ii, 82
Sura, the fortress and river, ii, 8
Susdalj, the principality, ii, 44
Svortzech, the town, i, 9
Svyadolt, urges Yaropolk to make war upon his brother, i, 13
Svyatopolk, aspires to the throne and kills his brother, i, 17
Svyatoslav', king of the Russians, i, 10; his warlike acts and military discipline, i, 11-13
Sweden, description of, ii, 103
Sylvius, Æneas, lxxiii
Syrna, i, 82
Szoret, the river, ii, 149
Szurnu, a musical instrument, i, 100

T.

Tachnin, the river, ii, 41
Tachtamich, king of the Tartars, i, 18
Tamenskii, the people, ii, 76
Tanas, the city, ii, 12
Tartars, their division into hordes, ii, 53; their mode of fighting, i, 98; ii, 55; war with the Muscovites, ii, 59; their proceedings in Russia, i, 18; their cruelty to aged captives, ii, 65; their origin, manners, and customs, ii, 49
Tartar kings, origin of the, ii, 78
Taurica, king of, crosses the Dnieper, and lays the country waste, i, 5
Taurimeni, the people, ii, 49
Temnick Manais, ii, 52
Tersack, the town, ii, 23
Teya, the river, ii, 144, 158
Thachamisch, king of the Tartars, lays Muscovy waste, ii, 52
Theft, punishment of, i, 56-101
Themerhoscha, kills his father, and is made king of the Tartars, ii, 51
Themirassack, invades Russia, ii, 52; obscurity of his origin, and how he obtained the regal dignity, ii, 52, 53
Themirkutlu, king of Savai, ii, 52
Theodosia, the city, ii, 78
Thomas, king of the Peloponnesus, i, 21
Thur, the river, ii, 85
Thurn, George von, lxxx
Tithes, i, 88
Toropecz, the fortress, i, 12; ii, 22

Torture, instruments of, i, 101
Trinity, Holy, feast of, i, 80; monastery of, in Moscow, i, 85
Troky, the castle, i, 79
Truce, form and ceremony of concluding a, in Muscovy, ii, 139-142
Trumpets, use of in battle, i, 100
Truvor, Prince of Plescov', i, 9
Tudela, Benjamin of, viii
Tula, the town, ii, 11
Tumen, the fortress, ii, 40; the kingdom, ii, 42
Turantum, the river, ii, 147
Turbervile, Master George, his letters in verse, cxlvii
Tver or Otwer, the principality, ii, 23; i, 151; Duchy of, i, 18; occupied by Ivan, i, 20; money of, i, 109
Tvertza, the river, ii, 23
Tyra, the river, i, 5
Tziptzan, ii, 82

U.

Uglitz, principality of, i, 19; town of, ii, 32
Ugra, the river, ii, 18
Ugritzschi, the people, ii, 40
Ulan, title of dignity among the Tartars, ii, 82
Uppa, the river, ii, 11
Uslad, the idol, i, 16
Ussa, the river, ii, 38, 149
Ustyug, the province, ii, 35, 36
Usury, prevalent among the Russians, i, 116

V.

Vaga, the river, ii, 35
Vandals, their language and power, i, 8
Varlamus, Prior of the monastery of Hutten, i, 55
Vasiley challenges Machmetgirei to battle, ii, 67
Vasiley, the Grand Duke, sent to Uglitz with his eyes put out, i, 20; his success in war, i, 25; his war with his brother for the duchy, i, 19; with the Tartars, ii, 39; his ingratitude towards the German bombardiers, ii, 65; his titles, i, 32
Vasilovogorod, ii, 9
Vedrosha, the river, i, 22
Vegetable productions of Muscovy, i, 208
Velia, the river, ii, 86
Velikareca, the river, ii, 28
Velikiluki, the city, ii, 23

Verasco, a faithful counsellor of Yaropolk, i, 16
Viatka, the province, ii, 44
Vidocha, the river, ii, 149
Viepers, the river, ii, 145
Viesma, the town and river, ii, 19, 20
Vilna, the city, ii, 86, 87, 146, 147
Vischora, the river, ii, 45
Vistula, the river, i, 6
Vitenen, Grand Duke of Lithuania, i, 45
Vithold, Grand Duke of Lithuania, i, 23, 45; ii, 20
Vitzechda, the river, ii, 45
Vladimir, son of Svyatoslav', is made Prince of Novogorod, i, 12; makes war upon his brother Yaropolk, i, 14, 15; marries Rochmida, daughter of Rochvolochda, i, 14; establishes many idols at Kiev, i, 16; institutes tithes, i, 88; his wives and concubines, i, 16; becomes sole monarch of Russia, i, 16; embraces Christianity, i, 17; dies, and is canonized, i, 17
——— the city, 17; is burnt, i, 18; description of, ii, 7; is laid waste, ii, 61
Vladislav', king of Poland, ii, 46
——— king of Hungary and Bohemia, i, 48; ii, 51
Vogolici, the people, ii, 39
Voguslaus, Duke of Stolpen and Pomerania, i, 47
Volchov', the river, i, 53; ii, 24, 27
Voldai, the lake, ii, 150
Voleslaus, Duke of Teschen, i, 47
Volga, the river, i, 6; ii, 7, 13-22, 31
Volga and Borysthenes, the rivers, do not spring from the same source, as some suppose, ii, 22
Volga, the lake, ii, 21
Volkonski, the wood, ii, 21
Vologda, the province, city, and fortress, ii, 25, 35
Vologda, the river, ii, 35
Volok, the lake, i, 53
Votska, the country, ii, 29

W.

Wagria, a province of the Vandals, i, 8
Waregan Sea, i, 8
Waregi, the people, i, 8
Waretzokoie Morie, i, 8
Warfare, diversity of amongst different nations, i, 98
Warlike exercises of the young men, i, 100
Warna, the lake, i, 46
Washings of the unclean, i, 78
Waywode, i, 5, 23
Wedrapusta, the town, ii, 151
Weissenkirchen, the town, ii, 157
Widowers not allowed to administer the sacraments, i, 56
Wife, a, desires her husband to show his love by beating her, i, 94
Wild beasts, ii, 95
Winter, extraordinary severity of the, ii, 2
Wisby, the city, ruins of, ii, 101
Women, their miserable condition among the Russians, i, 93; their amusements, i, 94
Wonderful drought, ii, 2
Worotin, the city and principality, ii, 15
Worotinski, Ivan, is deprived of his principality, ii, 15

Y.

Yaropolk, i, 12; is made monarch of Russia, i, 14; is betrayed by his councillor Blud, i, 15; wages war against his brother Oleg, i, 13

Z.

Zanebech, king of the Tartars, i, 18; ii, 51
Zapolski, John, i, 48
Ziegler, Jacob, i, 211

For EU product safety concerns, contact us at Calle de José Abascal, 56–1°, 28003 Madrid, Spain or eugpsr@cambridge.org.

www.ingramcontent.com/pod-product-compliance
Ingram Content Group UK Ltd.
Pitfield, Milton Keynes, MK11 3LW, UK
UKHW041951230426
12048UKWH00008B/270